DESKTOP PUBLISHING MADE EASY

USING MICROSOFT PUBLISHER

JAMES A KENNEDY

Gill & Macmillan

GILL & MACMILLAN LTD
HUME AVENUE
PARK WEST
DUBLIN 12
WITH ASSOCIATED COMPANIES THROUGHOUT THE WORLD
WWW.GILLMACMILLAN.IE

© 2003 JAMES A KENNEDY
0 7171 3537 3
PRINT ORIGINATION BY THE AUTHOR

SCREEN SHOTS REPRINTED BY PERMISSION FROM MICROSOFT CORPORATION
THE PAPER USED IN THIS BOOK IS MADE FROM THE WOOD PULP OF MANAGED FORESTS.
FOR EVERY TREE FELLED, AT LEAST ONE TREE IS PLANTED, THEREBY RENEWING NATURAL RESOURCES.

ALL RIGHTS RESERVED. NO PART OF THIS PUBLICATION MAY BE COPIED, REPRODUCED
OR TRANSMITTED IN ANY FORM OR BY ANY MEANS, WITHOUT PERMISSION OF THE PUBLISHERS.

A CATALOGUE RECORD IS AVAILABLE FOR THIS BOOK FROM THE BRITISH LIBRARY.

CONTENTS

About this Book

Acknowledgements

Introduction

Chapter 1:	Getting to Know Publisher	1
Chapter 2:	Setting up Publisher and Tips for Ease of Use	7
Chapter 3:	Designing a Form	15
Chapter 4:	Designing a Logo	37
Chapter 5:	Designing a Business Letterhead	59
Chapter 6:	Designing a Business Card	73
Chapter 7:	Designing a Compliment Slip	82
Chapter 8:	Designing a Greeting Card	89
Chapter 9:	Designing a Brochure	100
Chapter 10:	Document Analysis	119
Chapter 11:	Designing a Newsletter	133
	Index of Tutorials	172

ABOUT THIS BOOK

WHAT DOES THIS BOOK ACHIEVE?

It helps the learner to acquire a good knowledge of Desktop Publishing Design Principles and to put them into effect by designing properly a wide variety of publications. The tutorials on DTP skills and the completion instructions for each exercise make the task even easier for the learner.

WHO SHOULD READ THIS BOOK?

- Students completing the FETAC/NCVA Level 2 Desktop Publishing module (E20003).
  All the exercises from this module are comprehensively covered.
- All learners of Desktop Publishing.
  Tutorials on the skills needed for each exercise and numbered instructions for their completion help the learner to study DTP privately, making this book suitable not only for students covering specialised courses, but also for anyone wishing to learn the subject.

STRUCTURE OF THE BOOK

1. Chapter 1 helps the learner become familiar with the screen layout, the tools and the toolbars of the DTP package – Microsoft Publisher 2000. There is also a section devoted to some of the differences between Publisher 2000 and earlier versions of the program. Skip this chapter if you are familiar with the package.

2. Chapter 2 shows the learner how to set up Publisher to suit his/her needs. There is also a section on solutions to most of the common problems that learners encounter when covering the exercises. This can be used as a reference as you progress through the book.

3. Chapters 3-9 cover the designing of: (i) a form, (ii) a logo, (iii) a business letterhead, (iv) a business card, (v) a compliment slip, (vi) a greeting card and (vii) a brochure. Each of these chapters is structured as follows:
   - an exercise at the beginning of each chapter as a challenge to the learner
   - tutorials on the skills needed for each exercise
   - numbered instructions for the easy completion of each exercise
   - sketch sheets showing the final[1] design plan for each exercise
   - final printouts showing the end product
   - extra exercises at the end of each chapter which can be done using the same tutorials; these exercises help in the retention of information.

4. Chapter 10 helps the learner acquire a good knowledge of design principles. This is followed by an exercise on analysing a document page, which shows the learner how to make use of the knowledge acquired.

5. Chapter 11 covers the designing of a newsletter. It has the same structure as outlined in Chapters 3-9.

6. Index of tutorials.

[1]The preliminary sketch showing the design plan for each exercise may change during the creation of the exercise and the sketch will change accordingly.

ACKNOWLEDGEMENTS

I would like to thank those students in the Business Studies class who either wittingly or unwittingly tested some of the tutorials in this book.

I am also very grateful to the editorial team in Gill & Macmillan, whose professional advice was very valuable.

To the anonymous reviewers out there whose criticism was very constructive, I want to express my sincere gratitude. This was a source of great encouragement.

Finally, many thanks to my wife Veronica, whose encouragement and patience helped me finally complete the book.

INTRODUCTION

There are plenty of books on the market today which explain the concepts of Desktop Publishing. Some of these tend to be very technical and quite often the learner is overwhelmed by an excess of rules and regulations on good and bad design features. Other DTP books provide the learner with a wide range of exercises, but very little specific guidance on how to complete them. This book, however, provides the best of both worlds, as it offers the learner a collection of DTP exercises, tutorials on the skills needed for each exercise, instructions for their completion and a good knowledge of design principles.

DTP is essentially about design and DTP packages are merely the tools for design. While a knowledge of the tools is important, like any other tools they are only effective if placed in the right hands. However, with a knowledge of design principles, as discussed in 'Document Analysis', DTP is elevated to a new plateau. Chapter 10 lifts this book above and beyond a mere collection of DTP tutorials.

The book is structured so that the learner is given an exercise to complete in each chapter and tutorials on the skills needed for its completion. As the learner progresses from exercise to exercise he/she acquires the extra skills needed, so that by the time the last and largest exercise –'Designing a Newsletter' – is completed, the learner has become skilled in the use of virtually all the tools available in the DTP package. Numbered instructions also help the learner complete each exercise in a logical way. Extra exercises at the end of each chapter which can be done by using the same tutorials, offer a challenge to the learner, while at the same time helping him/her to retain the knowledge previously acquired. Sketch sheets are also included which show the final design plan for each exercise.

The exercises chosen in this book, with the exception of 'Designing a Greeting Card', are based on the *Collection of Work* and *Project* as outlined in the NCVA/FETAC – DTP Level 2 module descriptor (E20003). The exercises are very practical and wide-ranging and they demand the use of nearly all the DTP tools.

Even though the tutorials and completion instructions are based on Microsoft Publisher 2000, they can be adapted for use with any DTP program. There is a section in Chapter 2 devoted to some of the differences between Publisher 2000 and earlier versions of the program, which makes this book suitable for users of all versions of Microsoft Publisher.

Chapter 1

Getting to Know Publisher

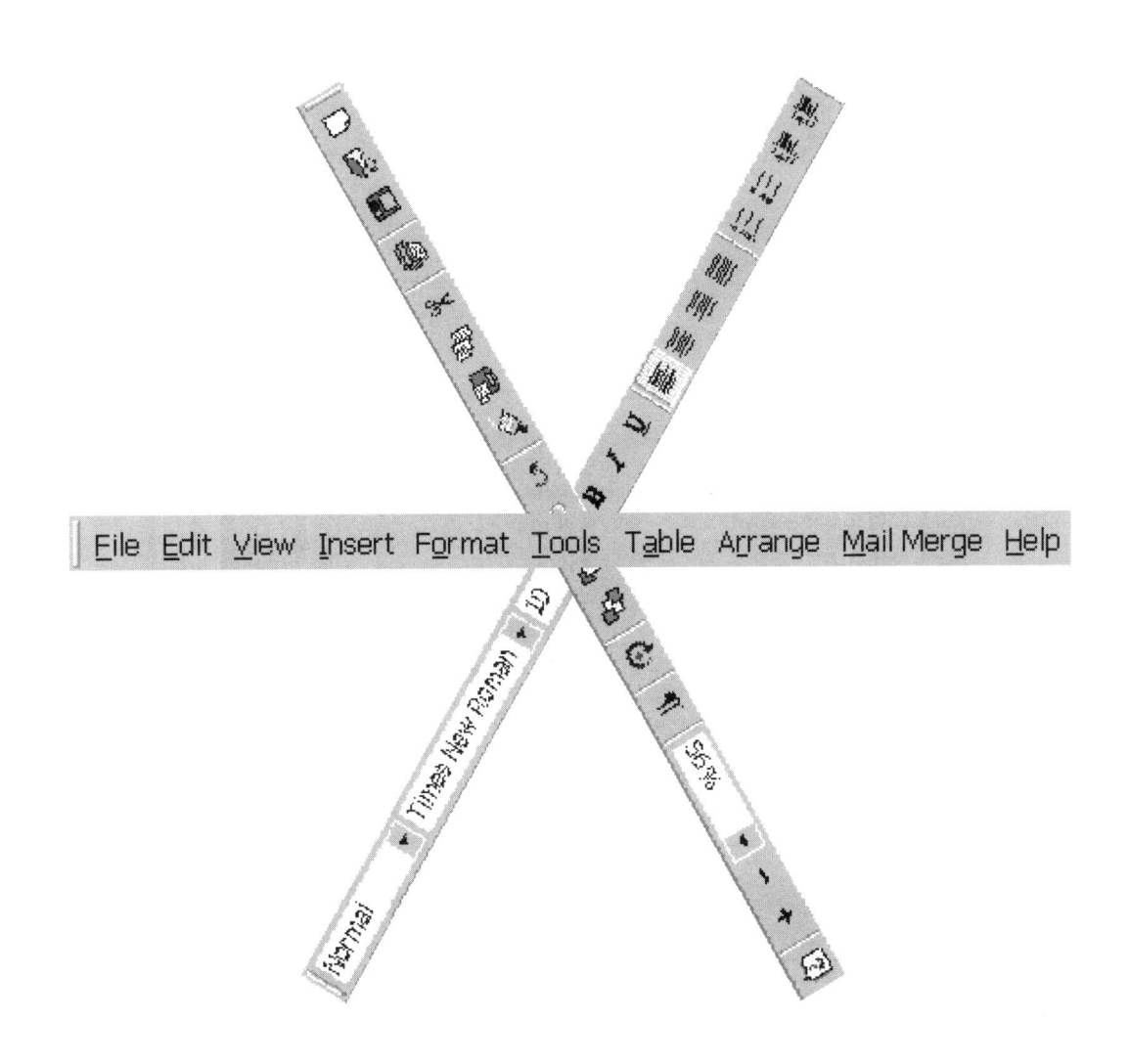

Getting to Know Publisher *Chapter 1*

MICROSOFT PUBLISHER 2000
SCREEN LAYOUT

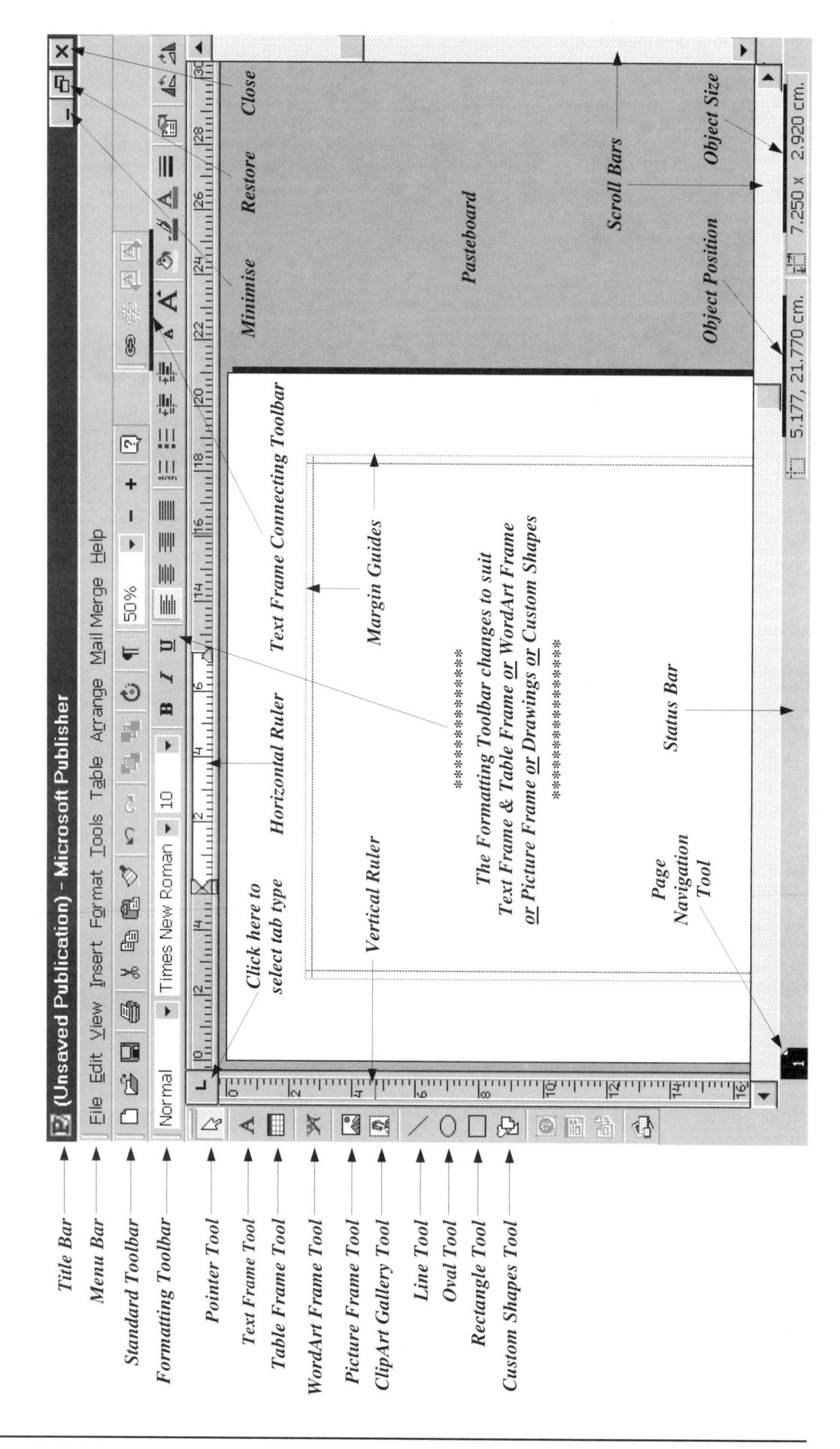

Labels pointing to screen elements:

- Title Bar
- Menu Bar
- Standard Toolbar
- Formatting Toolbar
- Pointer Tool
- Text Frame Tool
- Table Frame Tool
- WordArt Frame Tool
- Picture Frame Tool
- ClipArt Gallery Tool
- Line Tool
- Oval Tool
- Rectangle Tool
- Custom Shapes Tool

- Close
- Restore
- Minimise
- Pasteboard
- Scroll Bars
- Object Size
- Object Position
- Text Frame Connecting Toolbar
- Margin Guides
- Horizontal Ruler
- Click here to select tab type
- Vertical Ruler
- The Formatting Toolbar changes to suit
  Text Frame & Table Frame or WordArt Frame
  or Picture Frame or Drawings or Custom Shapes
- Status Bar
- Page Navigation Tool

Page 2 **Desktop Publishing Made Easy**

Chapter 1 — Getting to Know Publisher

MENU BAR

File — This allows you to:
- Create new publication
- Open existing publication
- Close publication
- Save publication
- Create Web Page
- Prepare document for another computer
- Set up page
- Set up printer for current publication
- Print
- Mail publication

View — This allows you to:
- See 2-page spread
- Go to specific page
- Go to master page(s)
- Ignore master page for current page
- Choose quality of picture display
- Show or hide special characters
- Choose toolbars
- Show or hide rulers
- Zoom

Format — This allows you to:
- Edit font
- Set character spacing
- Set line spacing
- Set indents
- Set tabs
- Use drop caps
- Align text vertically
- Autofit text in frame
- Change frame colour
- Set line/border style
- Shadow frame
- Set text frame properties
- Create text style
- Format paint

Table — This allows you to:
- Insert rows or columns
- Delete rows or columns
- Merge or split cells
- Divide cells
- Autoformat table
- Select table, row, column or cell
- Fill cells down or right
- Grow cell(s) to fit text

File Edit View Insert Format Tools Table Arrange Mail Merge Help

Edit — This allows you to:
- Undo or redo last action
- Cut, copy and paste object
- Paste special
- Delete object
- Delete page
- Highlight whole story (all text within frame and connected frames)
- Select all objects on a page
- Find text (letter(s), word(s) or groups of words)
- Replace text (letter(s), word(s) or groups of words)
- Edit story in Microsoft Word

Insert — This allows you to:
- Insert text file into frame
- Insert picture into frame
- Insert Design Gallery object
- Add selection to Design Gallery
- Insert object
- Insert Form Control
- Insert HTML Code
- Insert symbol
- Insert date and time
- Insert page numbers
- Insert page

Tools — This allows you to:
- Check spelling
- Turn on or off hyphenation
- Allow automatic correction and formatting
- Check design
- Connect text frames
- Snap to guides, ruler marks and objects
- Set program options

Arrange — This allows you to:
- Set layout guides – margins
- Add or clear ruler guides
- Bring to front, send to back, bring forward or send backward
- Send object to master page
- Nudge object
- Rotate or flip object

Using Microsoft Publisher — Page 3

Getting to Know Publisher — Chapter 1

STANDARD TOOLBAR

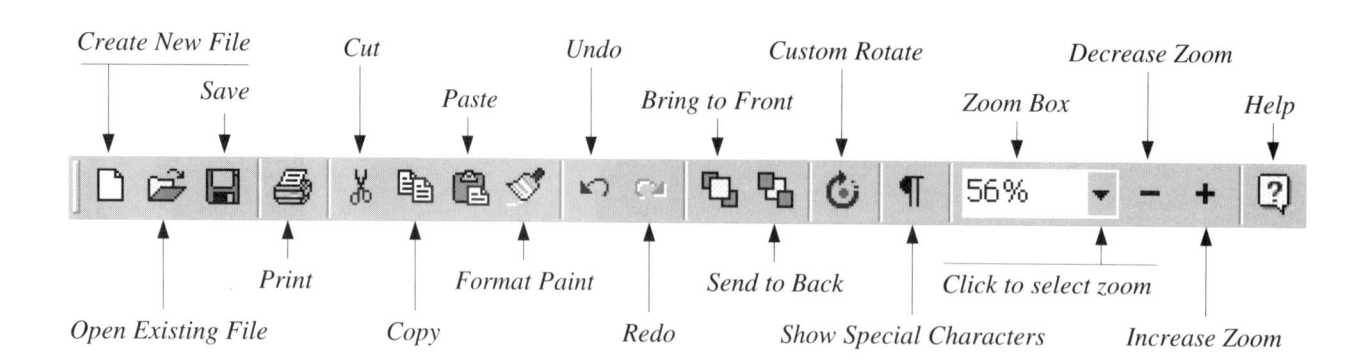

Labels (top): Create New File, Save, Cut, Paste, Undo, Bring to Front, Custom Rotate, Zoom Box, Decrease Zoom, Help

Labels (bottom): Open Existing File, Print, Copy, Format Paint, Redo, Send to Back, Show Special Characters, Click to select zoom, Increase Zoom

FORMATTING TOOLBAR (TEXT & TABLE)

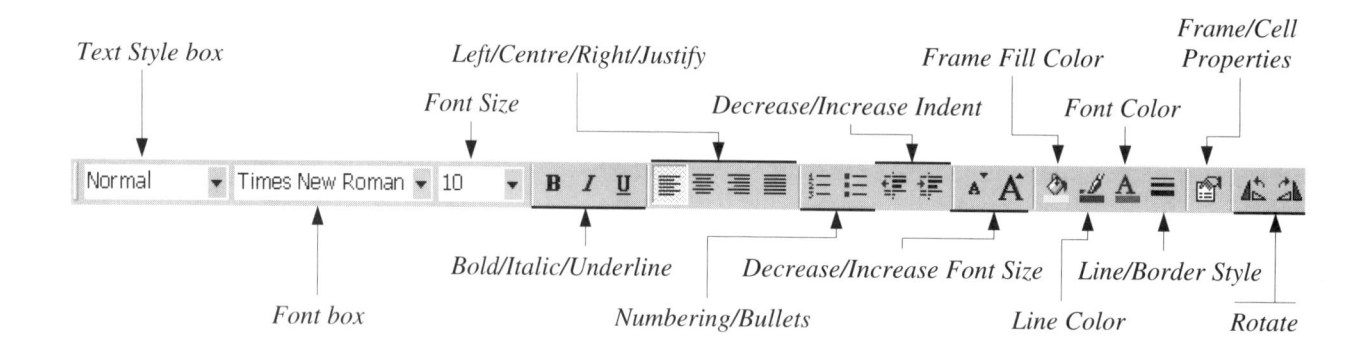

Labels (top): Text Style box, Font Size, Left/Centre/Right/Justify, Decrease/Increase Indent, Frame Fill Color, Font Color, Frame/Cell Properties

Labels (bottom): Font box, Bold/Italic/Underline, Numbering/Bullets, Decrease/Increase Font Size, Line Color, Line/Border Style, Rotate

FORMATTING TOOLBAR (PICTURE)

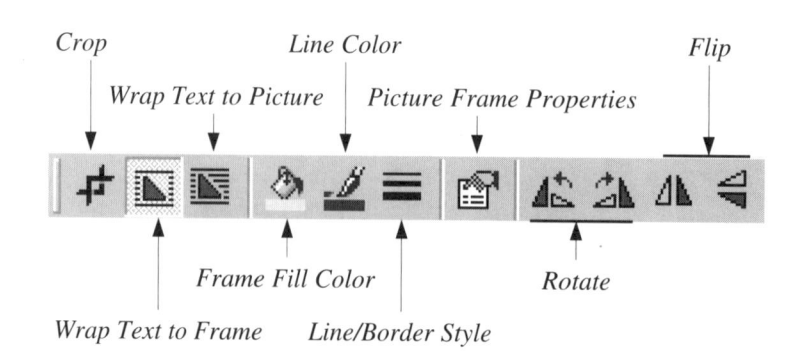

Labels (top): Crop, Wrap Text to Picture, Line Color, Picture Frame Properties, Flip

Labels (bottom): Wrap Text to Frame, Frame Fill Color, Line/Border Style, Rotate

Desktop Publishing Made Easy

Chapter 1   *Getting to Know Publisher*

FORMATTING TOOLBAR (WORDART)

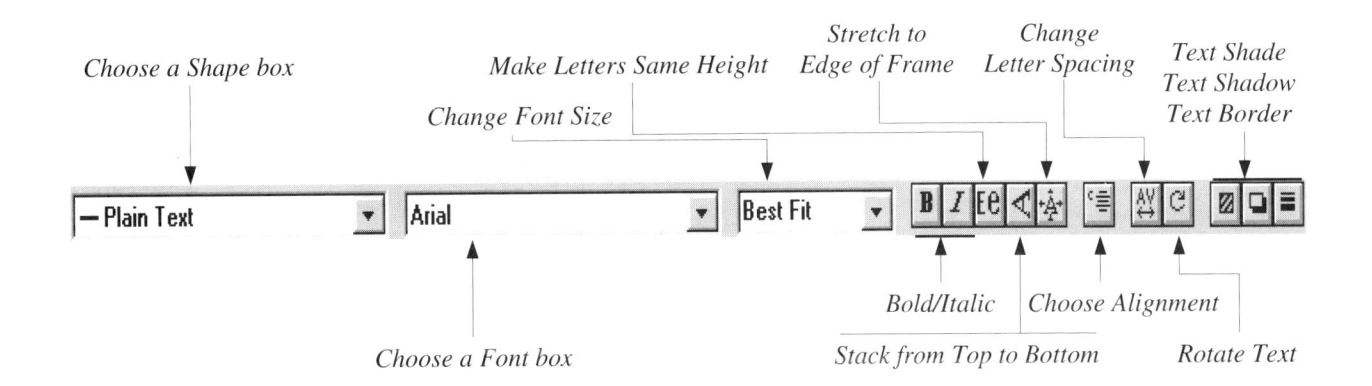

Labels (top): Choose a Shape box; Make Letters Same Height; Change Font Size; Stretch to Edge of Frame; Change Letter Spacing; Text Shade, Text Shadow, Text Border

Labels (bottom): Choose a Font box; Bold/Italic; Stack from Top to Bottom; Choose Alignment; Rotate Text

FORMATTING TOOLBAR
(CUSTOM SHAPES + DRAWINGS)

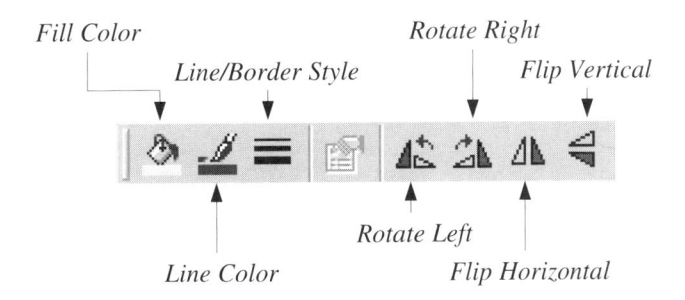

Labels (top): Fill Color; Line/Border Style; Rotate Right; Flip Vertical

Labels (bottom): Line Color; Rotate Left; Flip Horizontal

FORMATTING TOOLBAR (LINE)

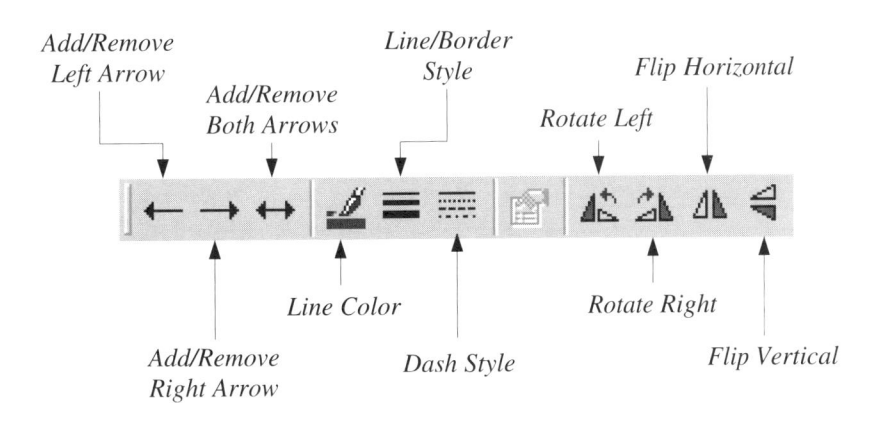

Labels (top): Add/Remove Left Arrow; Add/Remove Both Arrows; Line/Border Style; Rotate Left; Flip Horizontal

Labels (bottom): Add/Remove Right Arrow; Line Color; Dash Style; Rotate Right; Flip Vertical

Setting Up Publisher   *Chapter 1*

PUBLISHERS 97 AND 98

As far as the course outlined in this book is concerned, Microsoft Publisher 2000 has a few menu items that Microsoft Publisher 97 lacks.

Publisher 97 does not allow you to *Align Text Vertically* from the *Format* menu.

You can do it as follows in Publisher 97.

1. Click *Text Frame Properties* from *Format* on the Menu Bar.
2. Increase the value in the *Top Margin* box (see the illustration below).
3. Click *OK*.
4. If the text isn't centrally aligned from top to bottom in frame, repeat the process until it is.

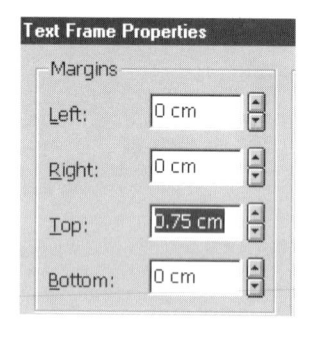

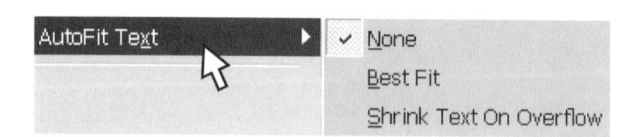

Another feature lacking in Publisher 97 is *AutoFit Text* from *Format* on the Menu Bar. Even though I have not made use of it in the exercises, it is nevertheless very useful.

By clicking *Best Fit* the text is shrunk or expanded to suit the size of the text frame.

Making text fit in text frames is dealt with in Chapter 11 of this book.

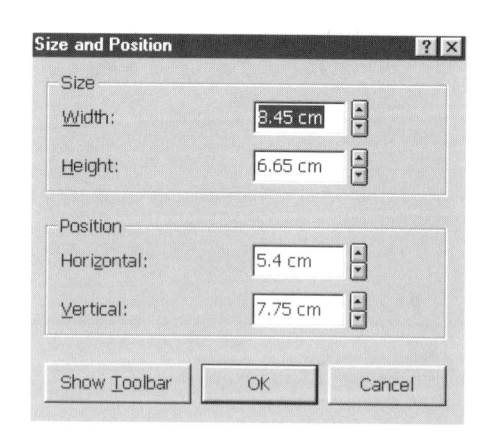

Publisher 97 also does not have the *Size and Position* feature from *Format* on the Menu Bar.

However, it is not necessary, as the position of the object on the page and the object size can be seen on the right of the Status Bar of Publisher 97.

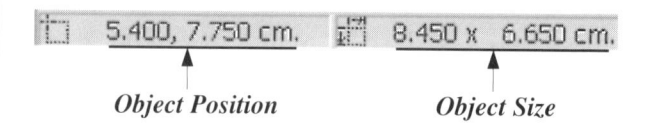

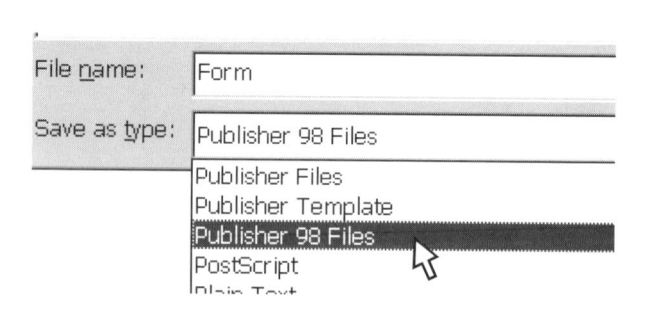

Object Position   *Object Size*

Microsoft Publisher 2000 allows you to save in Publisher 98 format. This is useful if you are working with both versions. If you save a file in Publisher 98 format you can open it in Publisher 2000. However, it doesn't work the other way around.

To save in Publisher 98 format:

1. Click *File* on the Menu Bar.
2. Click *Save As*.
3. Choose the file destination and the file name.
4. Before you click *Save* choose *Publisher 98 Files* in the *Save as type* box.
5. Click *Save*.
6. Click *OK* to the message warning about the loss of formatting.

Chapter 2

Setting Up Publisher
and
Tips for Ease of Use

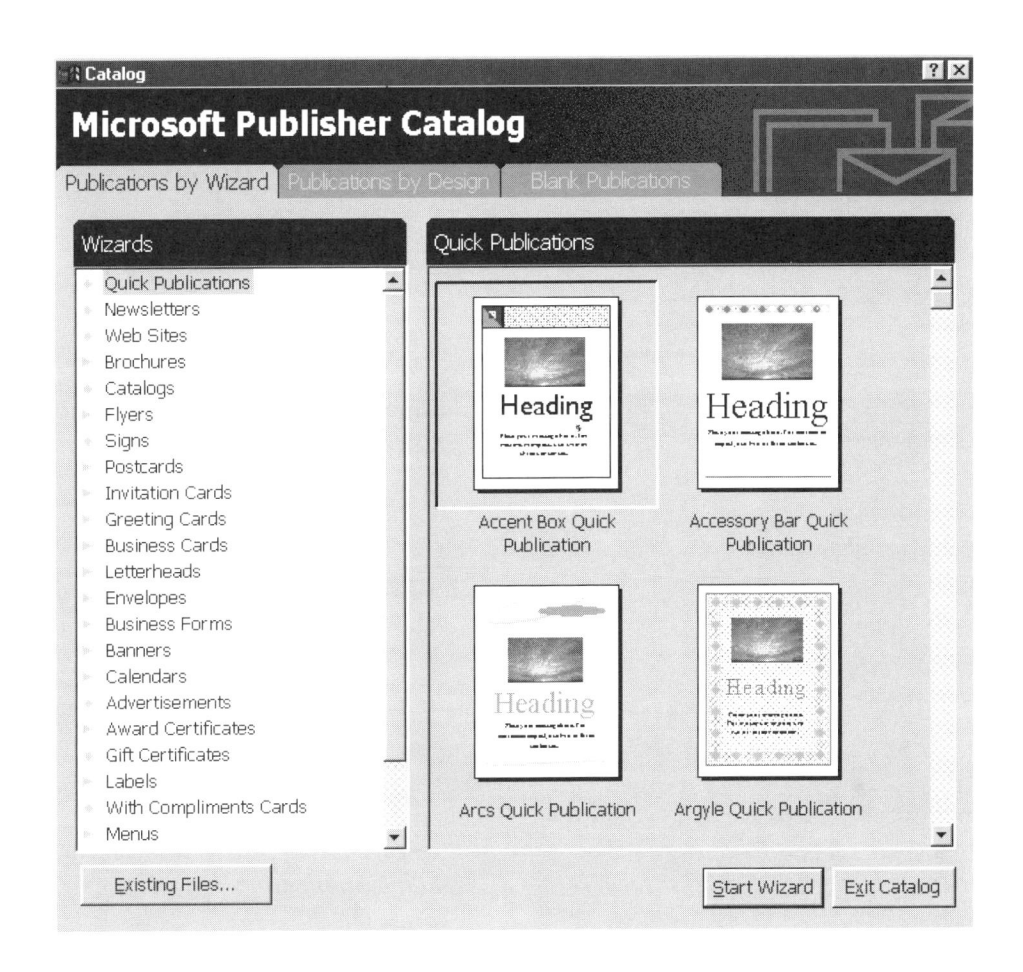

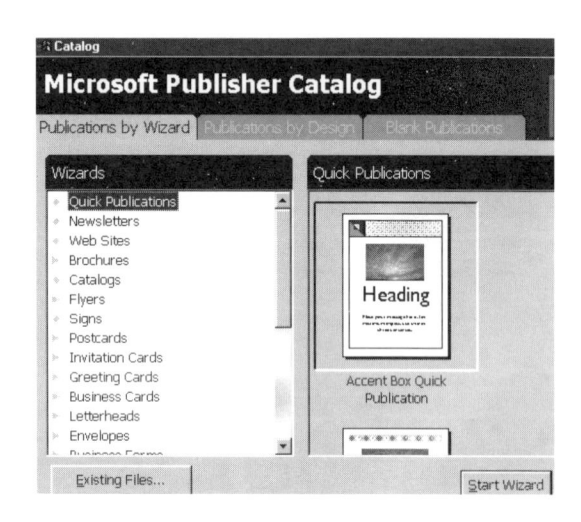

Setting Up Publisher   *Chapter 2*

Above is the default opening screen for Microsoft Publisher 2000.

This allows you to create *Publications by Wizard*, *Publications by Design* or *Blank Publications*.

Since the tasks outlined in this book are created from a blank page, we shall always start with a blank A4 page.

To go straight to a blank A4 page:

1. Click the *Blank Publications* tab at the top of *Microsoft Publisher Catalog* window.
2. Choose *Full Page* in the right of window.
3. Click *Create*.

This opens a new A4 page, which can be used to create a publication or can be altered from the Menu Bar to create a custom page for the creation of other publications.

4. Click the *Hide Wizard* tab on bottom left of screen to give you more space to work from.

SETTING UP PUBLISHER FOR EASE OF USE

Publisher 2000 can be set up to go directly to the new A4 page without going to the default opening screen. The wizard can also be hidden to allow more screen space to work from.

To do this:

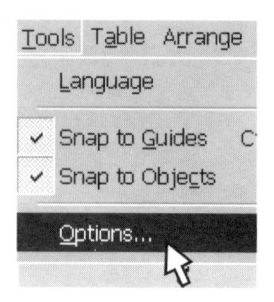

1. Click *Tools* on the Menu Bar.
2. Click *Options*.

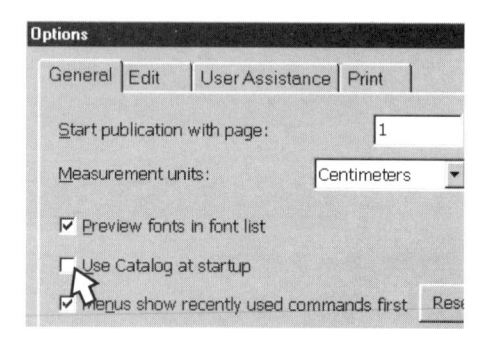

3. Click the *General* tab in the *Options* window.
4. Click the *Use Catalog at startup* box to remove the check mark.

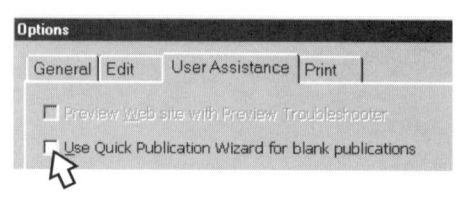

5. Click the *User Assistance* tab in the *Options* window.
6. Click the *Use Quick Publication Wizard for blank publication* box to remove check mark.
7. Click *OK*.

The default opening screen is now disabled and the wizard is hidden.

Page 8   *Desktop Publishing Made Easy*

Chapter 2 *Setting Up Publisher*

By clicking **Options** from the **Tools** menu, other settings can be changed. Experiment with them to see if they suit you.

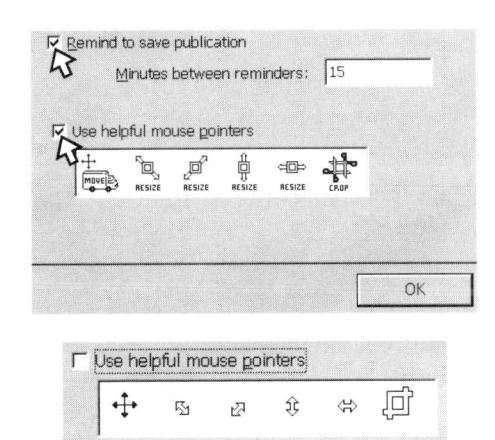

1. Click the **User Assistance** tab in the **Options** window.
2. Enable **Use helpful mouse pointers** by clicking the box to insert the check mark, if it has not already been inserted.

This is useful as the action word accompanies the pointer, e.g. **MOVE, RESIZE** etc. It helps to identify the action.

The lower of the two illustrations above shows the **Use helpful mouse pointers** box unchecked and the pointers without the action word.

3. Enable **Remind to save publication** by clicking the box to insert the check mark, if it has not already been inserted.
4. Enter a value in the **Minutes between reminders** box. I've entered 15 in this box.
5. Click **OK**.

In the example above there will be a reminder to save the publication every 15 minutes.

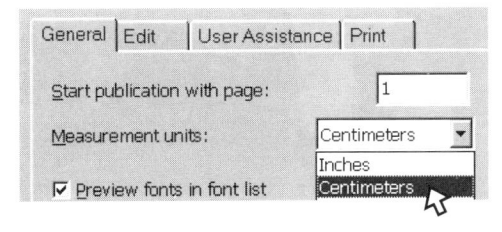

To change the measurement units:

1. Click the **General** tab in the **Options** window.
2. Choose a suitable unit in the **Measurement units** box.
3. Click **OK**.

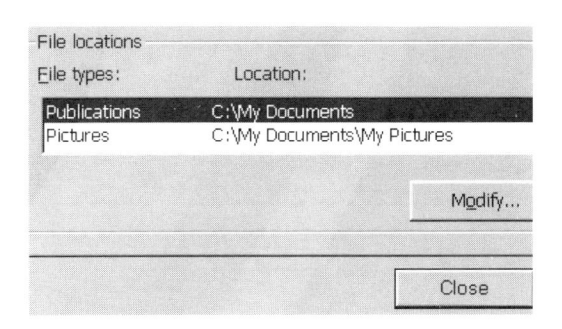

To change the default location for saved publications:

1. Select **Publications** in the **File types Location** box.
2. Click **Modify**.
3. Click the appropriate drive in the **Look in** box of the **Modify Location** window.
4. Choose the appropriate folder in the main section of the window.
5. Click **OK**.
6. The default location for the pictures to be inserted can be set by selecting **Pictures** in the **File types Location** box and following the same procedure again.
7. Click **Close**.

Another useful feature for beginners of DTP is shown above:

1. Click the **Edit** tab in the **Options** window.
2. Enable **Use single-click object creation** by clicking the box to insert the check mark, if it has not already been inserted.
3. Click **OK**.

By choosing any tool from the Tool Palette and then clicking on the page the object is created. You don't have to drag to create the frame. You will then have to resize the object.

There are other settings you may like to change in the **Options** window. Experiment by clicking boxes to enable the settings or clicking again to disable them and then clicking **OK**.

Using Microsoft Publisher

Setting Up Publisher   **Chapter 2**

Learners may encounter some simple problems when completing the course outlined in this book. The solutions to these problems are listed below.

WHERE'S THE TOOLBAR?

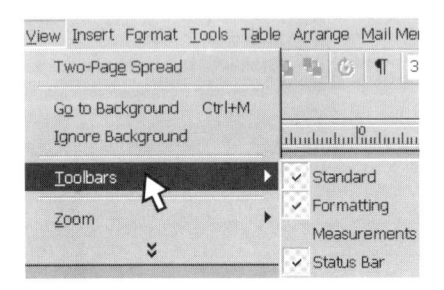

The most common problem relates to missing toolbars.

If it is a *Formatting Toolbar*:

1. Click the object. Every object has its own *Formatting Toolbar*. Before the toolbar will appear the object must first be selected.

If this doesn't work, make sure the toolbar is enabled. To do this:

2. Click *View* from the Menu Bar.
3. Click *Toolbars*.
4. If there is no check mark before the word *Formatting*, click it to enable it. Otherwise click *View* again to disable the menu.
5. If the *Standard Toolbar* or *Status Bar* is missing, the only way to retrieve it is by clicking *Toolbars* from the *View* menu.

The *Standard Toolbar*, *Formatting Toolbar* and *Status Bar* should always be enabled.

TOOL ON TOOLBAR IS GREYED!

If a tool is greyed out you cannot use it. Above are 3 tools on the Standard Toolbar, *Cut*, *Copy* and *Paste*. Only the *Paste* tool can be used as the other two are greyed out. Before you can use them click the object to select it.

No matter which toolbar is in use, the object usually has to be selected before a tool can be used.

CAN'T FIND THE TOOL!

Let's say you're looking for the *Font Color* tool on the Formatting Toolbar. There can be 2 reasons why that tool is missing:

You may have selected the wrong object. Every object has its own Formatting Toolbar.

1. Select a text frame or table frame before the *Font Color* tool appears.

Another reason why the tool may not be present is that there is no room for the tool across the screen top.

2. Click the *More Buttons* tool (see right and below).
3. Click the *Font Color* tool.

The *Font Color* tool appears on the Formatting Toolbar across the top of screen, replacing the first tool used.

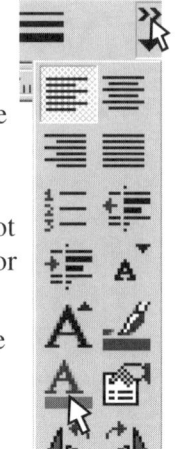

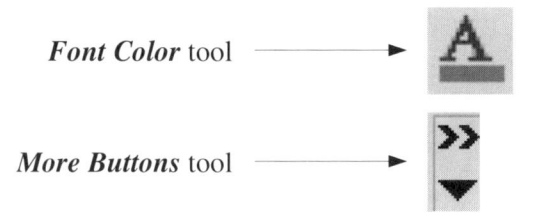

Font Color tool ⟶

More Buttons tool ⟶

CONFUSED BY TOOLS!

Students sometimes cannot distinguish one tool from another.

1. Bring the mouse pointer (arrow) over the tool without clicking the mouse. The tool name will be displayed as in the illustration above.
2. Click the tool to perform the action.

Chapter 2 — Setting Up Publisher

MADE A MESS!

Undo   *Redo*

The **Undo** and **Redo** tools on the Standard Toolbar are two of the most useful tools in Publisher.

If you make a mess of what you're doing, all you have to do is click the **Undo** tool. Clicking **Redo** will undo the **Undo** action.

Clicking **Undo** a number of times in succession will undo the actions in reverse order.

WHERE'S MY PICTURE?

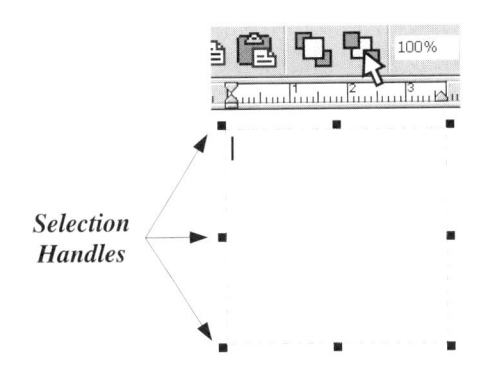

Selection Handles

Very often an object that you created on a page may be missing. This may be caused by creating another object and positioning it over the missing object. See **Layering Objects** in Chapter 4. In the illustration above a text frame is hiding a picture, which was created before it.

1. Click the text frame to select it. Selection handles will appear around the frame.
2. Click the **Send to Back** tool from the Standard Toolbar.

The text frame is sent to the back and the picture reappears as in the illustration below.

PROBLEMS WITH PICTURES!

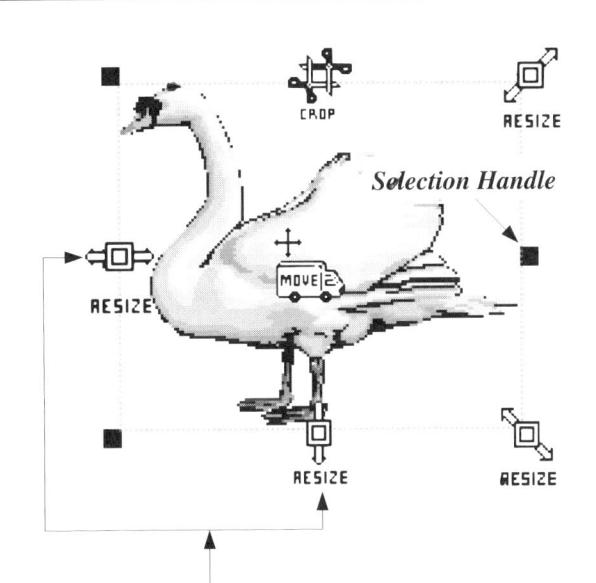

Selection Handle

Don't resize from middle selection handles as the picture will lose its shape

1. To move a picture, place the mouse pointer inside picture frame until it changes to **MOVE**.
2. Drag to where you want the picture positioned.
3. To resize a picture move the mouse pointer over a corner selection handle until it changes to **RESIZE**.
4. Drag until the picture is the correct size.

Resizing from any of the middle handles will distort the picture as in the illustrations below.

5. To crop the picture move the mouse pointer over a handle until it changes to **CROP**.
6. Drag in to remove part of picture or out to create more white space.

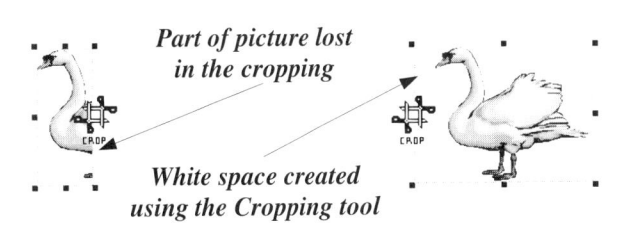

Pictures distorted as resizing is done from middle handles

Part of picture lost in the cropping

White space created using the Cropping tool

Setting Up Publisher Chapter 2

CAN'T MOVE TEXT FRAMES!

Ordinarily new *Insertion* :s of the Force must spe*Point* st three years on normal uniformed policing duties. After that, they are free to apply for any vacancies which may arise in specialist areas. Each section will have its own unique selection procedures.

1. To move a text frame, place the mouse pointer at the edge of the text frame and away from the selection handles.
2. When the mouse pointer changes to **MOVE**, drag the text frame to the required position.

Moving the mouse pointer inside a text frame changes it to an I-beam pointer. When clicked, an Insertion Point is created. This blinking Insertion Point invites you to to edit the text in the frame.

Remember that with a text frame there are two things you can edit – the frame and the text.

DID YOU RESIZE CORRECTLY?

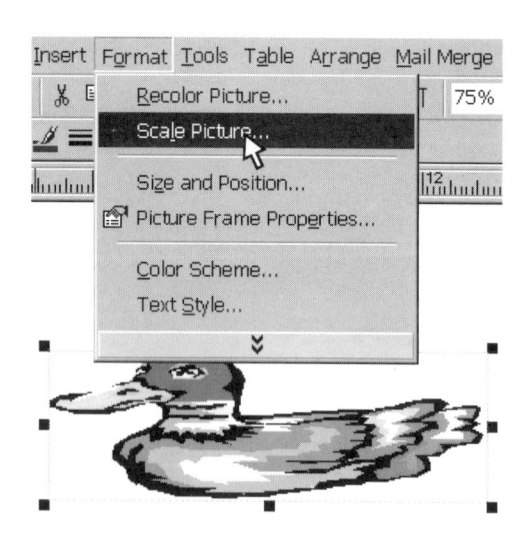

1. Click *Format* from the Menu Bar.
2. Click *Scale Picture*.

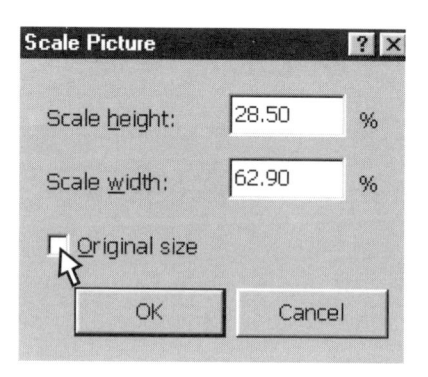

If the values in the *Scale height* and *Scale width* boxes are the same then the picture was resized correctly – from a corner handle. The values above show that the picture is distorted.

To rectify this:

1. Insert the same value in the boxes.
2. Click **OK**.

or

1. Click the *Original size* box to insert a check mark. The picture is given its full size – 100%.
2. Click **OK**.

LOST PAGE!

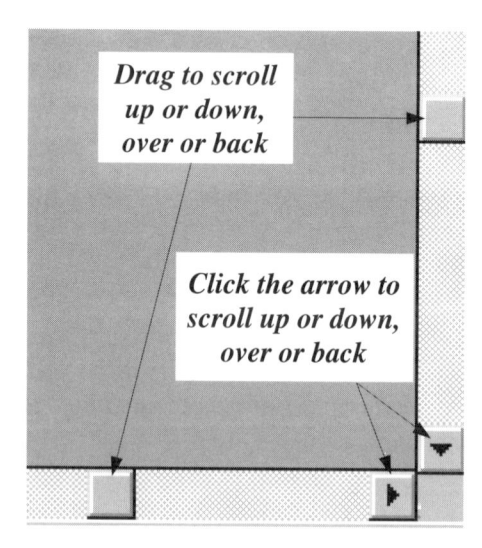

Sometimes due to excessively resizing an object or moving an object too quickly, you may lose the white electronic page and are left in the grey pasteboard area.

To find the page again:

1. Use the *Scroll Bars* on the bottom and right of the screen as in the illustration above.

Chapter 2   Setting Up Publisher

If you still cannot find the page using the scroll bars:

2. Click the down arrow to right of the **Zoom** box.
3. Click **Whole Page**.

The full page will now be available at a very low zoom. In order to work on this page you will have to increase the zoom.

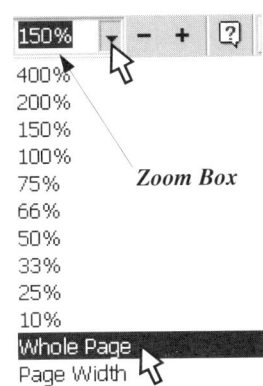

Zoom Box

I LOSE THE OBJECT WHEN I INCREASE THE ZOOM!

When a new page in Publisher is opened the whole page is seen. The page zoom is probably around 60%. You will have to increase the zoom to edit the objects.

To do this:

1. Select the object.
2. Click the down arrow to right of the **Zoom** box.
3. Choose a zoom value.

The secret is to select the object before zooming. Otherwise the zooming will not focus in on any object.

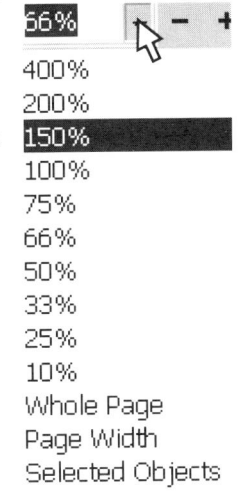

The handiest way to zoom to suit an object is to:

1. Right-click the object.
2. Choose **Selected Objects** from the menu that appears.

The object now takes up the full screen.

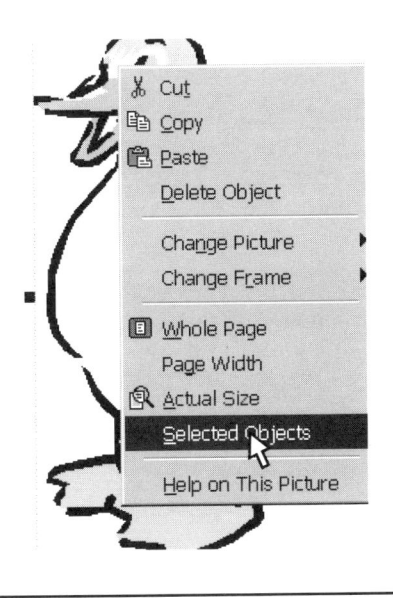

SELECTING ALL OBJECTS!

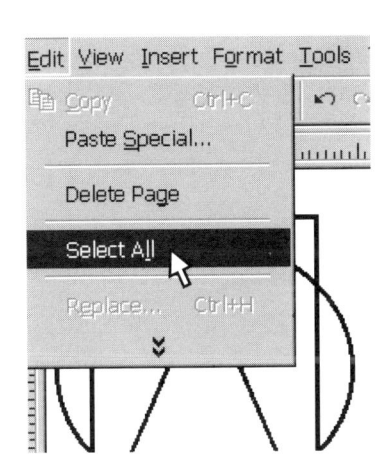

See Chapter 4 for multiple selection. However, to select all objects (all objects on a single page or facing pages):

1. Click **Edit** from the Menu Bar.
2. Click **Select All**.

See the result below.

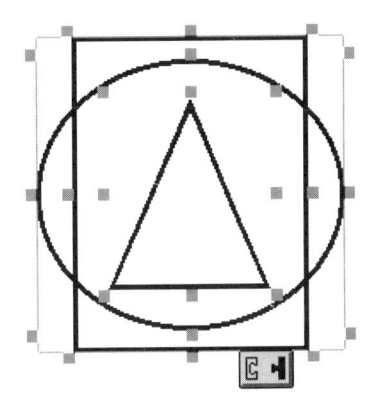

POSITION OR SIZE?

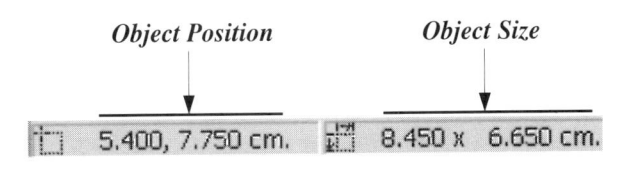

Object Position   *Object Size*

5.400, 7.750 cm.   8.450 x 6.650 cm.

Some students are always asking which of the 2 sets of measurements on the right of the Status Bar are for position and size.

Using Microsoft Publisher   Page 13

Setting Up Publisher   *Chapter 2*

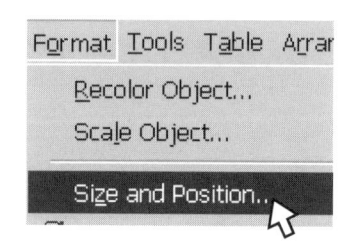

If you're in any doubt do the following:

1. Click the object to select it.
2. Click *Format* on the Menu Bar.
3. Click *Size and Position*.

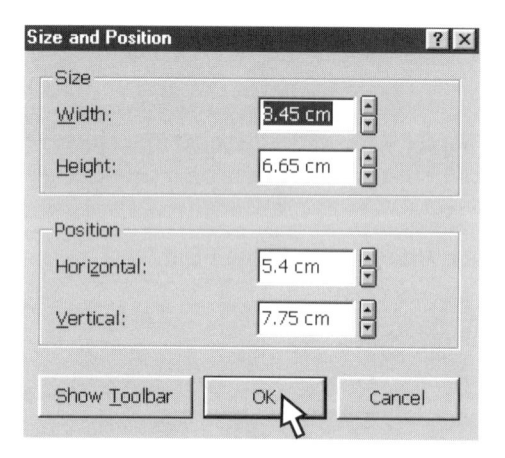

The *Size and Position* window shows you the size value and the position value.

4. Click *OK* or *Cancel*.

To change the position and size:

5. Type in values in the appropriate boxes.
6. Click *OK*.

Another way to distinguish between the sets of measurements is to remember that *P* (position) comes before *S* (size) in the alphabet.

NEED MORE HELP!

You can use *Microsoft Publisher Help* to learn on your own.

1. Click the *Microsoft Publisher Help* tool on the Standard Toolbar.

2. Click the *Index* tab at the top of window.
3. Type word in the *Type keywords* box.

The word appears in bottom section of window.

4. Click *Search*.

In the right section of the *Help* window you can choose from a list of topics as in the illustration below.

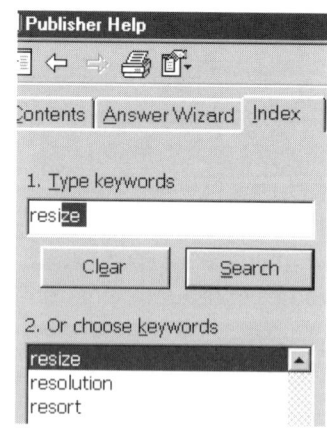

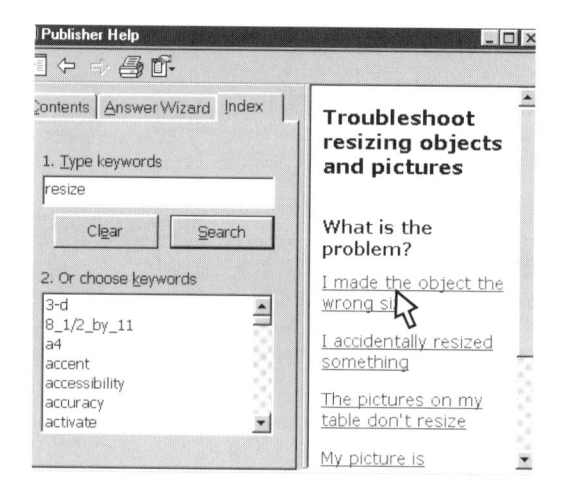

5. Click the topic in the right of the window.

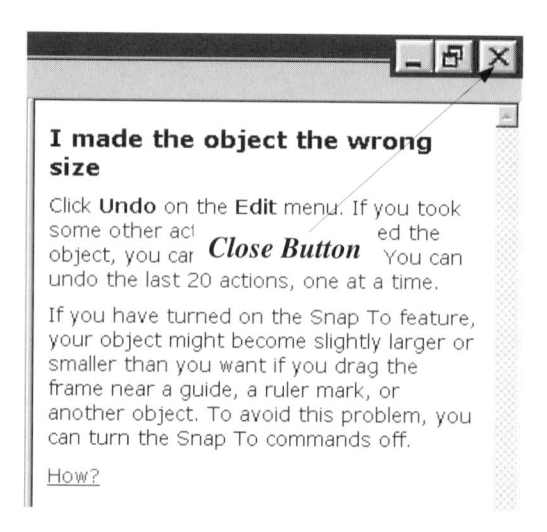

Use the scroll bar to see more of the help.

6. Click the *Close* button to exit *Help*.

Page 14   *Desktop Publishing Made Easy*

CHAPTER 3

DESIGNING A FORM

Designing a Form   Chapter 3

SETTING MARGINS

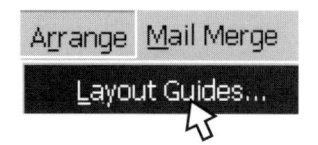

A margin is the space from the edge of the page to the area designated to contain the document.

1. Click **Arrange** on the Menu Bar.
2. Click **Layout Guides**.

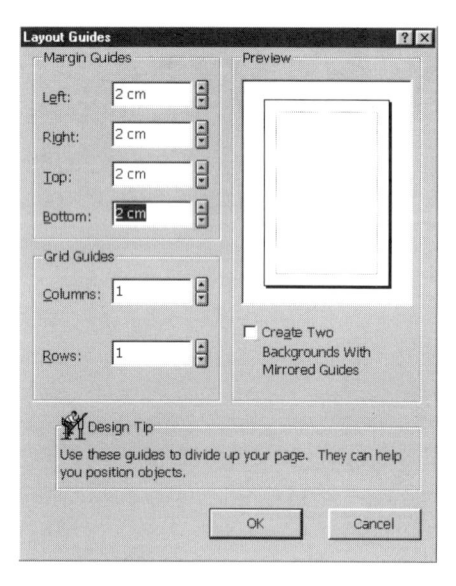

In the window that appears

3. Change the margins in the **Margin Guides** section if necessary. This can be done by clicking the up or down arrow beside each **Margin Guide** box or by clicking in the **Margin Guide** box and typing in the value.
4. Click **OK**.

Another way of stepping from box to box is by pressing the TAB key on the keyboard.

CREATING A TABLE

1. Click the **Table Frame** tool from the Tool Palette, which is situated on the left side of the screen.

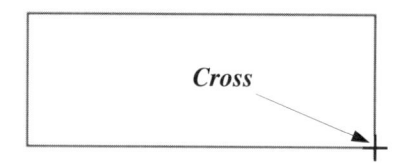

2. Bring the mouse pointer over onto the page.
3. When the pointer changes to a cross, drag over and down to create a table frame.

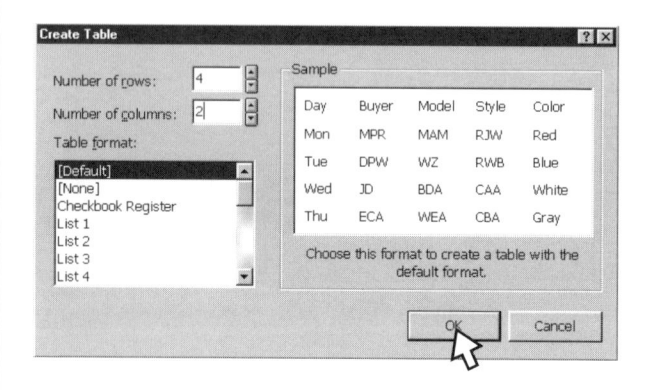

4. Insert a value in each of the **Number of rows** and **Number of columns** boxes.
5. Click **OK**.

A table with the specified number of columns and rows is created in the frame.

If the frame you created is too small to hold the required number of rows and columns, you will be invited to resize up the frame. Click **Yes**.

HIGHLIGHTING CELLS

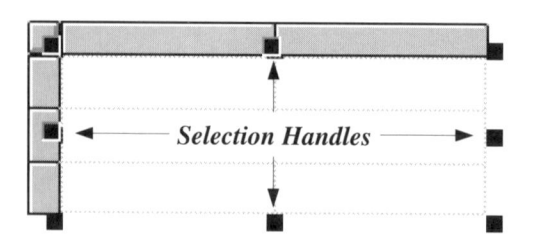

Before a table can be worked on it must first be selected. To select a table or any object:

1. Click on it.

Selection handles can be seen around it.

Page 16   Desktop Publishing Made Easy

Chapter 3   Designing a Form

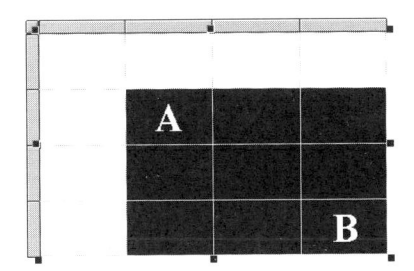

There are 2 ways of highlighting cells within a table:

2. Drag over and down from cell **A** to cell **B**. Release the mouse button.

or

2. Click in cell **A**, then with the SHIFT key on the keyboard pressed click in cell **B**.

HIGHLIGHTING COLUMN(S)/ROW(S)

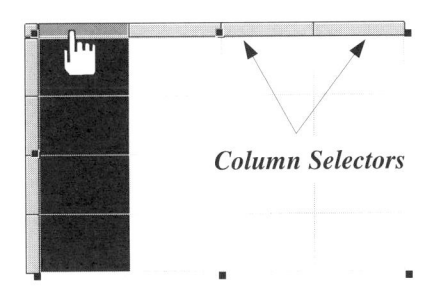

Column Selectors

To highlight a column:

1. Click the *column selector* (grey area) when the mouse pointer changes to a pointing finger.

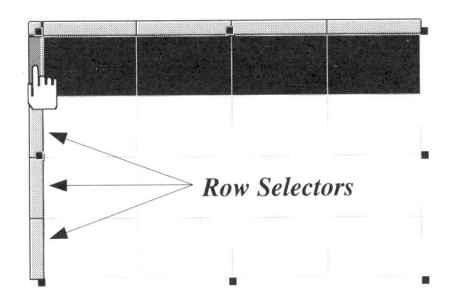

Row Selectors

To highlight a row:

2. Click the *row selector* (grey area) when the mouse pointer changes to a pointing finger.

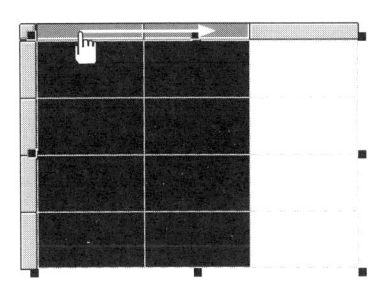

To highlight multiple columns or rows:

3. Drag across the *column selectors* or down the *row selectors* when the mouse pointer changes to a pointing finger.

HIGHLIGHTING A TABLE

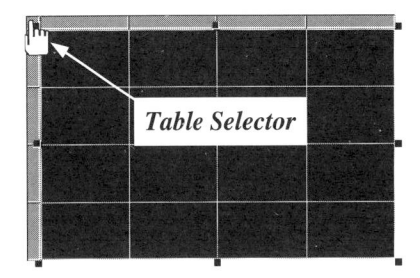

Table Selector

To highlight all the cells of a table:

1. Click the *table selector* (top left corner grey area) when the mouse pointer changes to a pointing finger.

HIGHLIGHTING ONE CELL

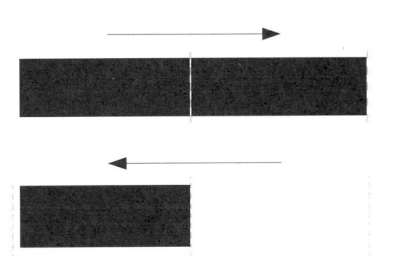

To highlight one cell:

1. Drag from the first cell over to an adjoining cell and then back to the first cell.

Using Microsoft Publisher   Page 17

Designing a Form   *Chapter 3*

ADDING A BORDER TO A TABLE

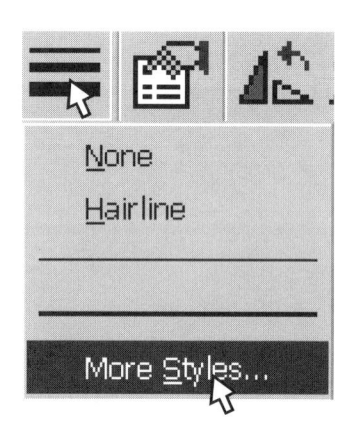

1. Highlight all the cells of the table.
2. Click the *Line/Border Style* tool from the Formatting Toolbar.
3. Click *More Styles*.

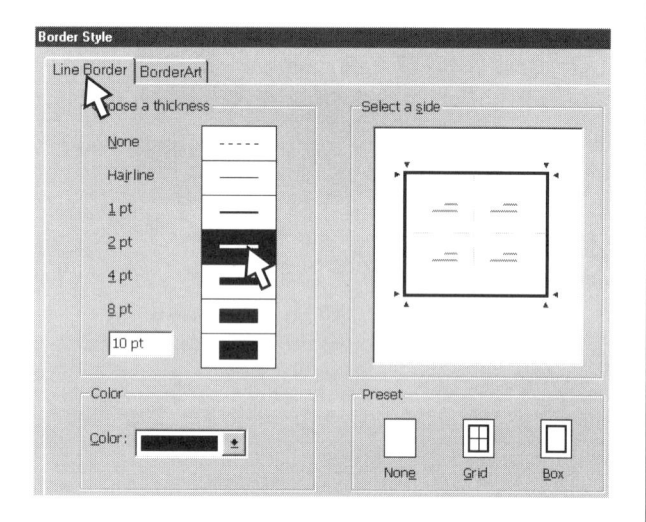

4. Click the *Line Border* tab.
5. Choose a point thickness box from the *Choose a thickness* section.
6. Click *OK* or *Apply*.

See the result below.

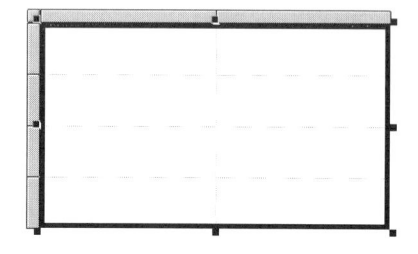

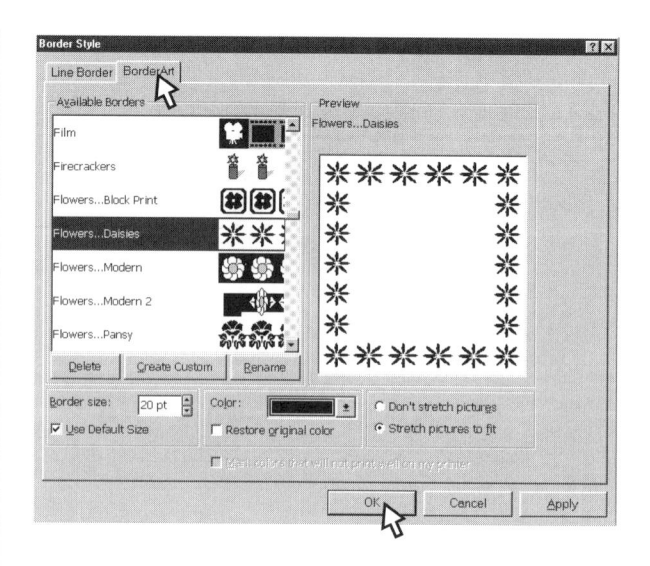

If you want a fancy border around the table:

7. Click the *BorderArt* tab.
8. Choose a border from the *Available Borders* section.
9. Choose a border size from the *Border size* box.
10. Click *OK* or *Apply*.

See the result below.

ADDING A BORDER TO A CELL

1. *Click* in the cell to select it.
2. Click the *Line/Border Style* tool from the Formatting Toolbar.
3. Click *More Styles*.
4. Click the *Line Border* tab.
5. Choose a point thickness box from the *Choose a thickness* section.
6. Click *OK* or *Apply*.

Chapter 3 — Designing a Form

ADDING A BORDER TO A RANGE OF CELLS

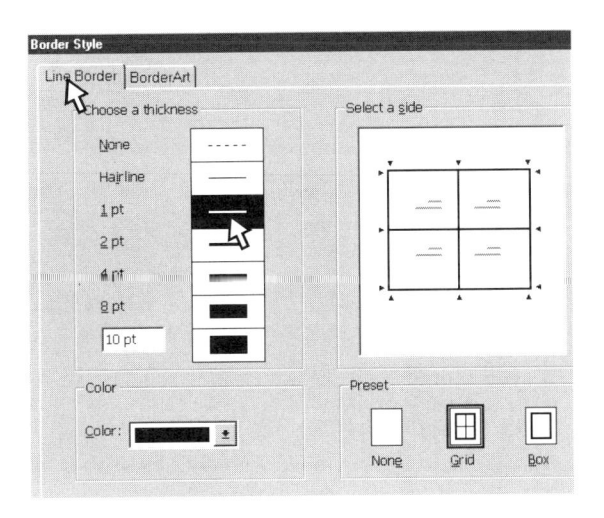

To add a border to a range of cells or to all the cells of a table:

1. Highlight the range of cells or the table.
2. Click the *Line/Border Style* tool from the Formatting Toolbar.
3. Click *More Styles*.
4. With the *Line Border* tab clicked, click the *Grid* box from the *Preset* section.
5. Choose a point thickness box from the *Choose a thickness* section.
6. Click *OK* or *Apply*.

Not only is there an outside border to the selected cells or table, but every selected cell has its own individual border.

See the result below.

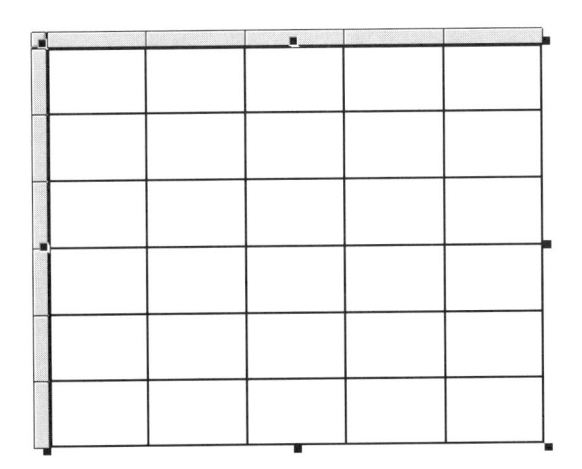

BORDERS OF DIFFERENT THICKNESS

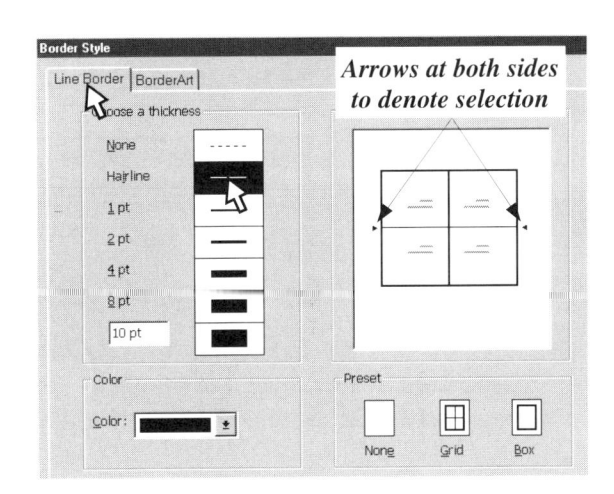

To add a 1 point outside border, 1 point vertical borders and hairline horizontal borders to a table:

1. Highlight the cells or the table.
2. Click the *Line/Border Style* tool from the Formatting Toolbar and click *More Styles*.
3. With the *Line Border* tab clicked, click the *Grid* box from the *Preset* section.
4. Click the *1 pt* thickness box from the *Choose a thickness* section.

This give a 1 pt thickness to all borders.

5. In the *Select a side* box click the horizontal middle line. You will now see an arrow at both sides of this line as in the illustration above.
6. Click the *Hairline* thickness box from the *Choose a thickness* section.
7. Click *OK* or *Apply*.

See the result below.

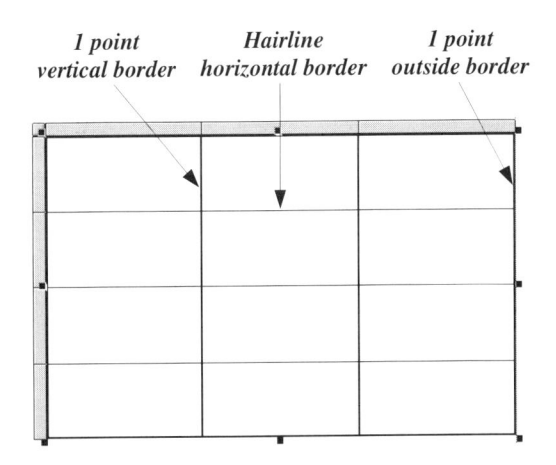

1 point vertical border   *Hairline horizontal border*   *1 point outside border*

Using Microsoft Publisher — Page 19

Designing a Form   Chapter 3

DELETING BORDERS

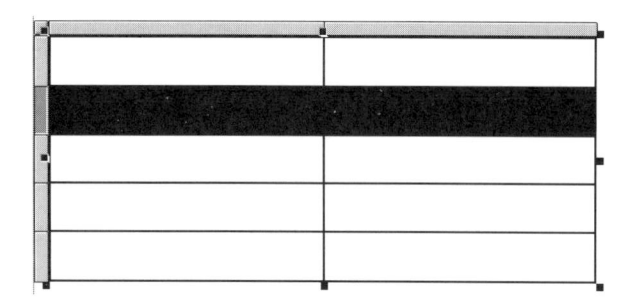

To delete the vertical borders from a row of cells:

1. Highlight the row by clicking the row selector.
2. Click the **Line/Border Style** tool from the Formatting Toolbar and click **More Styles**.

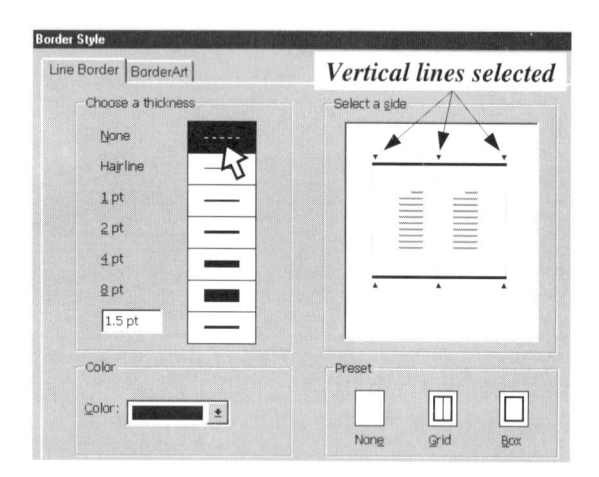

3. In the **Select a side** box click on any of the vertical lines. You will now see an arrow at both sides of this line.
4. While pressing SHIFT click on each of the other 2 vertical lines. Now the 3 vertical lines have been selected.
5. Choose **None** from the **Choose a thickness** section.
6. Click **OK** or **Apply**.

See the result below.

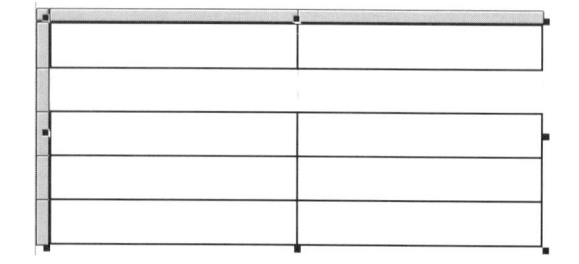

RESIZING A TABLE

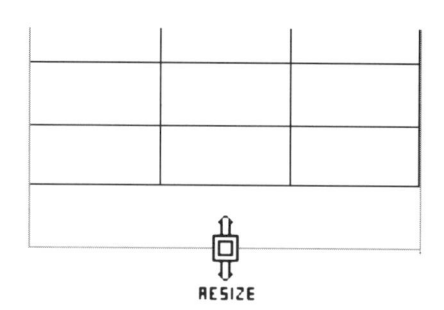

When you create a table, you may have to resize it to suit your needs.

To resize a table:

1. Click the table to select it.
2. Move the mouse pointer over any selection handle until it changes to **RESIZE**.
3. Drag to resize.

ADJUSTING ROWS AND COLUMNS

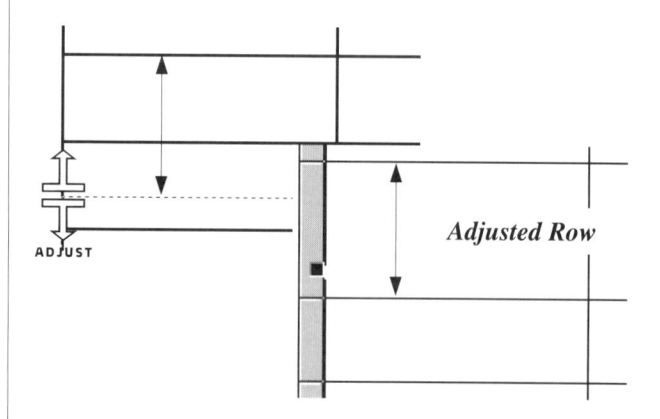

1. To adjust a row or column, first select the table by clicking on it.
2. Place the mouse pointer on the row selector between the row to be adjusted and the row beneath it <u>or</u> on the column selector between the column to be adjusted and the column to its right.
3. When the mouse pointer changes to **ADJUST** drag up or down for the row <u>or</u> over or back for the column.

Page 20   Desktop Publishing Made Easy

Chapter 3   Designing a Form

ADJUSTING MULTIPLE ROWS AND COLUMNS

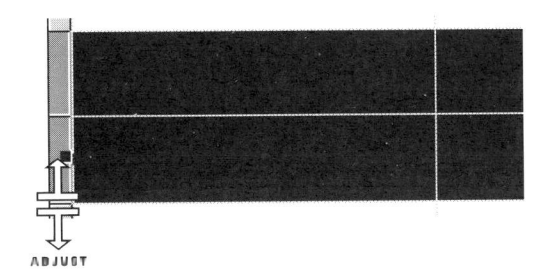

1. To adjust multiple rows or columns first highlight the rows or the columns.
2. Place the mouse pointer on the row selector between the bottom row to be adjusted and the row beneath it or on the column selector between the right column to be adjusted and the column to its right.
3. When the mouse pointer changes to *ADJUST* drag up or down for the rows or over or back for the columns.

See the result below.

SHADING CELL(S)

1. To shade one cell, click inside it.
2. To shade more than one cell, highlight them.

3. Click the *Fill Color* tool from the Formatting Toolbar.
4. Choose a colour from the available list.
5. To choose a different colour click *More Colors*.
6. Click the *Basic colors* or the *All colors* radio button.
7. Choose a colour.
8. Click *OK*.

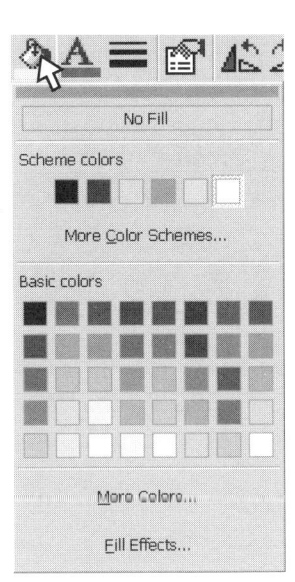

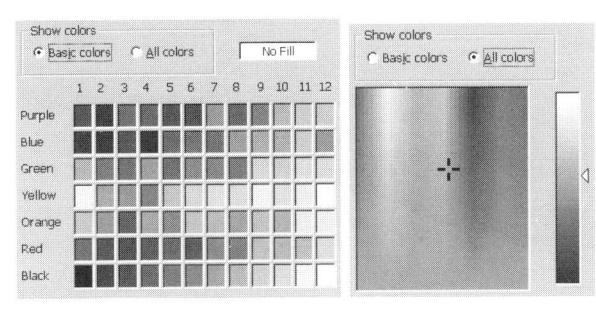

Basic colors   *All colors*

To shade cell(s) lightly, choose a percentage fill of that colour.

To make cell(s) transparent, choose a transparent fill.

9. To choose a percentage fill click *Fill Effects*.
10. From the *Style* section click the *Tints/Shades* button.
11. Choose a colour from the *Base color* box.
12. In the box containing the different percentage fills of the base colour scroll across until you have found a suitable fill and click it.
13. Click *OK*.
14. To choose a transparent fill click *No Fill*.

Using Microsoft Publisher   Page 21

Designing a Form   *Chapter 3*

15. From the *Style* section you could also have clicked the *Patterns* or *Gradients* button.
16. Choose a colour from the *Base color* and *Color 2* box.
17. Click *OK*.

A *Class 1A*

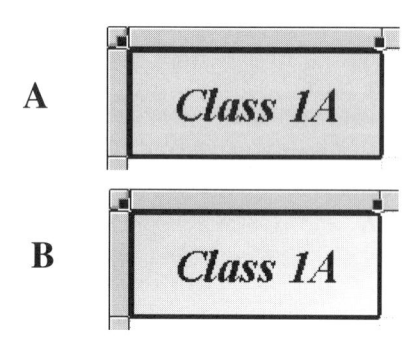

B *Class 1A*

Above are examples of different fills.

A = 20% of Black
B = *Gradients* (*Base color* is 20% Black, *Color 2* is White.

MERGING AND SPLITTING CELLS

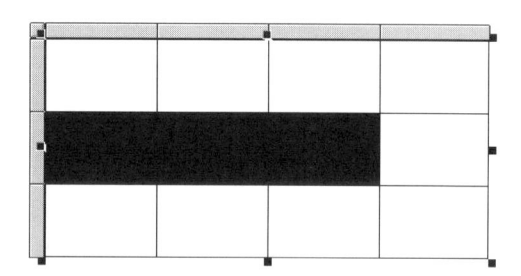

Merging cells means joining the cells together to make one larger cell. This allows more text to fit in them.

Widening or deepening the cells, by adjusting the columns or rows, will also allow more text to fit in them, but all the cells in the columns or rows are then adjusted.

Merging cells only affects the cells being merged.

To merge cells:

1. Highlight them. 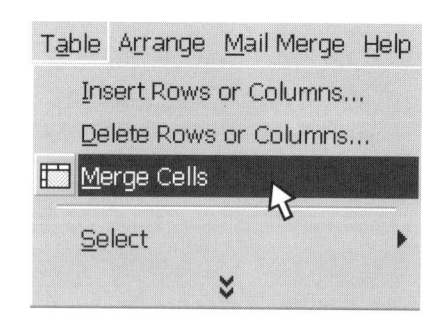
2. Click *Table* on the Menu Bar.
3. Click *Merge Cells*.

See the result below.

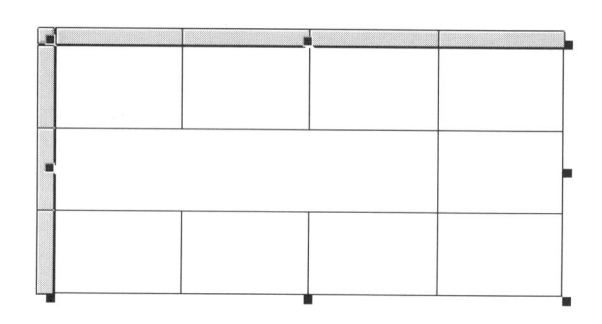

4. To split cells, highlight the merged cells.
5. Click *Table* on the Menu Bar.
6. Click *Split Cells*.

Splitting cells reverses the merging.

MOVING A TABLE FRAME

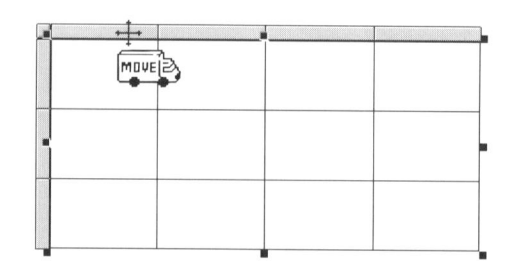

1. Select the table by clicking it.
2. Place the mouse pointer at any edge of the table and away from the selection handles.
3. When the pointer changes to *MOVE* drag to move.

If you place the mouse pointer inside the table you may affect the text rather than the frame.

Chapter 3   *Designing a Form*

ADDING ROWS AND COLUMNS

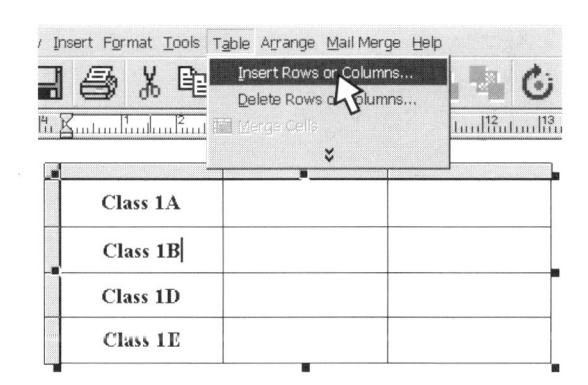

If you haven't created enough rows or columns, you can add some later.

To add a row or column:

1. In the table click any cell after which you want to add a row or column.
2. Click **Table** on the Menu Bar.
3. Click **Insert Rows or Columns**.

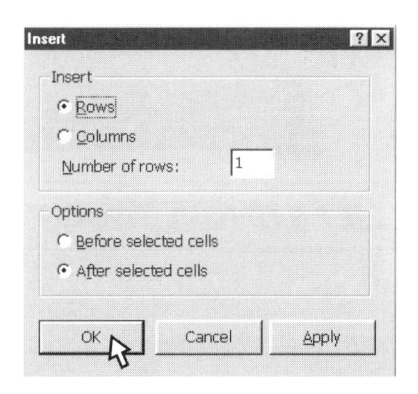

4. In the **Insert** window click either the **Rows** or the **Columns** radio button.
5. In the **Options** section click **After selected cells**.
6. Click **OK**.

In the example above one new row will be inserted after the selected cell.

See the result below.

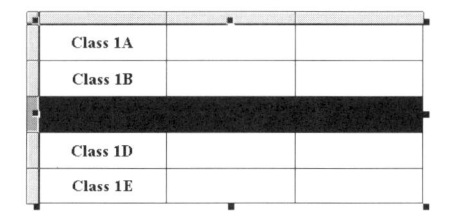

DELETING ROWS AND COLUMNS

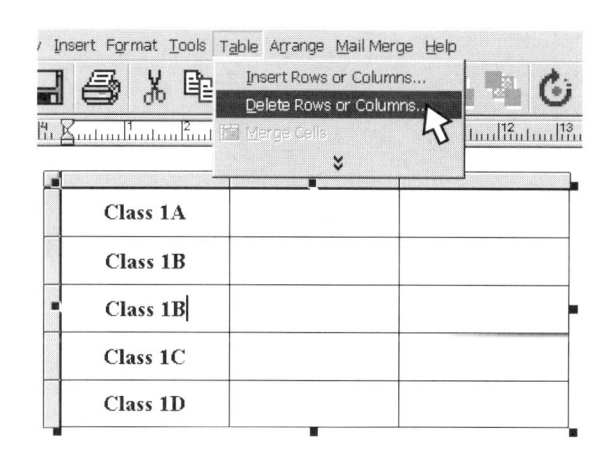

If you created too many rows or columns, you can delete some later.

To delete a row or column:

1. Click in any cell of the row or column which you want to delete.
2. Click **Table** on the Menu Bar.
3. Click **Delete Rows or Columns**.

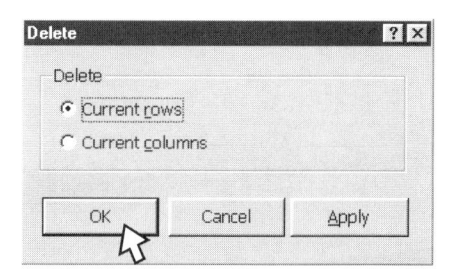

4. In the **Delete** section click either **Current rows** or **Current columns**.
5. Click **OK** or **Apply**.

In the example above the current row (3rd row) will be deleted.

See the result below.

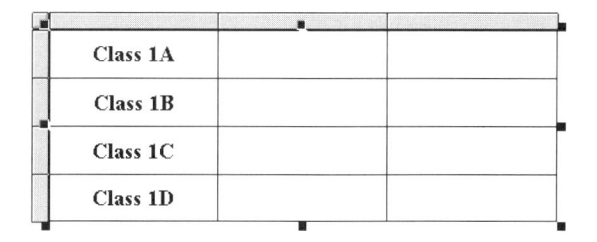

Using Microsoft Publisher   Page 23

INSERTING TEXT INTO CELLS

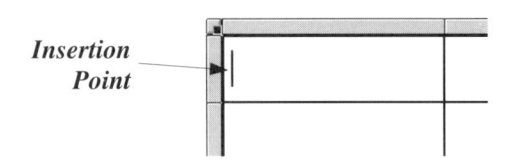

Insertion Point

1. Click inside the cell into which you want to enter the text.

The insertion point blinks, waiting for you to insert the text.

2. Insert the text by pressing the keyboard keys.

HIGHLIGHTING TEXT IN A CELL

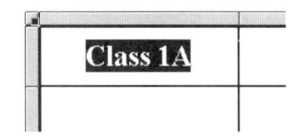

There are 2 methods of highlighting a block of text in a cell:

1. Starting at one side, drag across the text.
2. Click before the start of the text and then while pressing SHIFT click after the end of the text.

DELETING TEXT IN A CELL

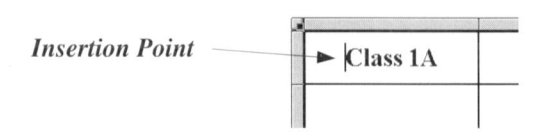

Insertion Point — Class 1A

There are 3 ways of deleting text:

1. Place the insertion point immediately before the text to be deleted.
2. Press the DELETE key on the keyboard for each character (letter, number, space etc.) to be deleted.

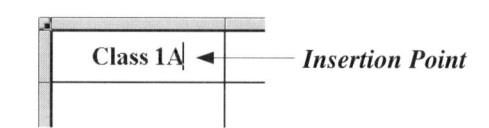

Class 1A — *Insertion Point*

or

1. Place the insertion point immediately after the text to be deleted.
2. Press the BACKSPACE key on the keyboard for each character (letter, number, space etc.) to be deleted.

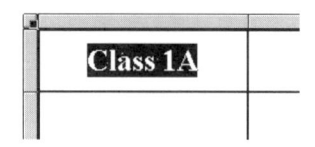

or

1. Highlight the text to be deleted by dragging over it.
2. Press the DELETE key on the keyboard or click the *Cut* tool on the Standard Toolbar.

Cut

DELETING A TABLE

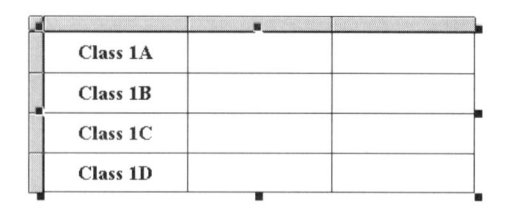

Class 1A		
Class 1B		
Class 1C		
Class 1D		

1. Click the table to select it.
2. Click the *Cut* tool on the Standard Toolbar.

If there is no text in the table when selecting it, pressing the DELETE key on the keyboard will delete the frame.

If you delete all the text in the table by pressing the DELETE key, then continuing to press the DELETE key will not delete the table. To delete the table click the *Cut* tool on the Standard Toolbar or click away from the table, select it again and then press the DELETE key.

Chapter 3 *Designing a Form*

CHANGING CELL PROPERTIES

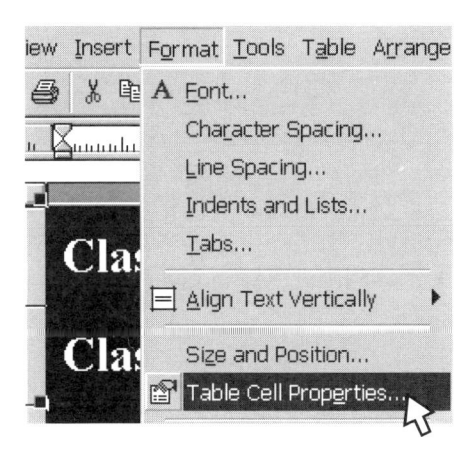

Text does not look well if it touches the border of a cell. You can set a specific space between the text and the cell's border by changing the margins in the *Table Cell Properties* window.

To do this:

1. Click in the cell or highlight the cells whose properties are to be changed.
2. Click *Format* on the Menu Bar.
3. Click *Table Cell Properties*.

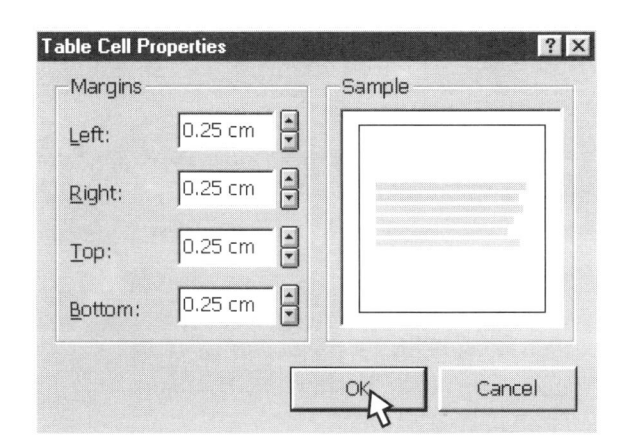

4. Change the margins in the *Margins* section. This moves the cell contents the set distance away from the edges of the cells.
5. Click *OK*.

The default setting in Microsoft Publisher is a margin of 0.1 cm. all around.

ALIGNING TEXT VERTICALLY

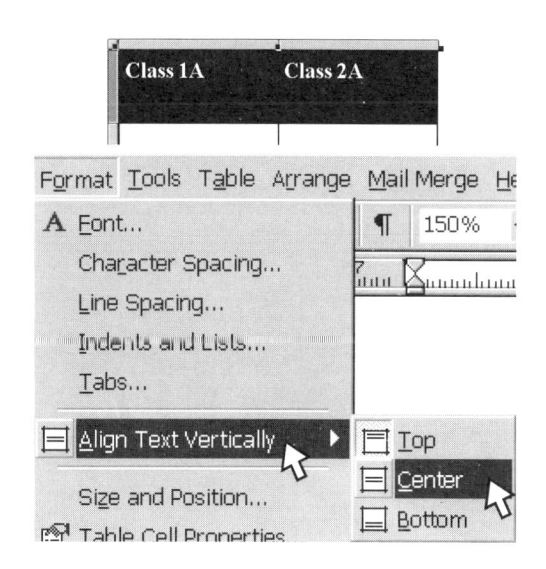

1. Click in the cell or highlight the cells.
2. Click *Format* on the Menu Bar.
3. Click *Align Text Vertically*.
4. Click whichever alignment you want. *Centre* is chosen above.

See the result below.

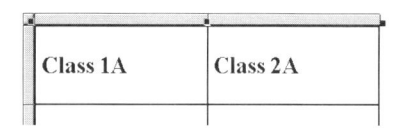

ALIGNING TEXT HORIZONTALLY

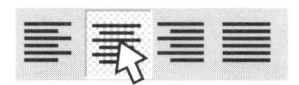

1. Click on text or highlight cell or cells or table.
2. Click the *Align Left*, or *Centre* or *Align Right* or *Justify* tools on the Formatting Toolbar.

Align Centre is chosen below.

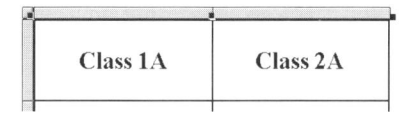

Using Microsoft Publisher

COPYING AND MOVING TEXT

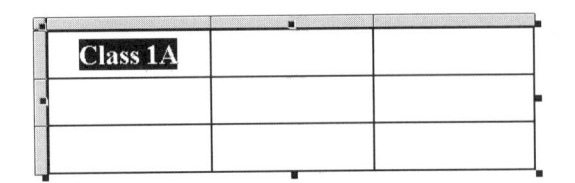

1. To copy text from one cell to another first drag across the text to highlight it.
2. Click **Copy** from the Standard Toolbar.

3. Place the insertion point in the cell into which you want to copy the text.
4. Click **Paste** from the Standard Toolbar.

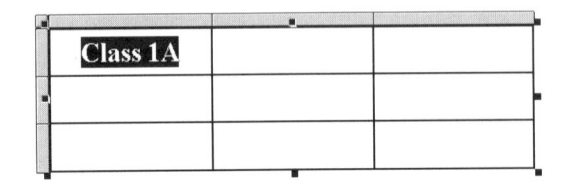

1. To move text from one cell to another first highlight the text.
2. Click **Cut** from the Standard Toolbar.

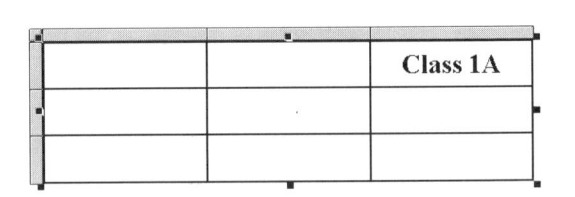

3. Place the insertion point in the cell into which you want to move the text.
4. Click **Paste** from the Standard Toolbar.

BOLD/ITALIC/UNDERLINE

Text can be emboldened or underlined or made italic to emphasise it.

To do it:

1. Highlight the text by dragging across it or highlight the cell or cells or table.
2. Choose **B** for bold, *I* for *italic* or <u>U</u> for underline on the Formatting Toolbar.

See the result below.

Click **B** or *I* or <u>U</u> again to remove the formatting.

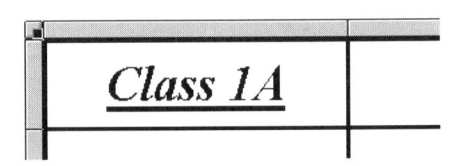

CHANGING A FONT IN A CELL

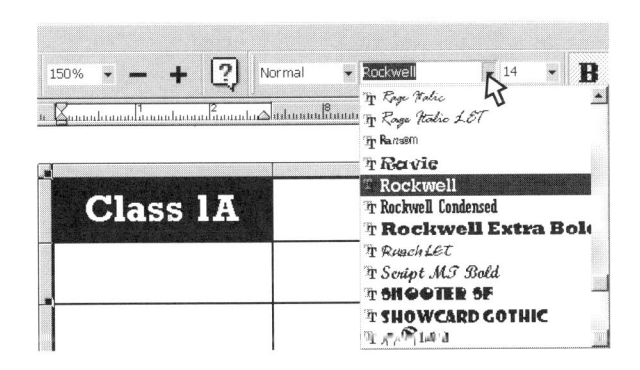

1. Highlight the text or cell or cells or table.
2. Click the **Font Box** on the Formatting Toolbar.
3. Choose a different font.

CHANGING THE FONT SIZE

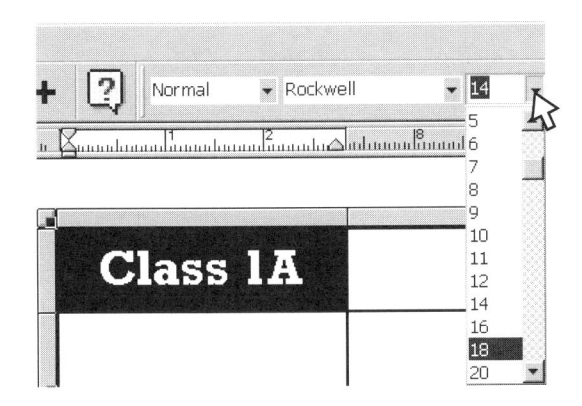

A font size is measured in *points*. Chapter 10 of this book explains all about fonts.

To change the font size:

1. Highlight the text or cell or cells or table.
2. Click the **Font Size** Box on the Formatting Toolbar.
3. Click a different font size.
4. You can choose a size which isn't available on the list by typing a number in the **Font Size** box and then pressing ENTER.

FORMAT PAINTING TEXT

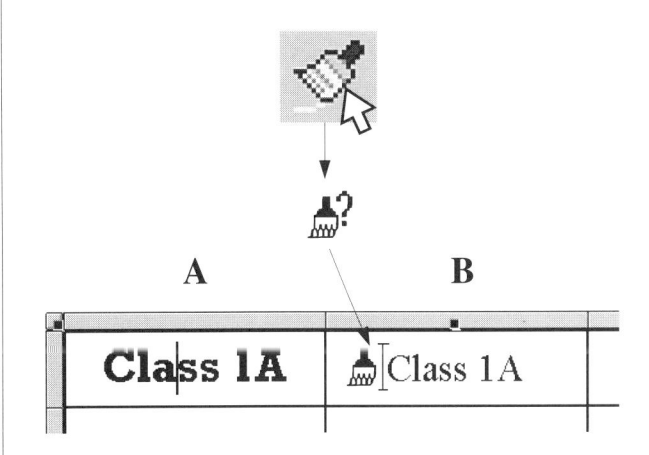

To format paint is to copy the formatting of text, a cell, or an object onto other text, cells or objects. This is handy for changing text formatting if there is a lot of text to be formatted in the same style.

To format paint contents of cell A to cell B above:

1. Click anywhere on the text in cell A.
2. Click the **Format Painter** tool on the Standard Toolbar.

The mouse pointer changes to a brush with a question mark to its right (see above).

3. Move this brush before the text to be format painted until it changes to a brush with an I-beam pointer (see above).
4. Drag across the text in cell B.

See the result below.

Once the format painting of the first block of text is done, you will have to click the **Format Painter** tool before you can format paint again.

Double-clicking the **Format Painter** tool will allow you to format paint as many blocks of text as you wish. To disable format paint when you're finished, click the **Format Painter** tool again.

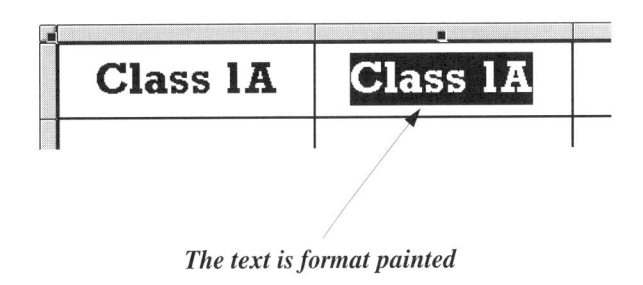

The text is format painted

Designing a Form   Chapter 3

FORMAT PAINTING A CELL

If you *format paint* cells, not only is the text formatting copied from one cell to another, but the cell formatting is also copied, e.g. cell borders, table cell properties, shading etc.

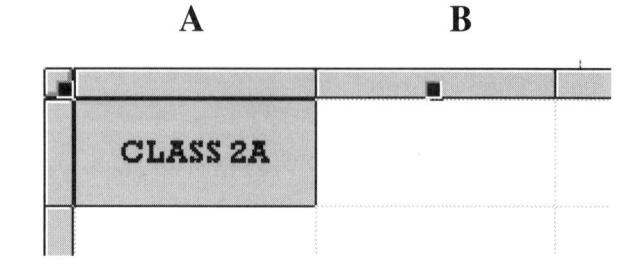

A   B

CLASS 2A

I have shaded cell A, given it a 1 pt border, changed the font style and centred it vertically and horizontally. Cell B has the default properties.

To format paint the properties of cell A to cell B:

1. Click in cell A.
2. Click the *Format Painter* tool from the Standard Toolbar.
3. Click in cell B.

See the result below.

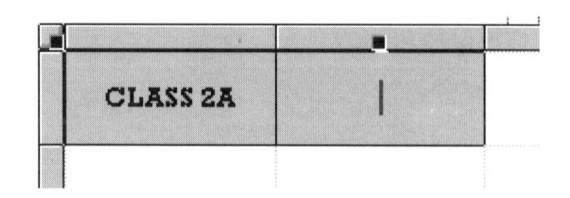

CLASS 2A

All of cell A's properties have been transferred to cell B. The insertion point is blinking, inviting you to type text with the new text formatting.

If there had been more than one word in cell B you would have had to drag across all the text to give it the new text formatting.

SNAPPING TO GUIDES ETC.

Tools Table Arrange Mail Merg
   Spelling
   Language
   Snap to Ruler Marks
   Snap to Guides   Ctrl+W
   Snap to Objects

Snapping to Guides allows you to snap frames against margin and ruler guides. This is very convenient for the placement of objects on a page.

1. Click *Tools* on the Menu Bar.
2. If there is no '✓' before *Snap to Guides* then click it. It is now enabled.
3. To snap off, click when there is a '✓' before it. The '✓' disappears.

Snap to Ruler Marks and *Snap to Objects* can also be enabled.

CHANGING PAGE ORIENTATION

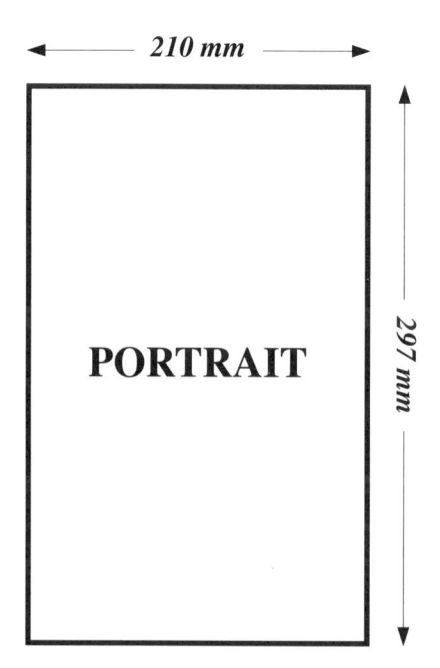

← 210 mm →

PORTRAIT

297 mm

The dimensions above represent an *A4* page with the narrowest side to the top. It is called *Portrait* orientation and is the default opening page in Microsoft Publisher.

Page 28   Desktop Publishing Made Easy

Chapter 3   Designing a Form

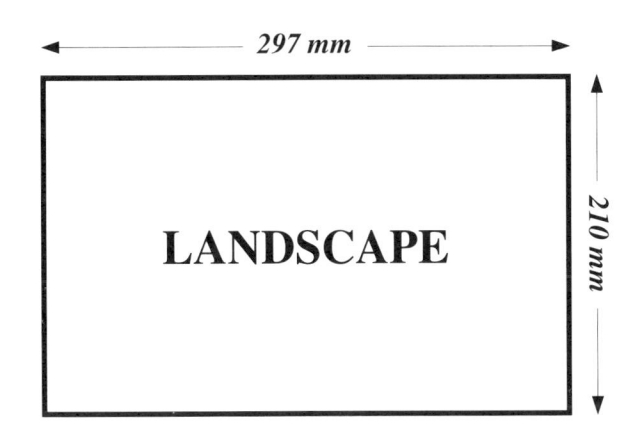

Page orientation can be changed from *Portrait* to *Landscape* to suit a publication you are creating. *Landscape* orientation is *Portrait* orientation turned on its side, with the widest side to the top.

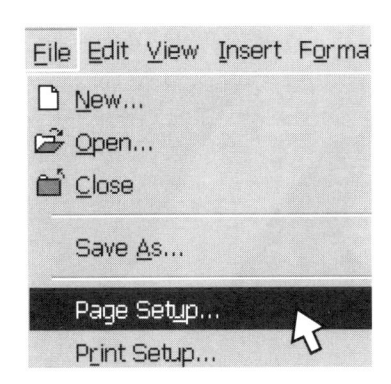

To change the orientation to *Landscape*:

1. Click *File* on the Menu Bar.
2. Click *Page Setup*.

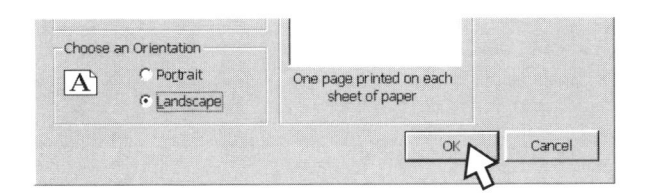

In the *Page Setup* window that appears:

3. Click the *Landscape* radio button.
4. Click *OK*.

The page is now *Landscape*. You will have to do more scrolling over and back rather than up and down to access your page.

SAVING A FILE

1. Click the *Save* tool on the Standard Toolbar.

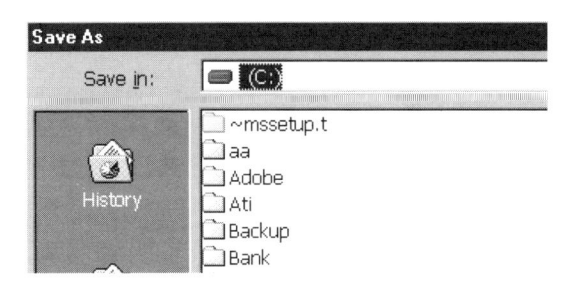

2. In the *Save in* box choose the drive in which you want to save the file. I've chosen Drive C in the illustration above.

3. Click the destination folder in the main part of window and click *Open*. It should now appear in the *Save in* box.
4. In the lower part of the window click in the *File name* box.
5. Type in the file name.
6. Click *Save*.

From now on no window will appear when you save this file by clicking the *Save* tool on the Standard Toolbar.

To change the file name or the destination folder, you must choose *Save As* from the *File* menu on the Menu Bar.

Using Microsoft Publisher   Page 29

Designing a Form   Chapter 3

OPENING A FILE

1. Click the *Open* tool on the Standard Toolbar.

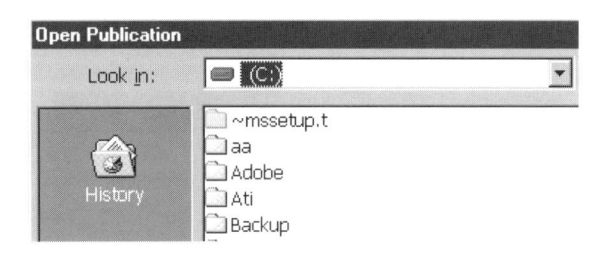

2. In the *Look in* box choose the drive which contains the folder.
3. In the main part of the window click the folder which contains the file.
4. Click *Open*.

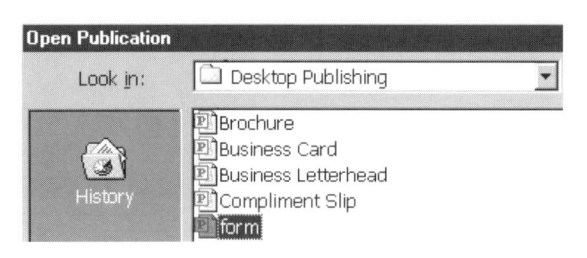

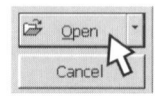

5. Click the appropriate file.
6. Click *Open*.

Another way to open a file:

If the file to be opened has been one of the last 4 worked on, then:

1. Click *File* from the Menu Bar.
2. If the file is listed in the bottom of the window, click to open it.

PRINTING

1. Click the *Print* tool on the Standard Toolbar.

Clicking the *Print* tool assumes that the proper printer has been set up for you and also assumes that you are printing the whole document – sometimes many pages.

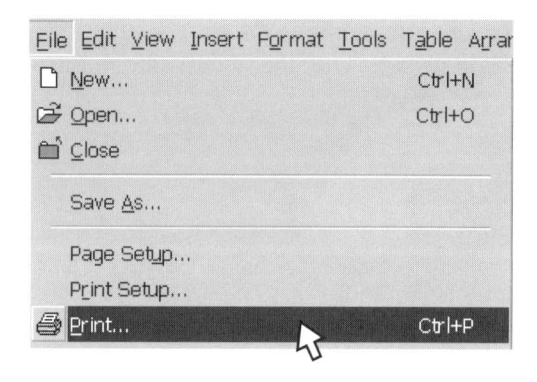

2. To have more control over your printing click *File* from the Menu Bar.
3. Click *Print*.

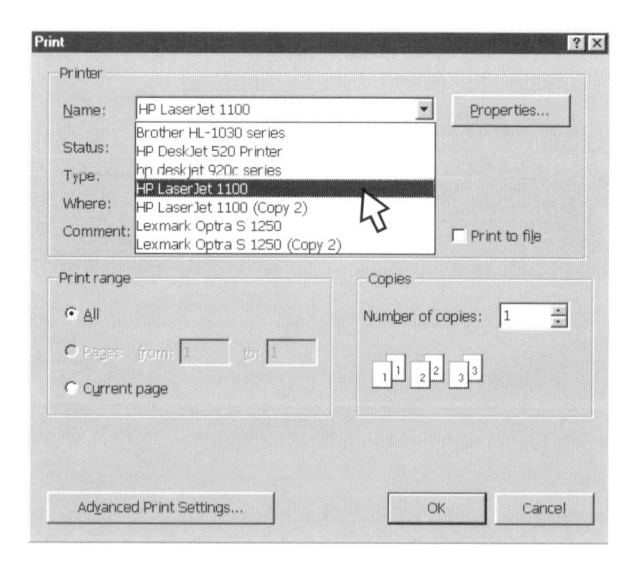

4. Clicking in the *Name* box enables you to choose another printer.
5. In the *Print range* section you can print the whole document by clicking *All*, a range of pages by clicking *Pages from* and the page you're working on by clicking *Current page*.

Page 30   Desktop Publishing Made Easy

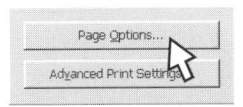

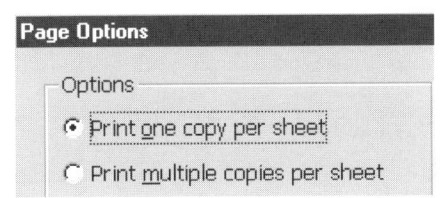

Chapter 3 — Designing a Form

If the electronic page being printed is less than half the size of the sheet in the printer, multiple copies may be printed on the one sheet.

To print only one copy per sheet:

6. Click the *Page Options* tab.
7. Click *Print one copy per sheet* to ensure only one copy will be printed per sheet.
8. Clicking *OK* will bring you back to the main *Print* window.

If the electronic page is smaller than the printer sheet you may want to print *crop marks* to show the exact limit of the page. We shall see more of this in later chapters. To enable crop marks:

9. Click the *Advanced Print Settings* in the main *Print* window.
10. Click the *Crop marks* box in the *Printer's marks* section.

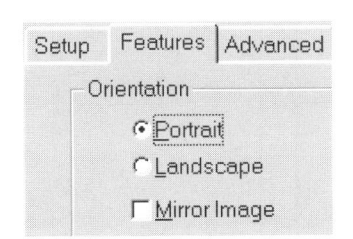

11. Click *Properties* in the *Print* window.
12. By clicking the various tabs in the top of the *Properties* window, you can choose either *Landscape* or *Portrait* orientation, *Paper Type*, *Paper Size* and *Print Quality*.

The appearance of the *Properties* window varies from printer to printer.

DESIGNING A FORM COMPLETION INSTRUCTIONS

See the illustration for *Exercise 3.1* on page 32 to help you with these instructions. I have numbered the rows and columns to facilitate the instructions.

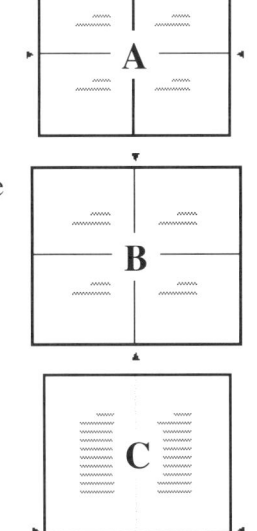

1. Change page orientation from *Portrait* to *Landscape*.
2. Save file as *Form*. Save regularly.
3. Set margins to 15 mm. all around.
4. Enable Snap to Guides.
5. Create a table covering size of the page with 23 rows and 22 columns.
6. If you need to resize the table to snap in against the margin guides, do so now.
7. Adjust rows 1 and 2 to allow for larger title and for the 2 boxed merged cells. This will increase the size of table.
8. Resize the table frame to snap back up against the bottom margin.
9. Highlight rows 5-21. Insert a 1 pt border around all these cells except the middle horizontal one, which is hairline. See *A* right.
10. Highlight the appropriate cells in columns 21-22. Change the 1 pt middle vertical border to hairline. Repeat this six more times to columns 9-10. See *B* right.
11. Highlight row 5 and change the bottom hairline border to 1 pt. See *C* right.
12. Merge the cells that are marked *Merge* in the illustration on page 32.
13. Give appropriate merged cells a 1 pt. border.
14. Shade appropriate cells – 10% fill of black.
15. Type text into appropriate cells.
16. Format text as appropriate.
17. Centre align text vertically.
18. Save.
19. Print.

Using Microsoft Publisher

EXERCISE 3.1

Create a table with 23 rows and 22 columns

All borders marked ☆ are hairline

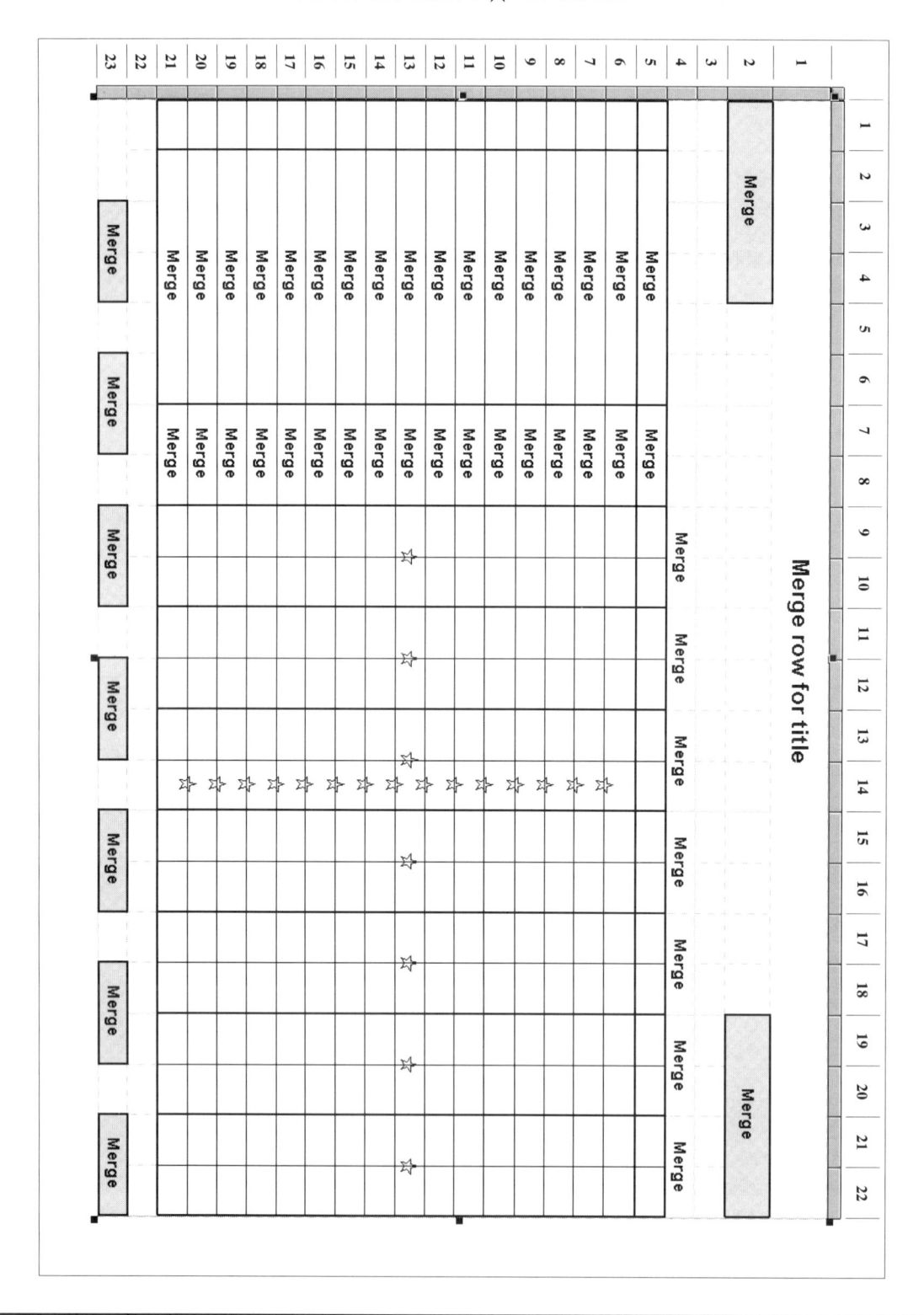

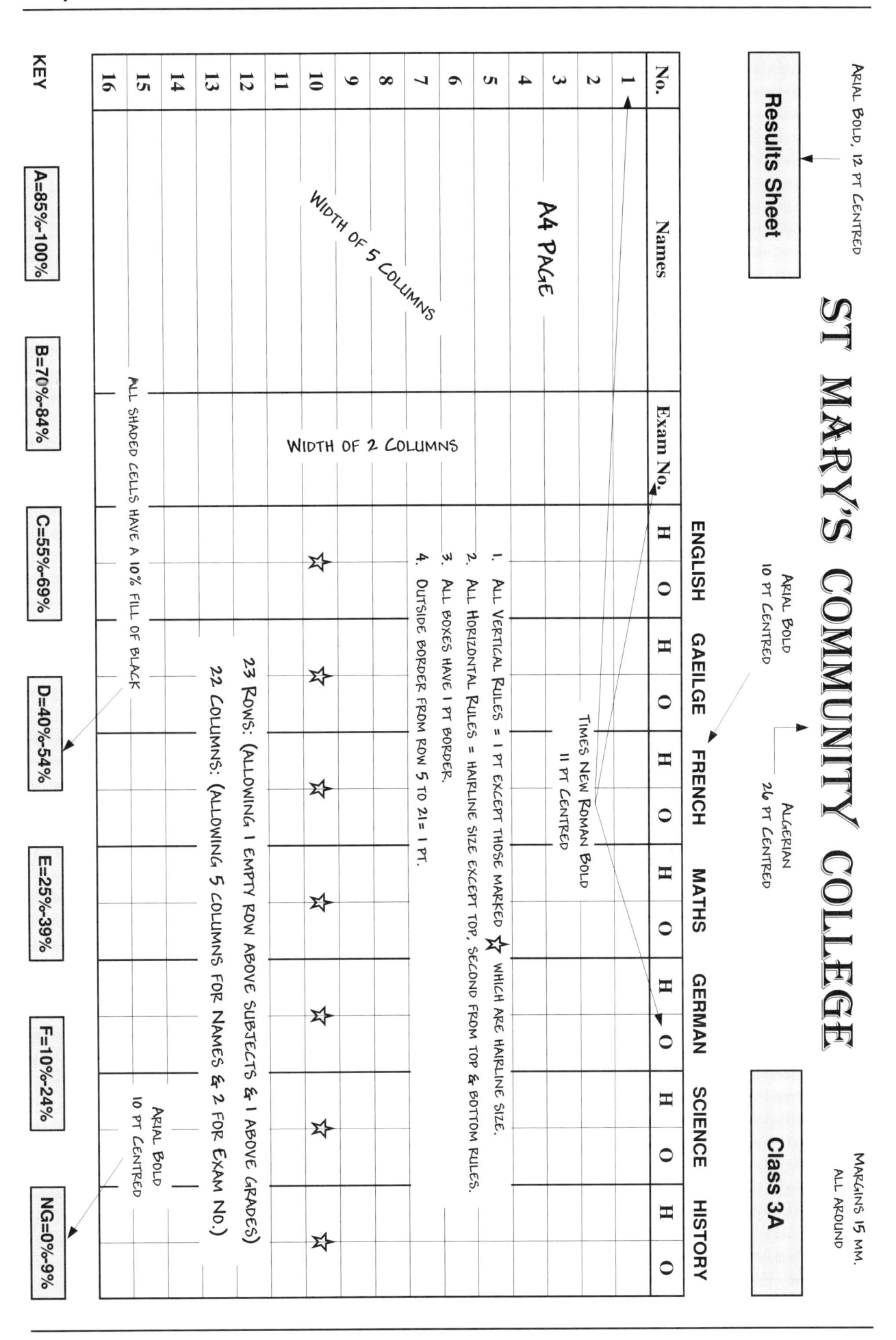

Chapter 3 *Designing a Form*

ARIAL BOLD, 12 PT CENTRED

Results Sheet

ST MARY'S COMMUNITY COLLEGE

ARIAL BOLD
10 PT CENTRED

ALGERIAN
26 PT CENTRED

Class 3A

MARGINS 15 MM.
ALL AROUND

No.	Names	Exam No.	ENGLISH		GAEILGE		FRENCH		MATHS		GERMAN		SCIENCE		HISTORY	
			H	O	H	O	H	O	H	O	H	O	H	O	H	O
1																
2																
3																
4																
5																
6																
7																
8																
9																
10			☆		☆		☆		☆		☆		☆		☆	
11																
12																
13																
14																
15																
16																

A4 PAGE

WIDTH OF 5 COLUMNS

WIDTH OF 2 COLUMNS

TIMES NEW ROMAN BOLD
11 PT CENTRED

1. ALL VERTICAL RULES = 1 PT EXCEPT THOSE MARKED ☆ WHICH ARE HAIRLINE SIZE.
2. ALL HORIZONTAL RULES = HAIRLINE SIZE EXCEPT TOP, SECOND FROM TOP & BOTTOM RULES.
3. ALL BOXES HAVE 1 PT BORDER.
4. OUTSIDE BORDER FROM ROW 5 TO 21 = 1 PT.

23 ROWS: (ALLOWING 1 EMPTY ROW ABOVE SUBJECTS & 1 ABOVE GRADES)
22 COLUMNS: (ALLOWING 5 COLUMNS FOR NAMES & 2 FOR EXAM NO.)

ARIAL BOLD
10 PT CENTRED

ALL SHADED CELLS HAVE A 10% FILL OF BLACK

KEY

| A=85%–100% | B=70%–84% | C=55%–69% | D=40%–54% | E=25%–39% | F=10%–24% | NG=0%–9% |

Using Microsoft Publisher Page 33

Exercise 3.2

Create a table with 26 rows and 6 columns

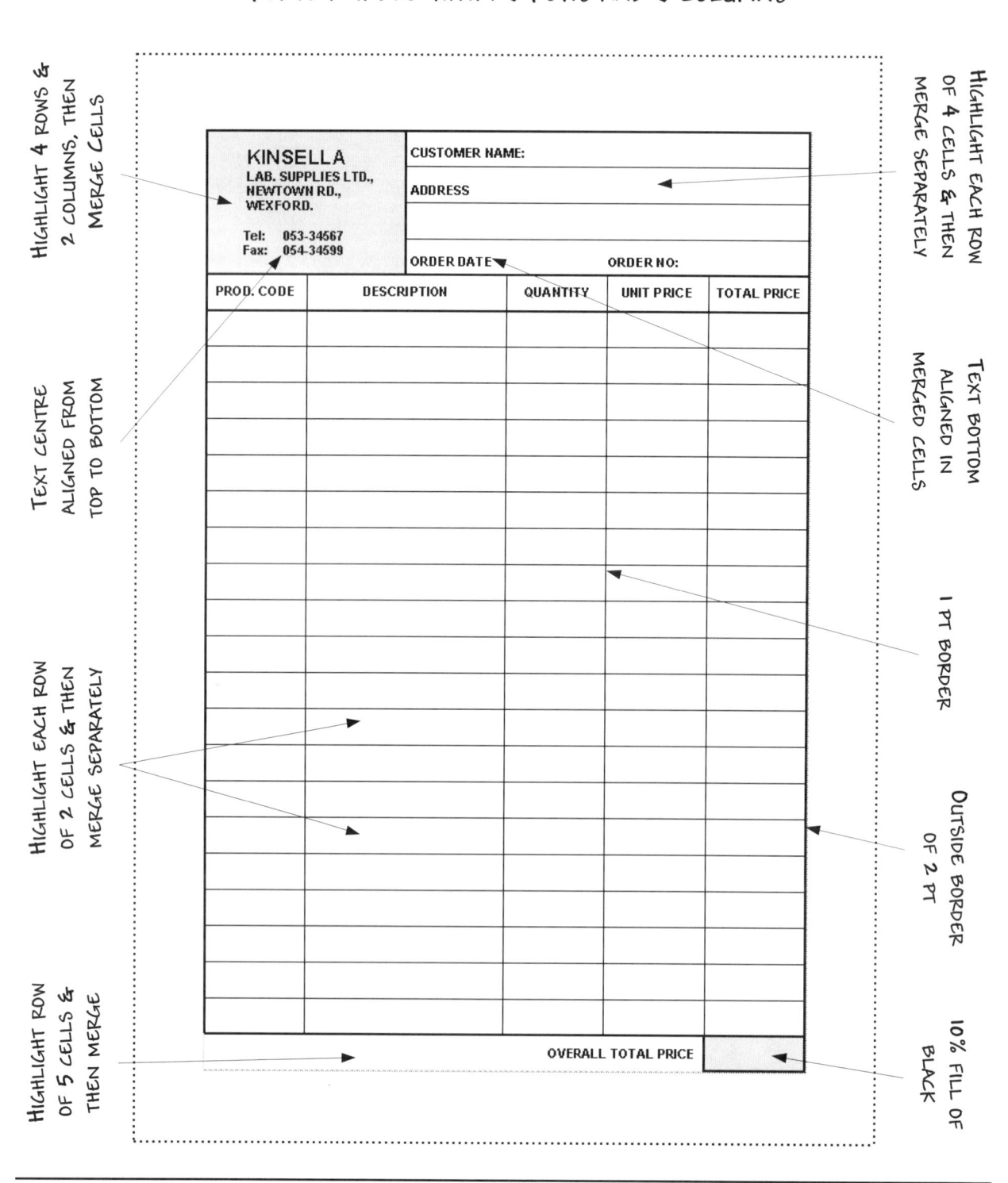

Highlight 4 rows & 2 columns, then merge cells

Highlight each row of 4 cells & then merge separately

KINSELLA
LAB. SUPPLIES LTD.,
NEWTOWN RD.,
WEXFORD.

Tel: 053-34567
Fax: 054-34599

CUSTOMER NAME:

ADDRESS

ORDER DATE   ORDER NO:

PROD. CODE	DESCRIPTION	QUANTITY	UNIT PRICE	TOTAL PRICE

Text centre aligned from top to bottom

Text bottom aligned in merged cells

1 pt border

Highlight each row of 2 cells & then merge separately

Outside border of 2 pt

Highlight row of 5 cells & then merge

OVERALL TOTAL PRICE

10% fill of black

Chapter 3 — Designing a Form

EXERCISE 3.3

CREATE A TABLE WITH 21 ROWS AND 9 COLUMNS

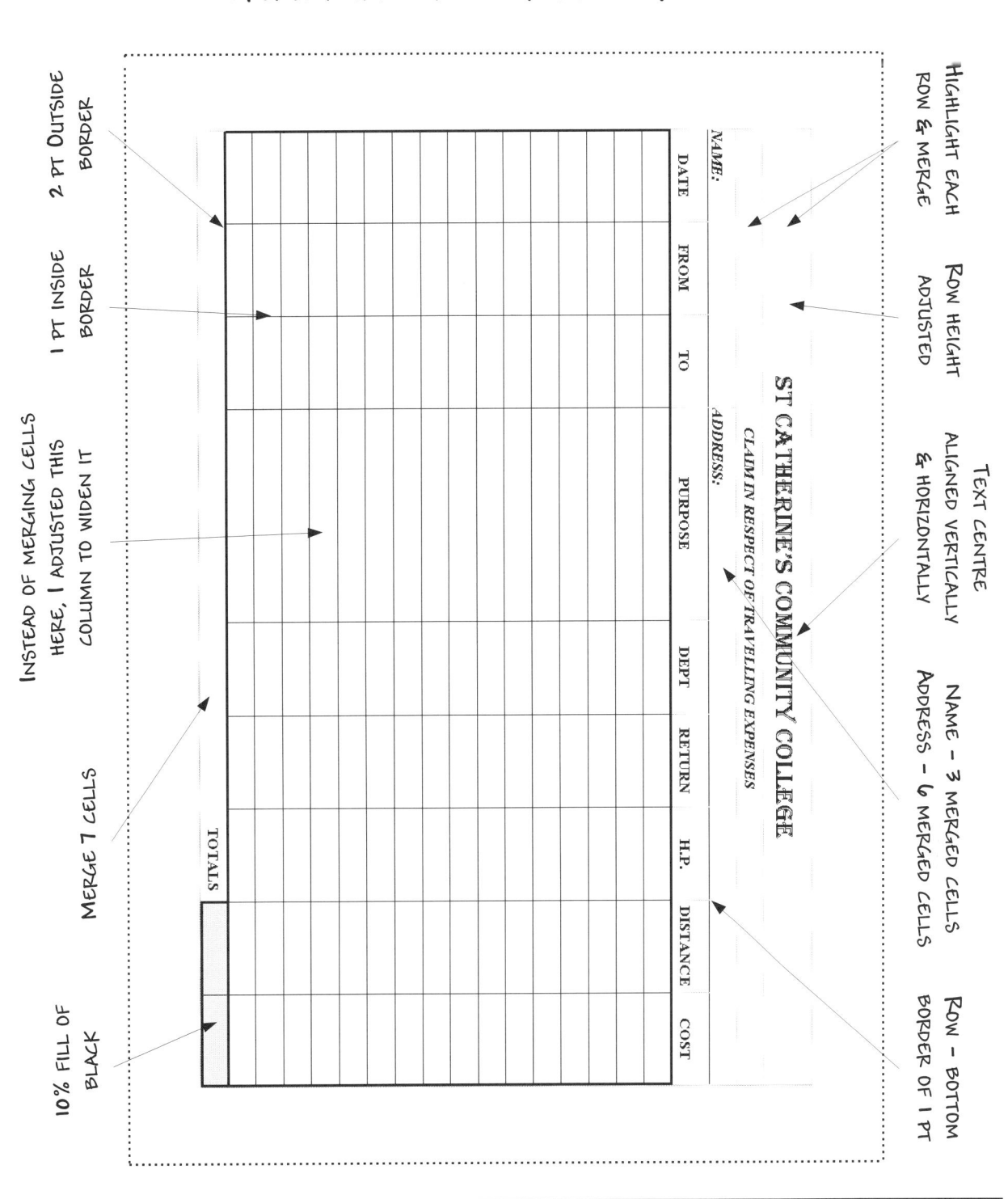

Annotations around the table:

- 2 PT OUTSIDE BORDER
- 1 PT INSIDE BORDER
- INSTEAD OF MERGING CELLS HERE, I ADJUSTED THIS COLUMN TO WIDEN IT
- MERGE 7 CELLS
- 10% FILL OF BLACK
- HIGHLIGHT EACH ROW & MERGE
- ROW HEIGHT ADJUSTED
- TEXT CENTRE ALIGNED VERTICALLY & HORIZONTALLY
- NAME – 3 MERGED CELLS
- ADDRESS – 6 MERGED CELLS
- ROW – BOTTOM BORDER OF 1 PT

Table headings: NAME: | DATE | FROM | TO | PURPOSE | DEPT | RETURN | H.P. | DISTANCE | COST

Title across table: ST CATHERINE'S COMMUNITY COLLEGE — *CLAIM IN RESPECT OF TRAVELLING EXPENSES*

ADDRESS:

TOTALS

Using Microsoft Publisher

IN CHAPTER 3 YOU HAVE DONE THE FOLLOWING:

- Set margins.
- Created tables.
- Highlighted cells, columns, rows and tables.
- Added borders to tables, cells and ranges of cells.
- Created borders of different thickness.
- Deleted borders.
- Resized tables.
- Adjusted rows and columns.
- Adjusted multiple rows and columns.
- Shaded cells.
- Merged and split cells.
- Moved table frames.
- Added rows and columns.
- Deleted rows and columns.
- Inserted text into cells.
- Highlighted text in cells.
- Deleted text.
- Deleted tables.
- Changed cell properties.
- Aligned text vertically.
- Aligned text horizontally.
- Copied text.
- Moved text.
- Made text bold, italic and underlined.
- Changed fonts.
- Changed font sizes.
- Format Painted text and cells.
- Snapped to guides, ruler marks and objects.
- Changed page orientation.
- Saved files.
- Opened files.
- Printed publications.

CHAPTER 4

DESIGNING A LOGO

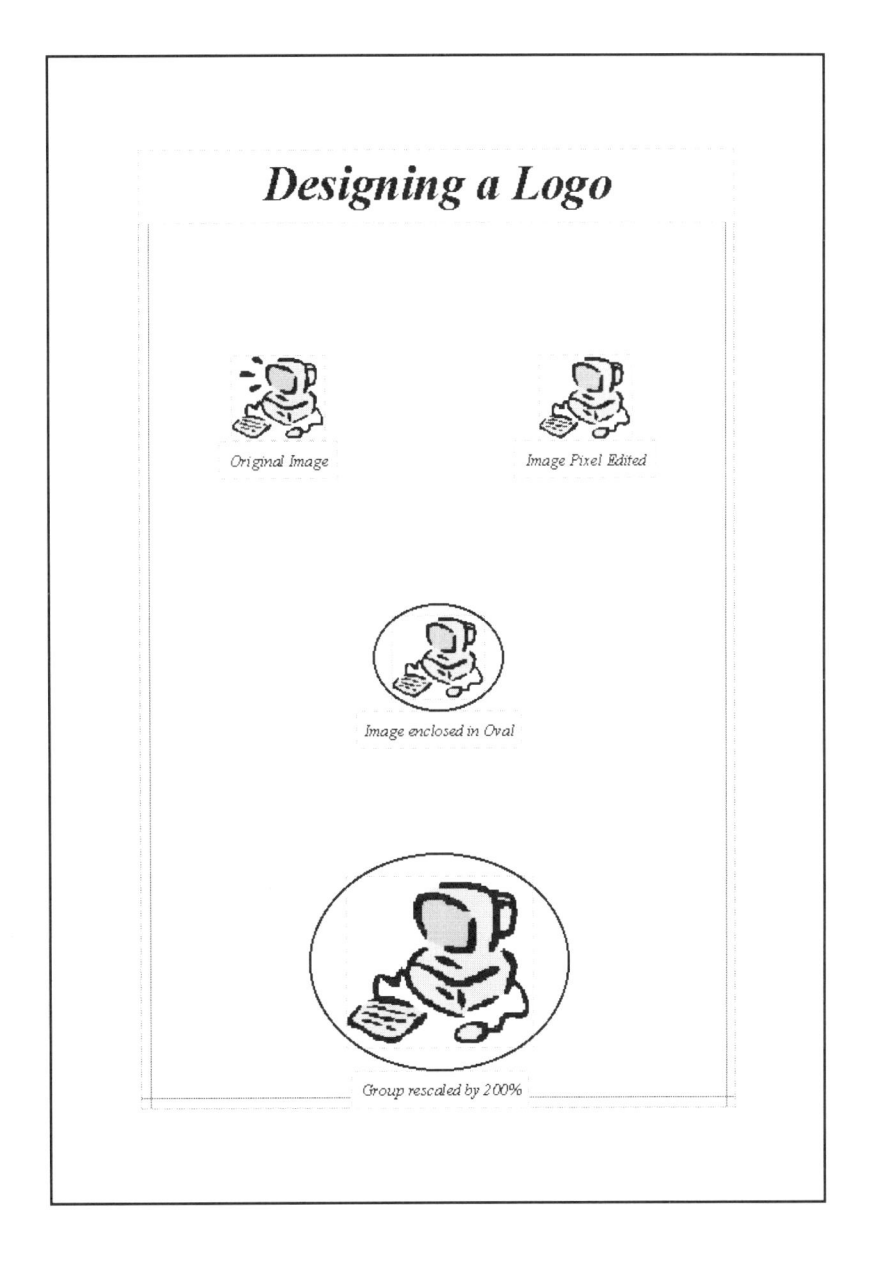

Designing a Logo   *Chapter 4*

OPENING A NEW FILE

1. If, while working on a publication you want to start a new one, click the *New* tool on the Standard Toolbar.
2. Unless the current file is saved, you will be asked to *Save* on exit. To keep your changes click *Yes*. Click *No* if you don't want to save or click *Cancel* to continue working in the current publication.

NUDGING OBJECTS

To move an object a short distance, it can be nudged for greater accuracy. Nudging an object means moving it a specific distance for each click. Nudging is very useful when placing one object in relation to another.

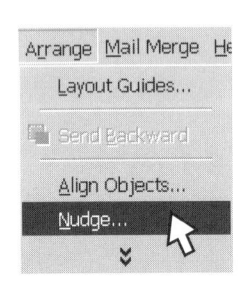

To nudge an object:

1. Click the object to select it.
2. Click Arrange on the Menu Bar.
3. Click *Nudge*.

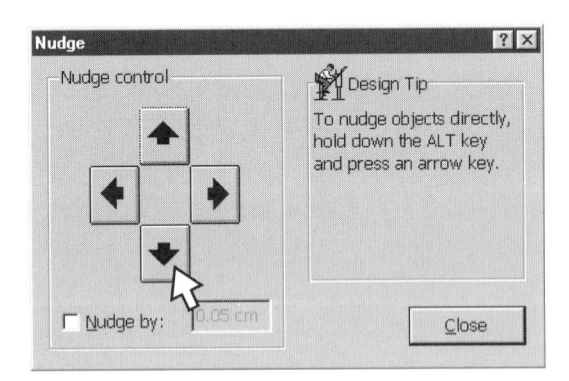

4. Click one of the arrows to move the object in a particular direction.

The value in the *Nudge by* box above means that the object will move 0.05 cm. (0.5 mm.) for each click. This is a very small value and the objects are placed with great precision.

This value can be changed.

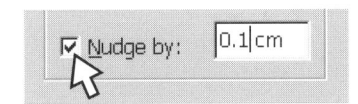

5. Click the *Nudge by* box to add a check mark.
6. Type a value in the box to the right.
7. When finished nudging, click *Close*.

In the example above the object will move 0.1 cm. or 1 mm. for each nudge.

There is another way to nudge an object:

1. Click the object to select it.
2. Holding down the ALT key on keyboard while pressing one of the keyboard arrow keys will nudge the object in a particular direction.

ZOOMING IN AND OUT

It is sometimes necessary to *zoom in* on an object in order to have more control when working on it (e.g. resizing accurately), or to *zoom out* in order to see how objects are balanced on a page.

1. Click the object to select it.
2. Click the down arrow to the right of the *Zoom* box on the Standard Toolbar.
3. Click the zoom you want or type in a percentage zoom and press ENTER.

Whole Page shows the complete page, *Page Width* shows the full width of the page, and *Selected Objects* zooms in on the object(s) selected at the highest possible zoom.

Right-clicking the object(s) will give the menu below, which contains zooming options. *Actual Size* gives a zoom of 100%.

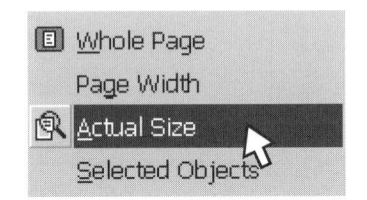

Page 38   *Desktop Publishing Made Easy*

USING RULER GUIDES

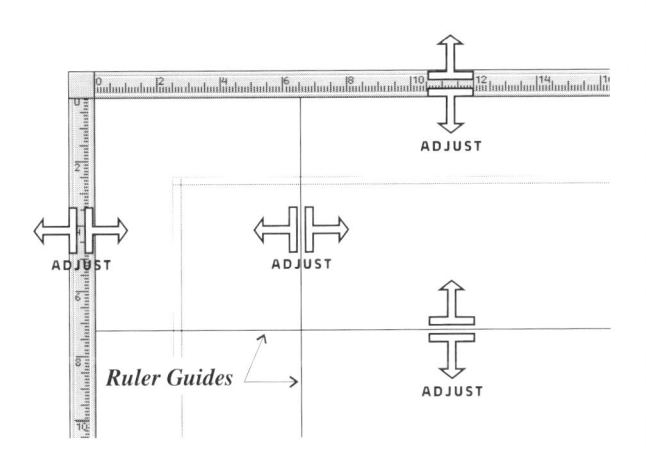

Ruler Guides

Ruler guides can be very useful for precision placement of objects on a page.

1. While pressing the SHIFT key on the keyboard bring the mouse pointer to either the vertical or horizontal ruler.
2. When the mouse pointer changes to *ADJUST* click and hold.
3. Drag across or down to where you want to place the ruler guide.
4. Release the mouse button.

CREATING A PICTURE FRAME

1. Click the *Picture Frame* tool from the Tool Palette.

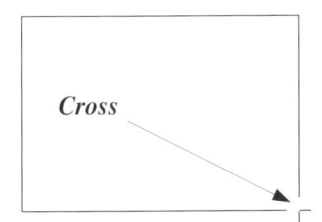

Cross

2. When the pointer changes to a cross, drag over and down on the page to create a picture frame.

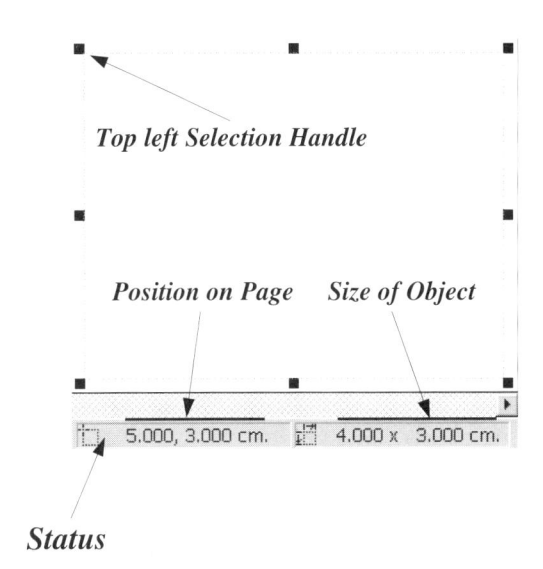

Top left Selection Handle

Position on Page   *Size of Object*

5.000, 3.000 cm.   4.000 x 3.000 cm.

Status

The position of the frame on the page and the frame size are displayed in the two sets of measurements on the Status Bar at the bottom right of the Publisher screen.

The top left selection handle in the illustration above is positioned 50 mm. in from the left of the page and 30 mm. down from the top of the page. The frame is 40 mm. wide and 30 mm. deep.

Get used to these sets of measurements because students very often read the first set as the size rather than the position of the object. One way of remembering it is that *P* (position) comes before *S* (size) in the alphabet.

INSERTING A PICTURE

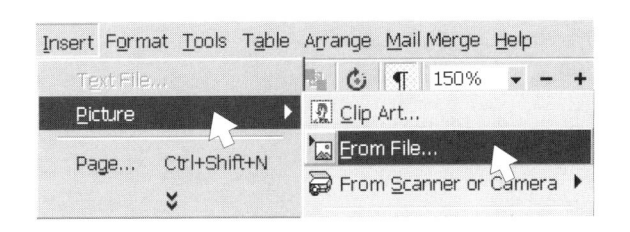

1. Create a picture frame or click an existing one to select it.
2. Click *Insert* from the Menu Bar.
3. Click *Picture*.
4. Click *From File*.

Designing a Logo Chapter 4

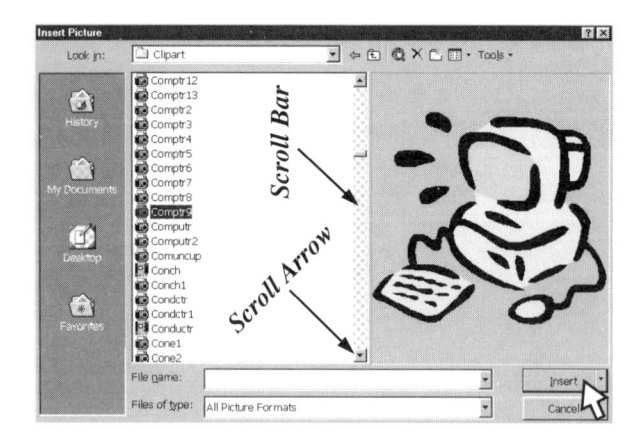

5. In the **Look in** box choose the appropriate drive.
6. In the main part of the window click the folder where the picture file is and click **Open**.
7. Use the scroll arrows (click on one of them) to locate the file.
8. Click the file and click **Insert**.

One of the frame dimensions has been changed to suit the shape of the picture.

Microsoft Publisher 2000 automatically resizes the frame you created to suit the picture.

Microsoft Publisher 97 will ask you if you want to change the frame to suit the picture before the picture is inserted.

RESIZING A PICTURE FRAME

When an image is inserted onto the page it is inserted in the right proportions, retaining its proper shape. Sometimes, though, you will have to resize it to suit a particular need – an article in a magazine or a newsletter etc. It should always be resized proportionately to avoid distortion.

To resize proportionately:

1. Place the mouse pointer on one of the corner selection handles.
2. When the pointer changes to **RESIZE** drag to resize. In Microsoft Publisher 97 press the SHIFT key on the keyboard as you drag, if you want to resize proportionately.

If you choose the middle selection handles to resize, you will change the shape of the picture.

MOVING A PICTURE FRAME

1. Place the mouse pointer inside the frame.
2. When it changes to **MOVE** drag the picture.

Chapter 4 *Designing a Logo*

Notice the first pair of measurements on the Status Bar. They signify the position of the top left frame selection handle of the moved picture. The first reading shows the distance the handle is from the left edge of the page and the second shows the distance from the top of the page.

Top left Selection Handle

Position of frame has changed

CREATING A TEXT FRAME
INSERTING TEXT
RESIZING A TEXT FRAME

---

1. Click the *Text Frame* tool from the Tool Palette.

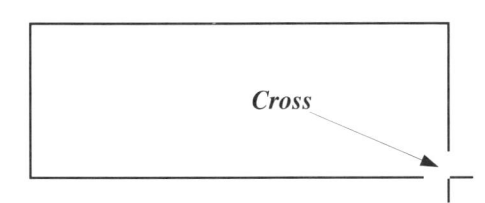

2. When the mouse pointer changes to a cross, drag over and down on the page to create a text frame.

The insertion point is blinking, waiting for you to insert the text.

3. Insert text by pressing keys on the keyboard.

The default font in Microsoft Publisher is Times New Roman, 12 pt regular. This will appear very small at a low zoom. Before you start typing text into a text frame or into a table frame you should increase the zoom to at least 75%.

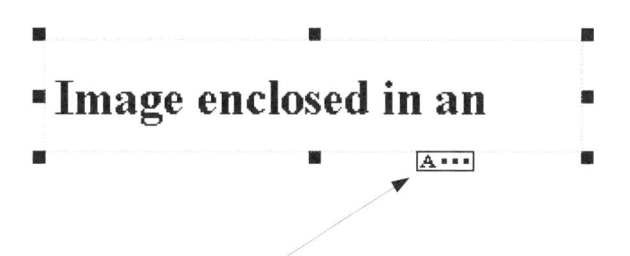

If the text frame is too small to fit all the text, then this tab appears at the bottom of the frame.

4. Resize the text frame to make the text fit.

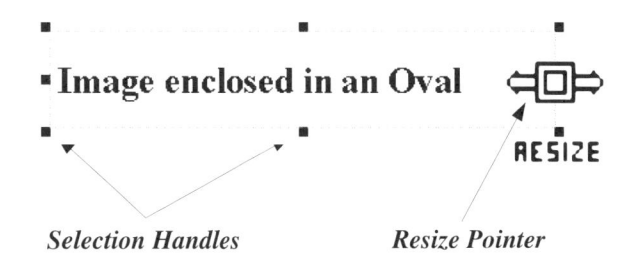

Selection Handles   *Resize Pointer*

To resize a text frame:

5. Place the mouse pointer on a selection handle until it change to a *RESIZE* pointer.
6. Drag over or back, up or down to resize.

The text now fits and the tab disappears from the bottom right of the text frame.

Using Microsoft Publisher — Page 41

Designing a Logo   *Chapter 4*

HIGHLIGHTING TEXT IN A TEXT FRAME

Original Image

There are 2 ways to highlight a block of text:

1. Drag across the text.
2. Click before the start of the text and then while pressing the SHIFT key on the keyboard click after the end of the text.
3. To highlight a word double-click on it.
4. To highlight a paragraph treble-click anywhere within it.

Be very careful when text is selected as touching a key on the keyboard will very likely delete it. If you accidentally delete the text, click the **Undo** tool on the Standard Toolbar to recover the text. More about deleting text follows.

Read about the **Undo/Redo** tools in Chapter 2 of this book under the heading **Made a Mess!**

DELETING TEXT IN A TEXT FRAME

Insertion point is placed before the text to be deleted

The car has been in existence for more than for more than eighty years now.

There are 3 ways of deleting text:

1. Place the insertion point immediately before the text to be deleted.
2. Press the DELETE key on the keyboard for each character (letter, number, space etc.) to be deleted.

Insertion point is placed after the text to be deleted

The car has been in existence for more than for more than eighty years now.

or

1. Place the insertion point immediately after the text to be deleted.
2. Press the BACKSPACE key on the keyboard for each character (letter, number, space etc.) to be deleted.

Text to be deleted is highlighted

The car has been in existence for more than **for more than** eighty years now.

or

1. Highlight the text to be deleted by dragging over it.
2. Press the DELETE key on the keyboard or click the **Cut** tool on the Standard Toolbar.

Cut

If there is no text in the text frame when you select it, pressing the DELETE key on the keyboard deletes the frame.

However, if you delete all the text in the frame by pressing the DELETE key, continuing to press the DELETE key will not delete the frame.

To delete the text frame then click the **Cut** tool on the Standard Toolbar or click away from the text frame, select it again and then press the DELETE key on the keyboard.

COPYING AND MOVING TEXT

For *Copying and Moving Text* see Chapter 3.

TEXT FRAME PROPERTIES

Text Frame Properties tool

You can set a specific gap between the text and the edges of text frame by changing the margins in the *Text Frame Properties* window.

To do this:

1. Click the frame to select it.
2. Click *Format* from the Menu Bar.
3. Click *Text Frame Properties*.
4. Change the margins.

You could also have clicked the *Text Frame Properties* tool on the Formatting Toolbar.

In the example to the right I changed the top margin to 0.25 cm. This means that the text is pushed down 0.25 cm. from the top edge of the frame.

This can be done for a number of reasons – moving text in a caption away from a picture, moving body text further away from a heading etc.

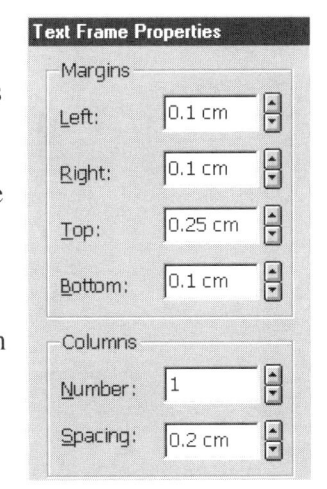

Inserting text in a tinted frame demands that there is a gap between the text and edges of the frame.

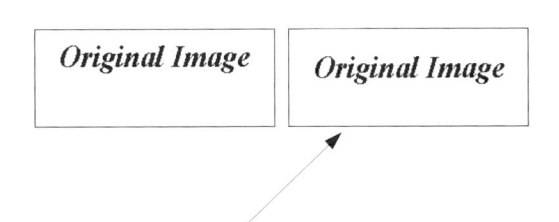

Original Image   *Original Image*

The text in the right text frame has been pushed down from the top edge of the frame.

MOVING A TEXT FRAME

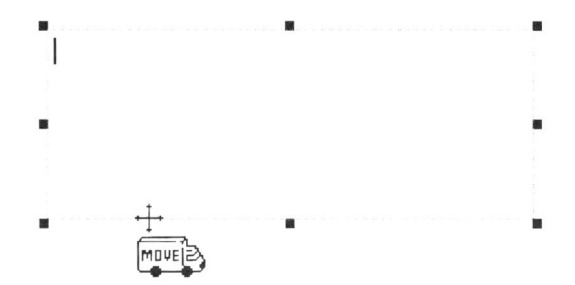

When moving a text frame or a table frame the mouse pointer must be placed on the frame's edge and away from the selection handles. Otherwise the program assumes you want to edit the text or resize the frame.

1. Place the mouse pointer as shown above.
2. When it changes to *MOVE* drag the text frame to move it.

DELETING OBJECTS

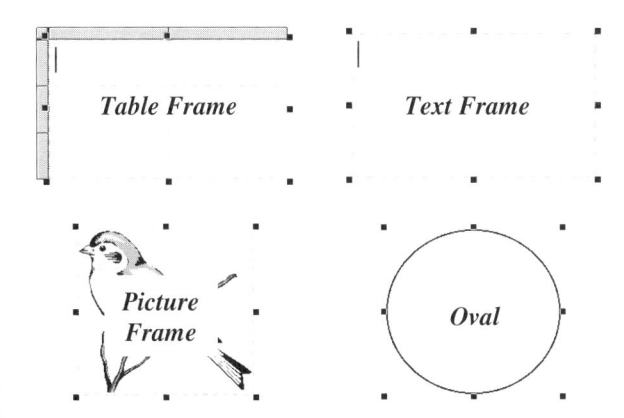

Table Frame   *Text Frame*

Picture Frame   *Oval*

1. Click the object to select it.
2. Press the DELETE key on the keyboard or click the *Cut* tool on the Standard Toolbar.

Note

If there is text in either the table frame or the text frame, clicking the *Cut* tool on the Standard Toolbar is the only way to delete the frame.

Designing a Logo   Chapter 4

CREATING AN OVAL

1. Click the *Oval Frame* tool from the Tool Palette.

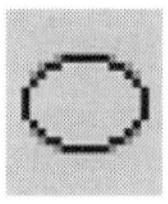

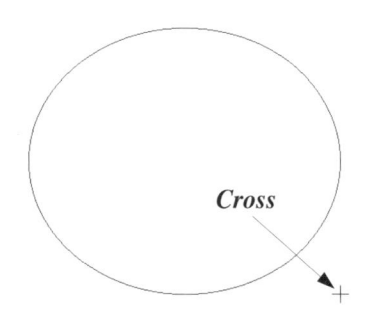

2. When the mouse pointer changes to a cross, drag over and down on the page to create an oval.
3. To draw a perfect circle press the SHIFT key on the keyboard while dragging.

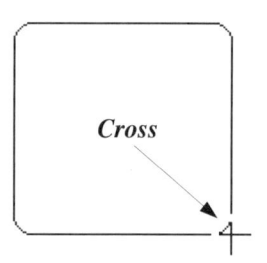

3. When the mouse pointer changes to a cross, drag over and down on the page to create a custom shape.

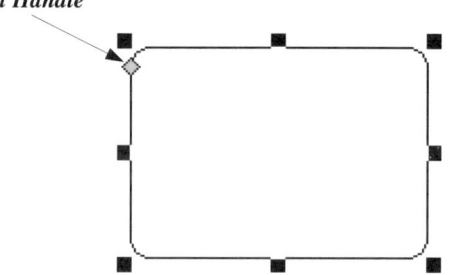

Adjust Handle

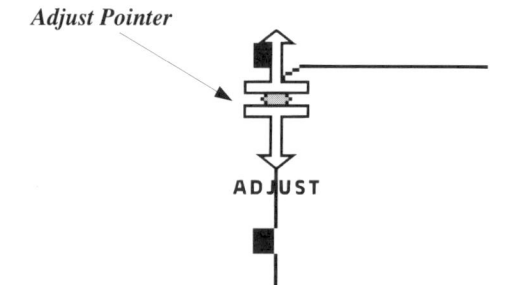

Adjust Pointer

CREATING CUSTOM SHAPES

1. Click the *Custom Shapes* tool from the Tool Palette.

2. Click a shape. In the illustration above I've clicked the first shape in the first row.

4. Position the mouse pointer over the adjust handle until it changes to an adjust pointer.
5. Drag up or down to edit the shape.

See the result below where I adjusted down to make the corners more rounded.

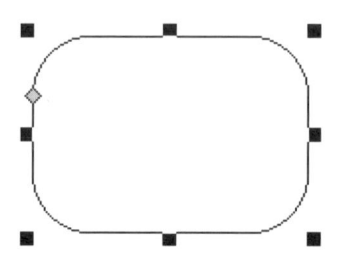

Page 44   Desktop Publishing Made Easy

Chapter 4   Designing a Logo

MULTIPLE SELECTION

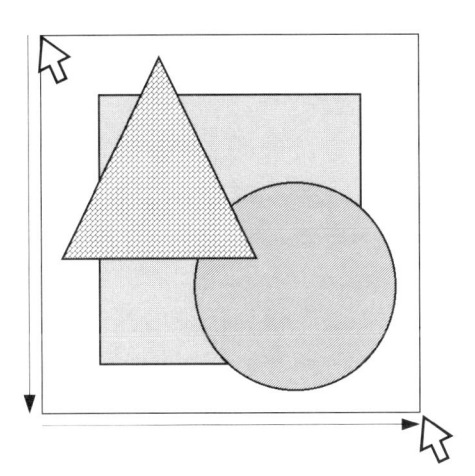

There are 2 ways to multiple-select:

1. Click on the first object.
2. With the SHIFT key on the keyboard pressed, click on each of the other objects.

or

1. Place the mouse pointer above the highest object and to left of the furthest left object.
2. Drag to below the lowest object and well to the right of the furthest right object.

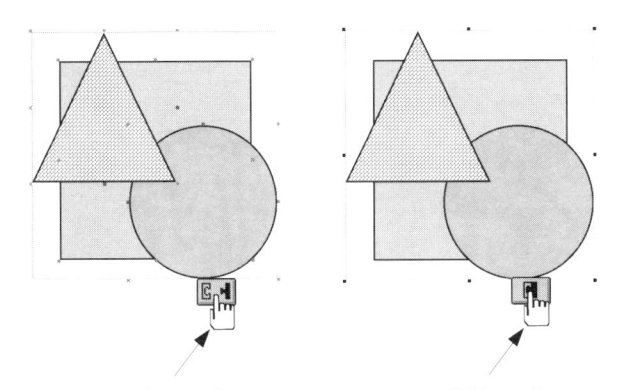

Group Objects button   *Ungroup Objects button*

The *Group Objects* button at the bottom indicates that the objects have been selected and are ready to be grouped. The *Ungroup Objects* button shows that they are grouped. Click to ungroup.

Click the *Group Objects* button to group the objects and click the *Ungroup Objects* button to ungroup them.

Grouped objects are treated as one object. When one of the grouped objects is moved, resized etc., the others are moved, resized too. All the grouped objects retain their position within the group.

ALIGNING OBJECTS

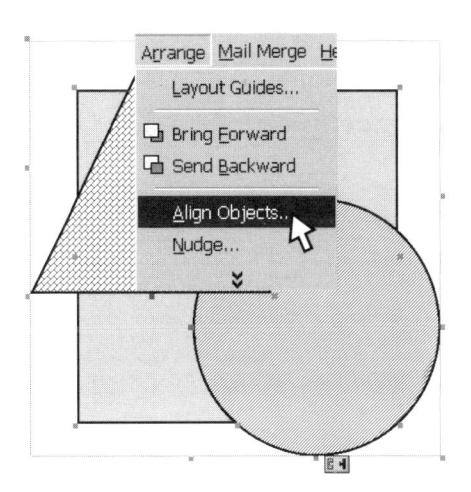

1. Draw any three objects and shade them differently as above.
2. Multiple-select the 3 objects.
3. Click *Arrange* from the Menu Bar.
4. Click *Align Objects ...*

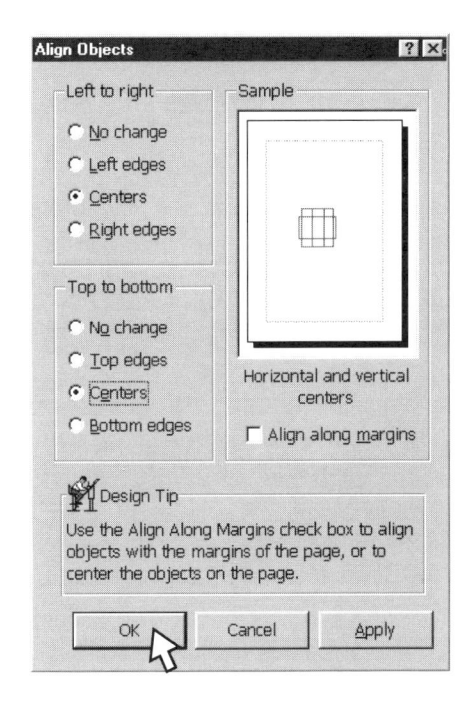

5. Choose an alignment from *Left to right* or from *Top to bottom* or both options.
6. Click *OK* or *Apply*.

Centers have been chosen for both options. You can see the thumbnail in the *Sample* section.

Using Microsoft Publisher   Page 45

Designing a Logo *Chapter 4*

Group Objects button

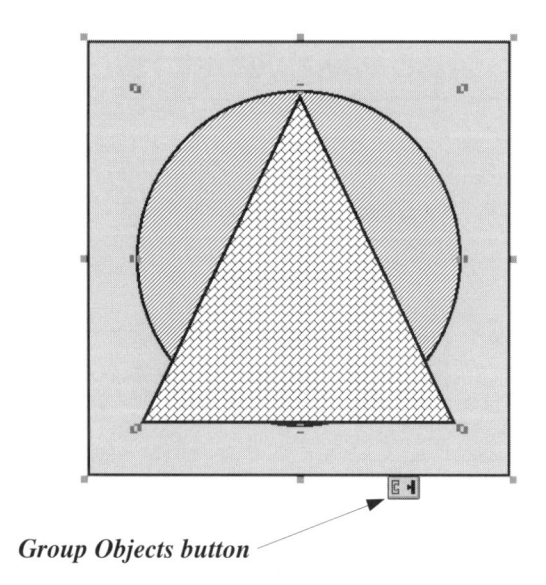

The objects above have been centred horizontally and vertically in relation to each other. The two smaller objects (triangle and oval) have been centred in relation to the larger object (rectangle).

Clicking the ***Align along margins*** box will also align the centred objects in relation to the page.

Clicking on the ***Group Objects*** button groups the objects, treating them as one object and preserving each object's position within the group.

If only one object is selected, it is always aligned in relation to the page. Remember that a grouped object is considered to be one object.

LAYERING OBJECTS

Layering objects is like playing with a deck of cards. Objects can be stacked in layers, with the first object at the bottom of the stack and the last object at the top. This means that if one object occupies the same area on the page as another, one of the objects at least partially hides the other.

In the tutorial ***Aligning Objects*** the rectangle was the first object drawn as it is at the bottom of the stack, followed by the oval and then the triangle.

One way of making the first object visible is to select the second object, by clicking it, and clicking ***No Fill*** from the ***Fill Color*** tool on the Formatting Toolbar.

Read ***Changing the Layering*** to see another way.

CHANGING THE LAYERING

Bring to Front Tool   *Send to Back Tool*

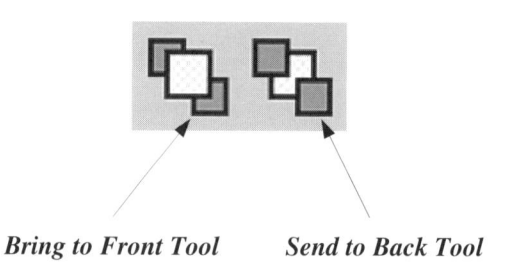

The 2 tools above are found on the Standard Toolbar.

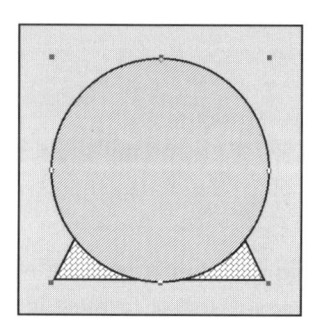

1. To bring the triangle to the front select it.
2. Click the ***Bring to Front*** tool. See below.

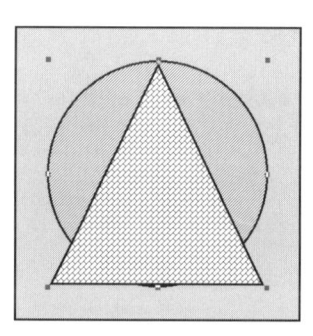

3. To send the triangle to the back select it.
4. Click the ***Send to Back*** tool. See below.

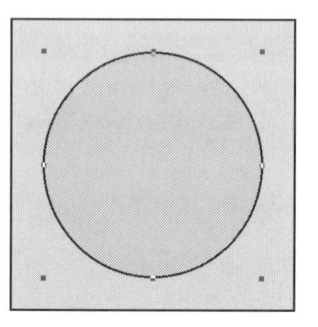

Page 46   Desktop Publishing Made Easy

Chapter 4   Designing a Logo

There is another way to change the layering.

5. Click **Arrange** from the Menu Bar.

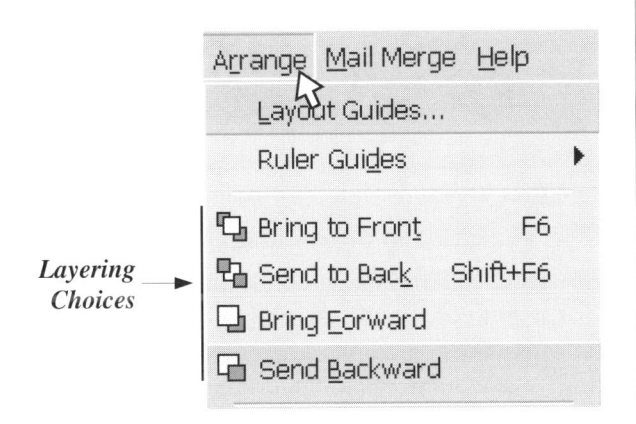

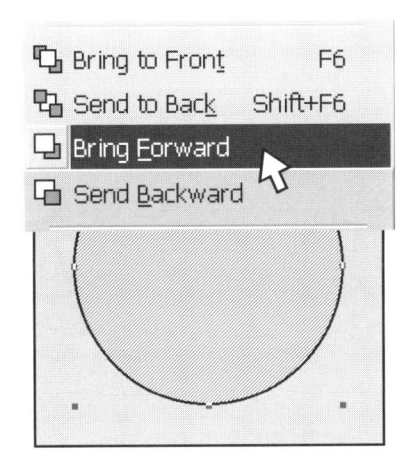

Layering Choices →

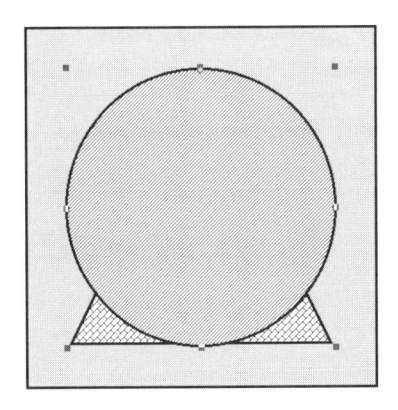

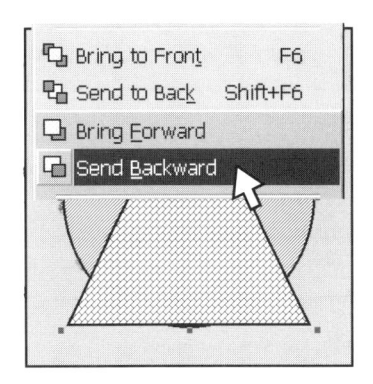

7. To send the oval back one layer click it to select it.
8. Click **Send Backward**. See the result above.

Even though the triangle was sent to the back it is still selected – unless you clicked away from it.

6. To bring it forward one layer click **Bring Forward**. See the result below.

COPY AND PASTE OBJECTS

Copy and *Paste* creates a second copy of the original object. This can be done within one publication or from one publication to another.

To do it:

1. Select the object by clicking it.
2. Click the *Copy* tool on the Standard Toolbar.

3. Click the *Paste* tool on the Standard Toolbar.

Using Microsoft Publisher   Page 47

Designing a Logo	Chapter 4

CUT AND PASTE OBJECTS

Cut and *Paste* deletes the original object and makes a copy of it. It can be done within one publication or from one publication to another. However, moving the object is more appropriate if done on the same page.

Cut

To do it:

1. Select the object by clicking it.
2. Click the *Cut* tool on the Standard Toolbar.
3. Click the *Paste* tool on the Standard Toolbar.

PIXEL EDITING

There are 2 types of images – *vector* and *bitmap*. A vector based image is one created in a *Draw* program, one that stores its components (lines, curves, circles etc.) as mathematical formulae. They are much easier to rescale than bitmaps as no distortion takes place.

A bitmap is one created in a *Paint* program, one that is made up of a set of bits (dots), each bit being independent of the others. When a vector based image is copied into a *Paint* program it becomes a bitmap. When it is rescaled up, the independent bits are increased in size and the edges of the image become jagged.

Pixel editing is done to smooth the image. This is done by zooming in on the image – making it seem at least 300% its original size – so that each pixel (screen dot) that makes up the image can be seen, and finally editing the image by adding or deleting the pixels. *Pixel editing* can also be used to smooth rescaled bit-mapped fonts.

See the difference between a rescaled *vector* and rescaled *bit-mapped* image below.

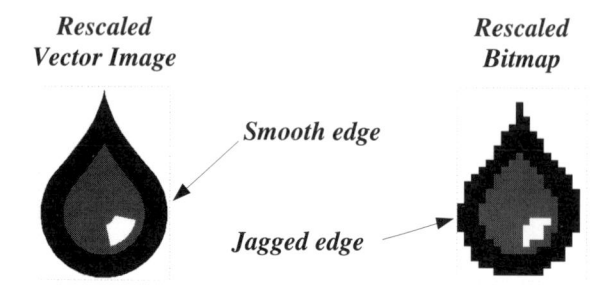

Rescaled Vector Image   *Rescaled Bitmap*

Smooth edge

Jagged edge

To pixel edit:

1. Insert a picture – a vector based image.

Most of the clip art images in Microsoft Publisher are vector based images.

2. Copy and paste the picture.
3. Move the copied picture to the right.
4. If you want to retain the original picture, then copy the pasted picture.
5. Deselect the pasted picture by clicking away from it on the empty page space.

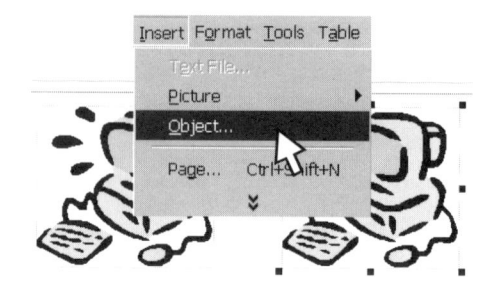

6. Click *Insert* from the Menu Bar.
7. Click *Object*.

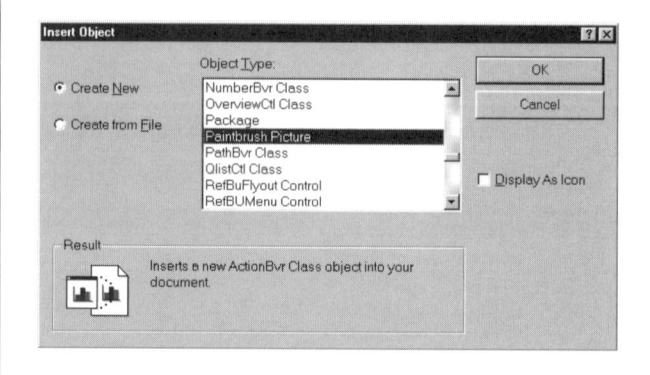

8. With the *Create New* button selected scroll down and select *Paintbrush Picture*.
9. Click *OK*.

Page 48	Desktop Publishing Made Easy

Chapter 4   Designing a Logo

Resize bitmap area to make smaller

Resize Paintbrush Picture frame to make bigger

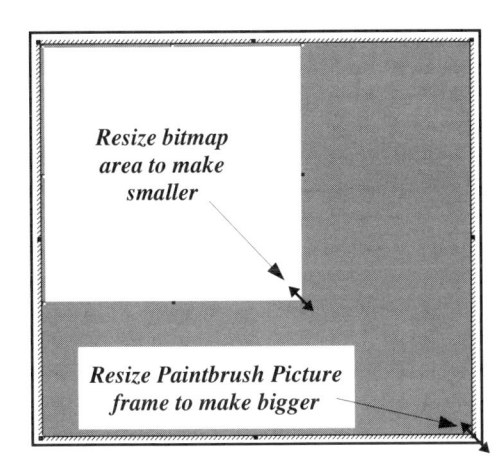

The white background (bitmap area) is the area in which the picture will be pasted. This area should be decreased in size so that it will be too small for the picture. It will later be resized upwards on pasting to exactly fit the picture.

10. Resize the *Paintbrush Picture* frame to make it larger. See the illustration above.
11. Resize the white bitmap area to make it smaller. See the illustration below.

The resizing is done the same way as in Publisher.

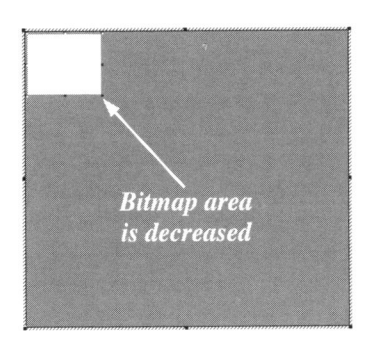

Bitmap area is decreased

12. Click *Edit* from the Menu Bar.
13. Click *Paste*.
14. If you made the bitmap area smaller you will get the message below. Click *Yes* to enlarge the bitmap.

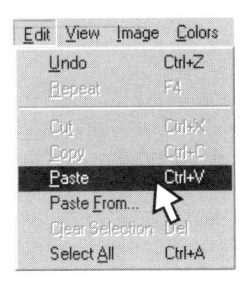

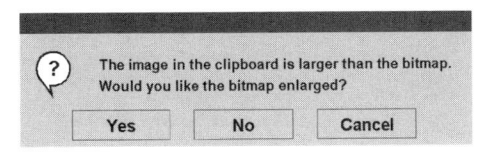

The picture above is exactly the size of the white bitmap area. When the picture is copied into the Paintbrush program it changes from being a *vector* image to a *bitmap* – a picture made up of a set of independent bits.

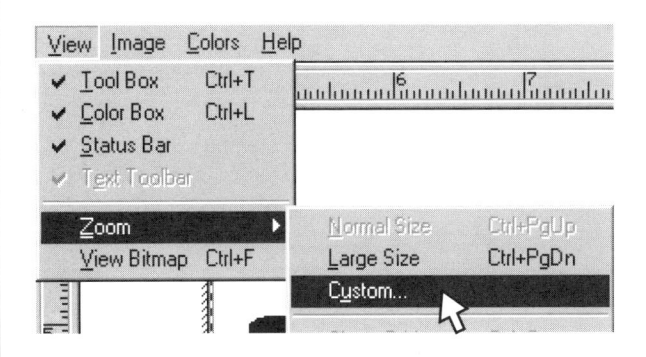

15. Click *View* from the Menu Bar.
16. Click *Zoom*.
17. Click *Custom*.

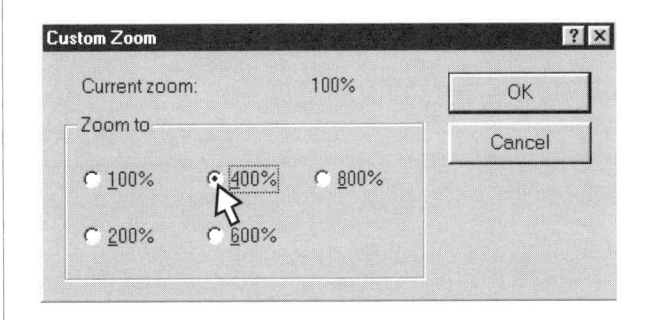

18. Click the *400%* zoom radio button.
19. Click *OK*. See the result on the next page.

Using Microsoft Publisher   Page 49

Designing a Logo   *Chapter 4*

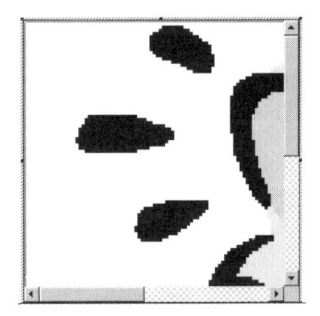

The picture is at a 400% zoom.

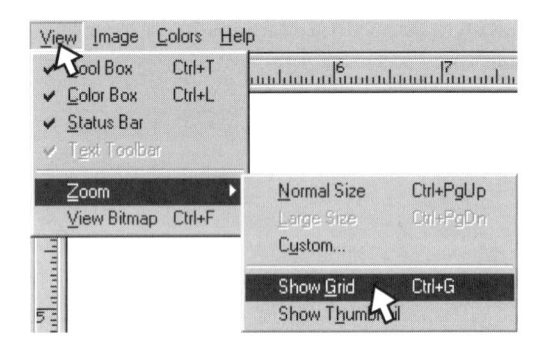

20. Click *View* from the Menu Bar.
21. Click *Zoom*.
22. Click *Show Grid*.

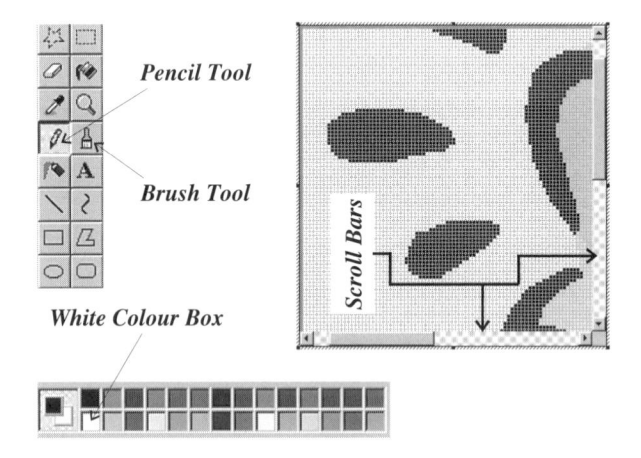

Scroll bars are used to scroll around the picture.

I want to edit this picture by getting rid of the large black dots. I will change the foreground colour to white and make the black dots white.

23. Click the white colour in the colour palette.
24. Click the *Pencil* tool in the Tool Box.

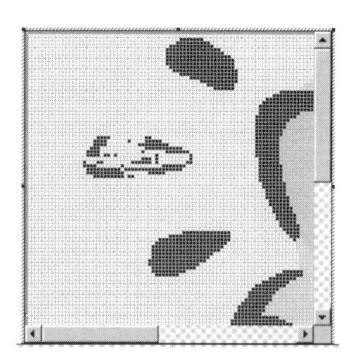

25. Click onto one of the black dots. One of the pixels has changed to white.
26. Repeat until all the dots have gone.

Because the dots above are so large and are not awkward to get at, you could really have used the *Brush* tool to edit more than one pixel at a time.

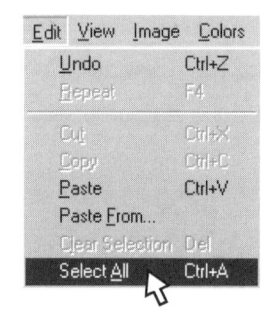

27. Having finished the pixel editing click *Edit* from the Menu Bar.
28. Click *Select All*.

Select All selects the whole bitmap. If the bitmap (white area) is larger than the pixel edited picture, then when the bitmap is copied and pasted back to Publisher, the picture will not fill the entire frame. An illustration of this is shown at the end of this *Pixel Editing* tutorial on the next page.

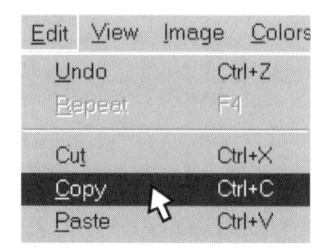

29. Click *Edit* from the Menu Bar.
30. Click *Copy* (copies the bitmap).

Page 50   *Desktop Publishing Made Easy*

Chapter 4   Designing a Logo

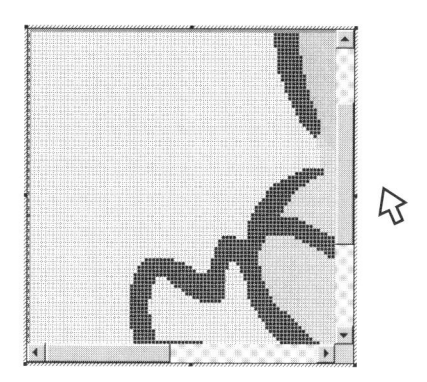

31. Click away from Paintbrush area – out to the side as in the illustration above. This inserts the pixel edited picture back into Publisher.

We could accept this pixel edited picture and resize it down to the size of the original. However, it is more convenient to click on the pasted picture and paste the pixel edited one into its frame. This will ensure that both the original and the pixel edited pictures have the same dimensions.

Move large picture out of the way

32. Click the large pixel edited picture and move it out of the way of the other two.

33. Click the original pasted picture on the right.

34. Click the *Paste* tool from the Standard Toolbar. The pixel edited picture replaces the original pasted picture and is also the same size.
35. Delete the larger pixel edited picture which you moved out of the way by clicking the *Cut* tool from the Standard Toolbar.

If we had not decreased the bitmap area (see steps 11-14 in this tutorial), and instead left it larger than the picture, the pasted pixel edited picture would only fill a section of the frame as in the illustration above right. The frame represents the bitmap area.

It is a good idea to resize down the white bitmap area of the *Paintbrush Picture* frame before pasting the Publisher image into it.

ENCLOSING AN OBJECT IN AN OVAL GROUPING AND RESIZING THEM

The purpose of this exercise is to see how a vector and a bit-mapped image are displayed when rescaled. First of all we select the images and then group them. It is when the grouped images are rescaled up that we notice the smooth edge of the vector based image – the oval – and the jagged edge of the bitmap – the pixel edited image.

Using Microsoft Publisher   Page 51

Designing a Logo   *Chapter 4*

1. Draw a picture frame and insert a picture.
2. Draw an oval making it slightly larger than the picture.
3. Give the oval a 2 point thickness by clicking the **Line/Border Style** tool, clicking **More Styles** and choosing **2 pt** in the **Choose a thickness** box.

4. Drag the oval over the picture.
5. Resize the oval until you're satisfied that the picture can fit inside the oval without touching its border.

If the picture is inserted after the oval, part of the oval will be hidden. In that case select the picture and send it to the back.

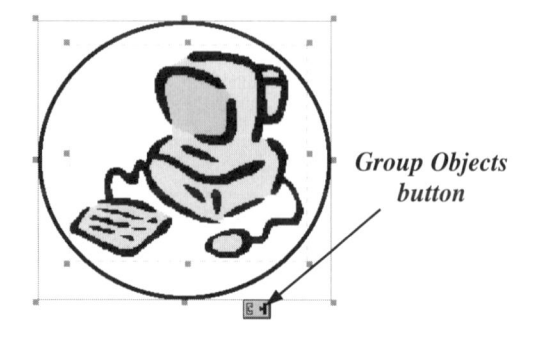

Group Objects button

6. Multiple-select the picture and the oval.
7. Centre them horizontally and vertically in relation to each other.
8. Group the objects by clicking the **Group Objects** button.

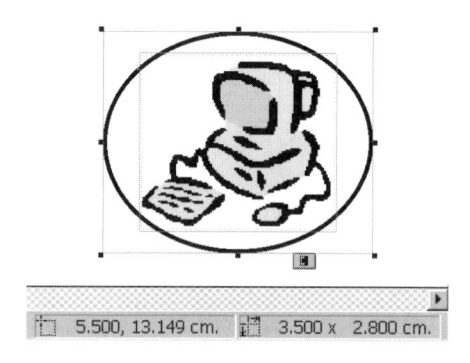

The objects are grouped and are now treated as one object. Take note of the group's size – the second set of measurements on the Status Bar.

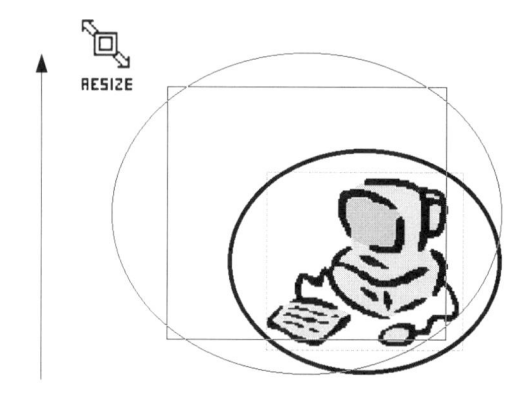

9. Rescale the grouped object proportionally from a corner handle.

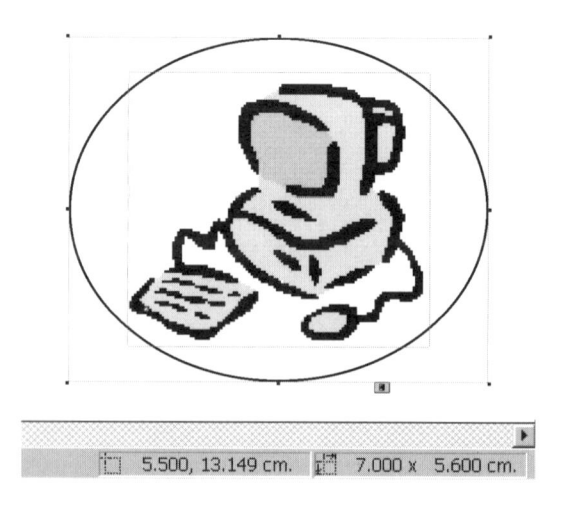

The second set of measurements on the Status Bar shows that the grouped object has been rescaled proportionally by 200%.

Being a vector image, the oval resizes smoothly, but the picture becomes jagged as it is a bitmap. Vector images are easier to edit than bitmaps.

Chapter 4   *Designing a Logo*

EXERCISE 4.1

COMPLETION INSTRUCTIONS

Carry out the instructions in numerical order

See the sketch sheet on the next page

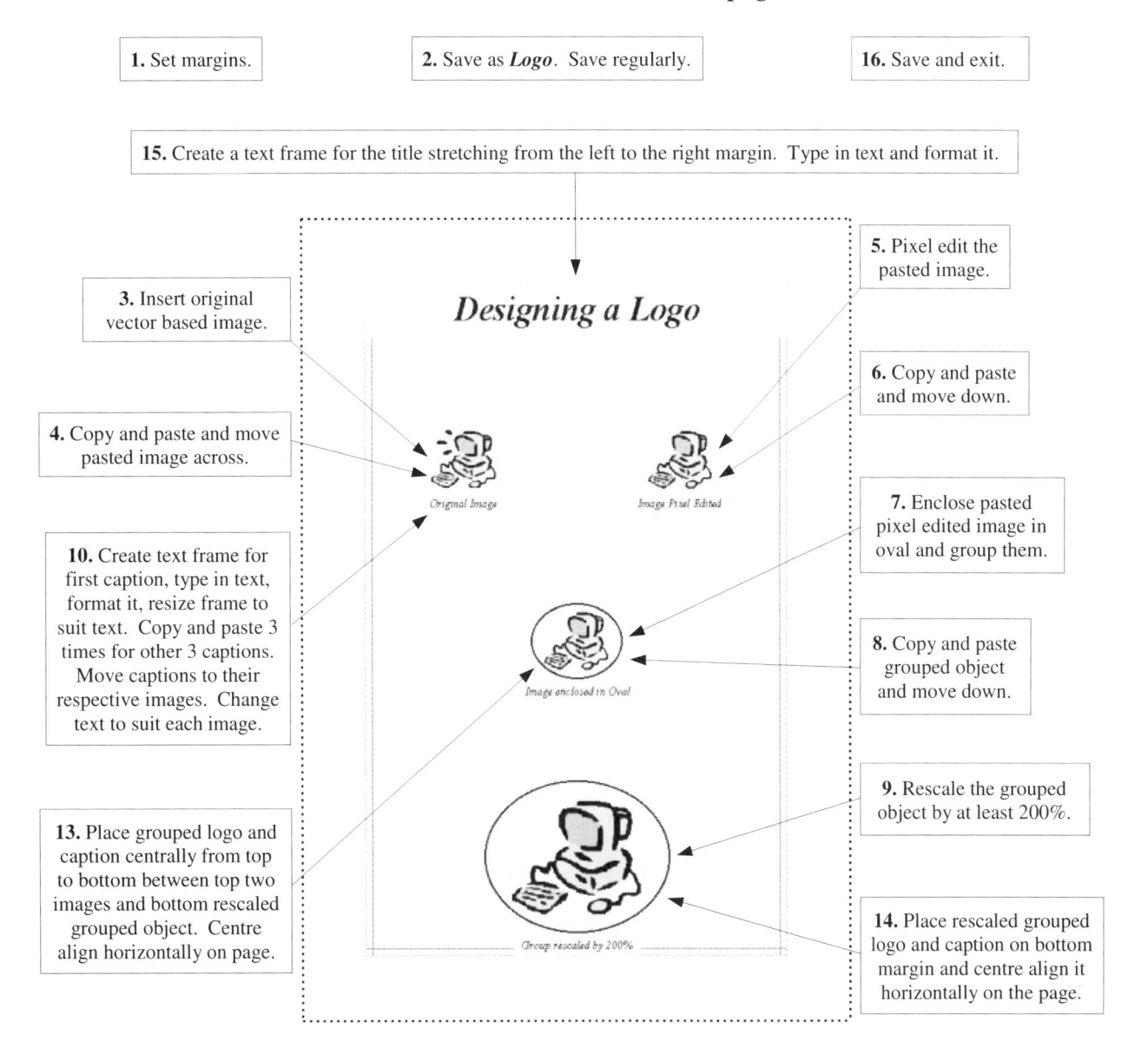

1. Set margins.

2. Save as *Logo*. Save regularly.

16. Save and exit.

15. Create a text frame for the title stretching from the left to the right margin. Type in text and format it.

3. Insert original vector based image.

5. Pixel edit the pasted image.

6. Copy and paste and move down.

4. Copy and paste and move pasted image across.

7. Enclose pasted pixel edited image in oval and group them.

10. Create text frame for first caption, type in text, format it, resize frame to suit text. Copy and paste 3 times for other 3 captions. Move captions to their respective images. Change text to suit each image.

8. Copy and paste grouped object and move down.

9. Rescale the grouped object by at least 200%.

13. Place grouped logo and caption centrally from top to bottom between top two images and bottom rescaled grouped object. Centre align horizontally on page.

14. Place rescaled grouped logo and caption on bottom margin and centre align it horizontally on the page.

11. With *Snap to Objects* enabled, move each caption until it snaps in against the bottom of its appropriate picture. Nudge the caption down the same number of steps away from each picture for consistency. Multiple-select each image and caption. Centre align them horizontally in relation to each other. Group them.

12. Place the 2 top grouped objects about 80 mm. from the top of the page and about 60 mm. apart. Centre align them vertically in relation to each other. Group them and centre align them horizontally on the page. *You could also have brought down a ruler guide in order to align the objects vertically.*

Designing a Logo Chapter 4

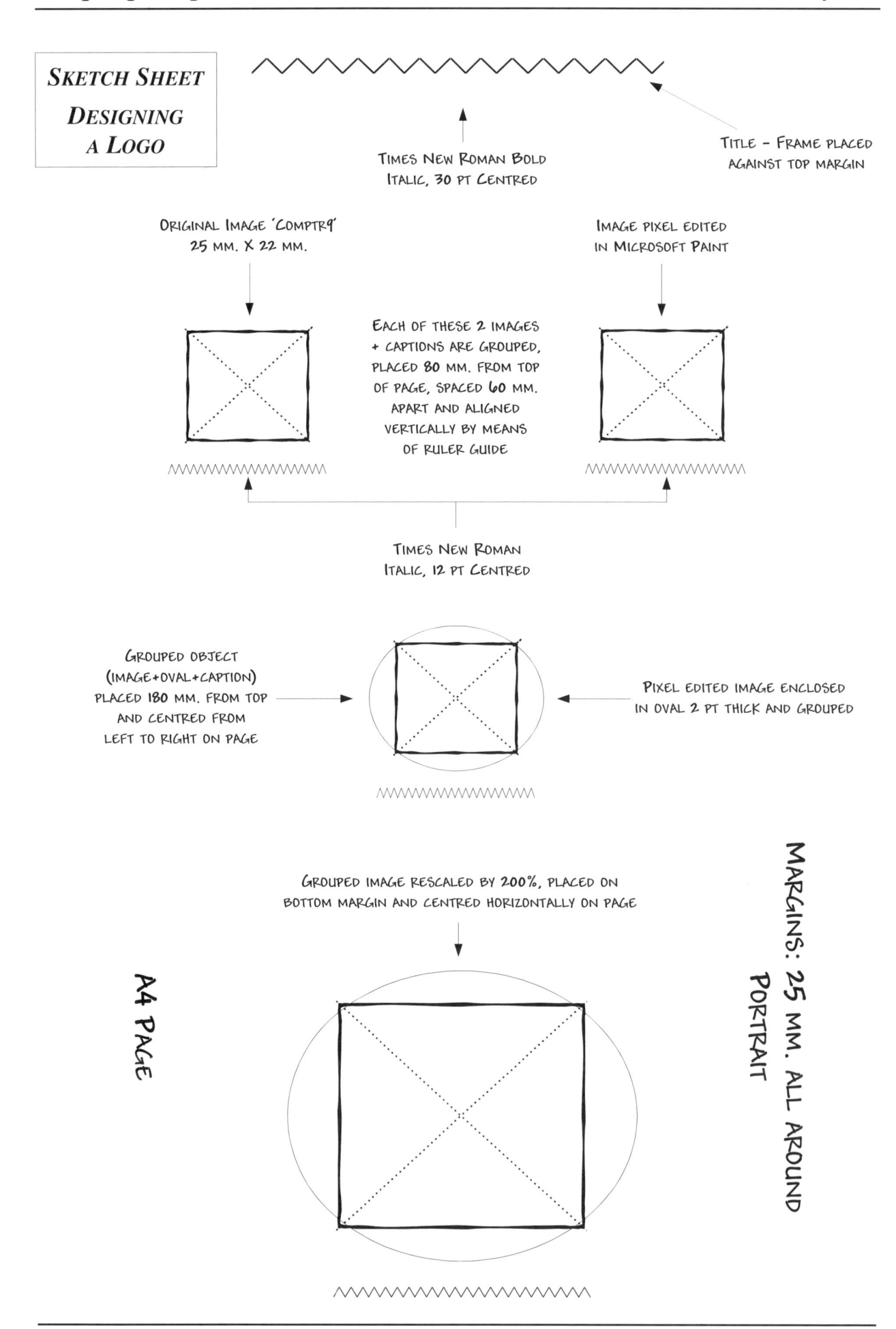

SKETCH SHEET
***DESIGNING**
A LOGO*

TIMES NEW ROMAN BOLD ITALIC, 30 PT CENTRED

TITLE – FRAME PLACED AGAINST TOP MARGIN

ORIGINAL IMAGE 'COMPTR9' 25 MM. X 22 MM.

IMAGE PIXEL EDITED IN MICROSOFT PAINT

EACH OF THESE 2 IMAGES + CAPTIONS ARE GROUPED, PLACED 80 MM. FROM TOP OF PAGE, SPACED 60 MM. APART AND ALIGNED VERTICALLY BY MEANS OF RULER GUIDE

TIMES NEW ROMAN ITALIC, 12 PT CENTRED

GROUPED OBJECT (IMAGE+OVAL+CAPTION) PLACED 180 MM. FROM TOP AND CENTRED FROM LEFT TO RIGHT ON PAGE

PIXEL EDITED IMAGE ENCLOSED IN OVAL 2 PT THICK AND GROUPED

GROUPED IMAGE RESCALED BY 200%, PLACED ON BOTTOM MARGIN AND CENTRED HORIZONTALLY ON PAGE

A4 PAGE

MARGINS: 25 MM. ALL AROUND PORTRAIT

Page 54 Desktop Publishing Made Easy

Chapter 4   **Designing a Logo**

Designing a Logo

Original Image   *Bitmap Image Pixel Edited*

Image enclosed in Oval

Group rescaled by 200%

Exercise 4.2

Design a logo for a Garage House Style

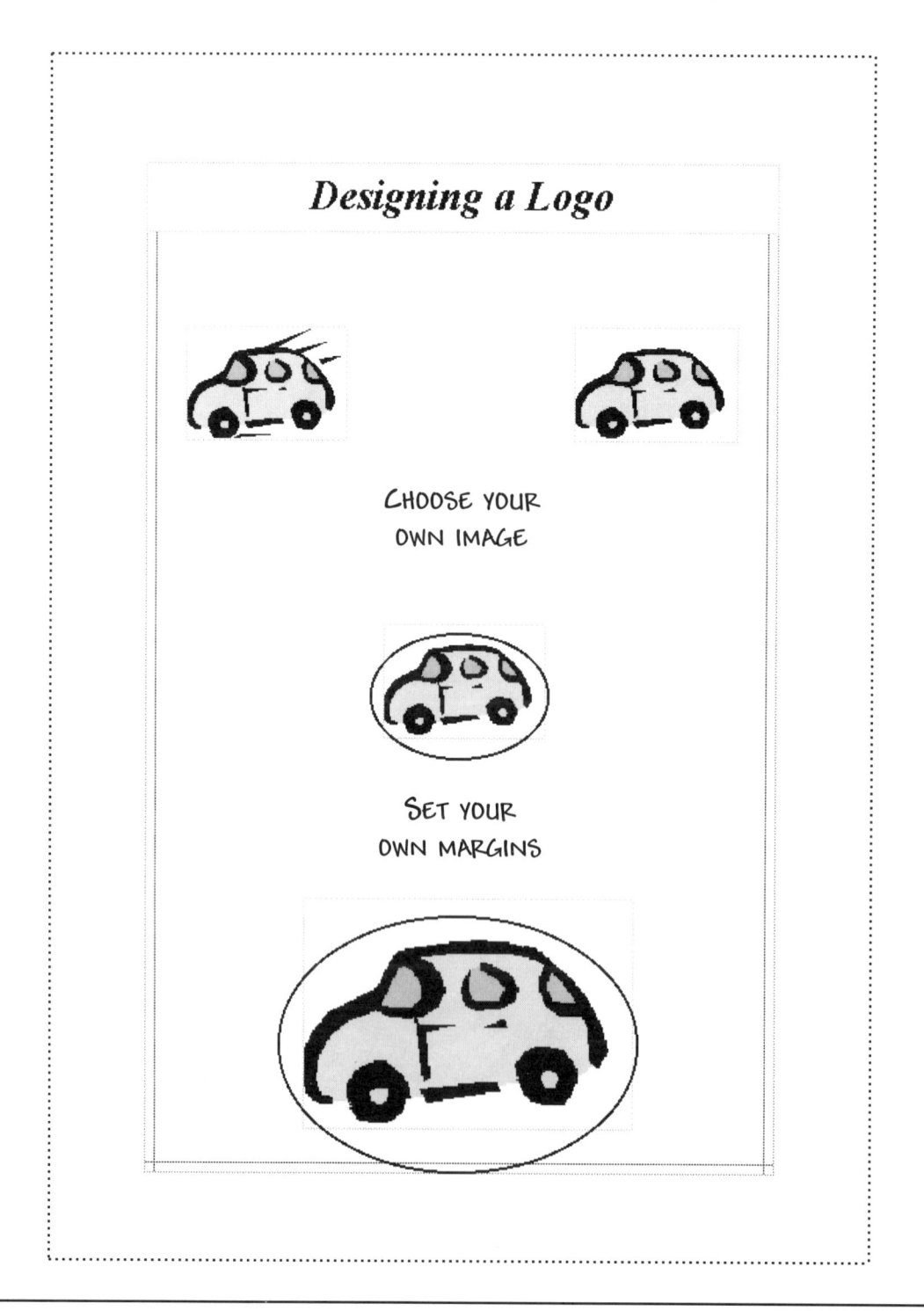

Exercise 4.3

Design a logo for a Building Contractor's House Style

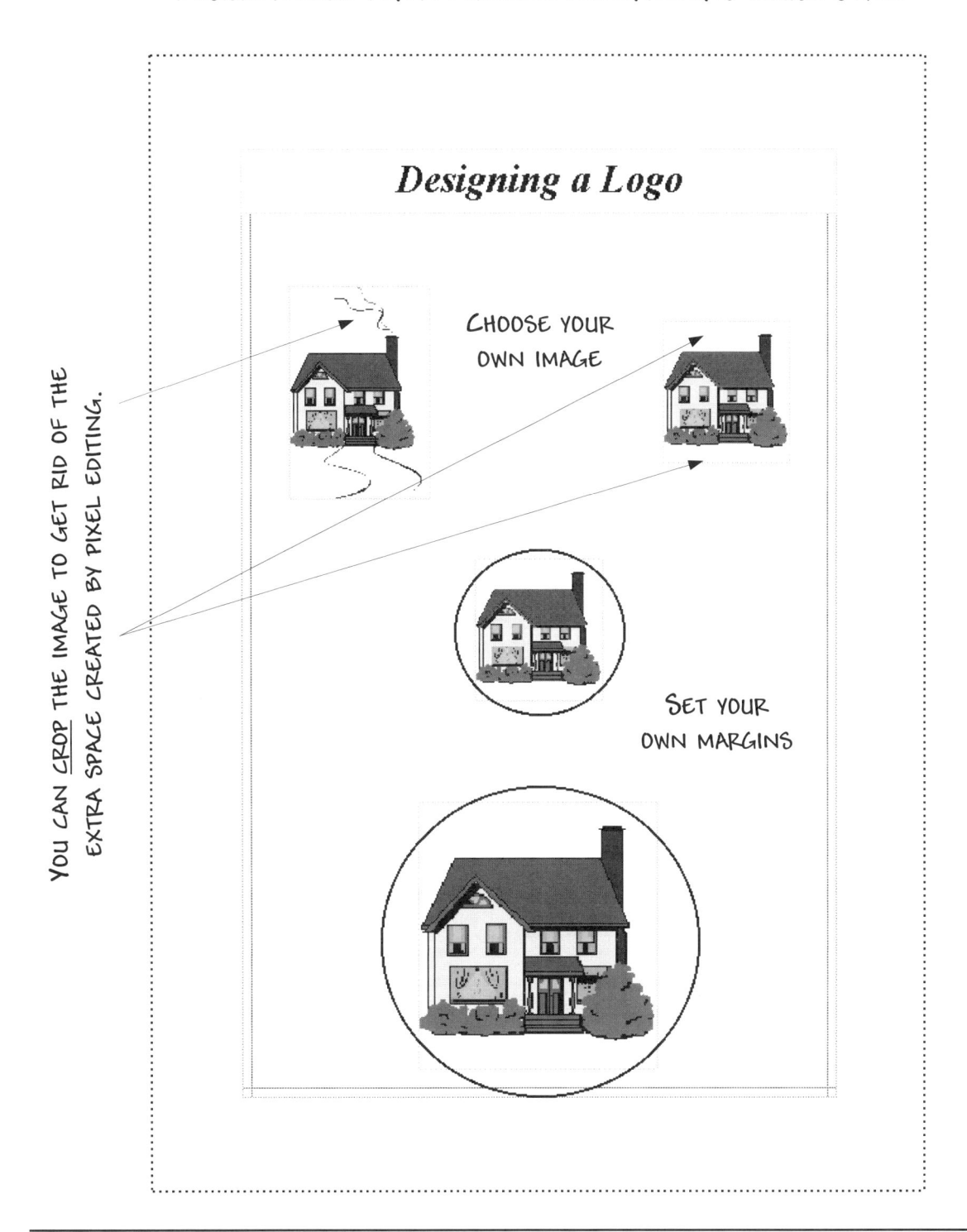

Designing a Logo

Choose your own image

You can crop the image to get rid of the extra space created by pixel editing.

Set your own margins

Cropping Pictures is explained on page 162.

IN CHAPTER 4 YOU HAVE DONE THE FOLLOWING:

- Opened new files.
- Nudged objects.
- Zoomed in and out.
- Used ruler guides.
- Created picture frames.
- Inserted pictures.
- Resized picture frames.
- Moved picture frames.
- Created text frames.
- Inserted text in text frames.
- Resized text frames.
- Highlighted text in text frames.
- Changed text frame properties.
- Deleted text in text frames.
- Moved text frames.
- Deleted objects.
- Created ovals.
- Created custom shapes.
- Made multiple selections.
- Aligned objects.
- Layered objects.
- Changed the layering.
- Copied and pasted objects.
- Cut and pasted objects.
- Pixel edited.
- Enclosed objects in ovals.
- Grouped objects.
- Resized grouped objects.

CHAPTER 5

DESIGNING A BUSINESS LETTERHEAD

Designing a Business Letterhead   Chapter 5

TEMPLATE (STYLE SHEET, MASTER PAGE)

The next exercise requires the use of a *template*, *style sheet* or *master page*. These three terms have the same meaning – a publication that you want to use as a basis for other similar publications, such as a report that you produce weekly, a newsletter that you produce regularly or a letterhead.

In Publisher we use the term *template* rather than either of the other two. In a template for a letter we shall set up specification for material that is required many times and will be presented in the same format – business letterhead (address, logo, company name etc.) and a text frame for the letter.

Having created the template for the letter, opening it will open a copy of the template rather than the actual template itself. All we have to do then is write the text of the letter, as the rest of the letter is there – the letterhead (logo, title, address etc.).

When we make the changes by writing the letter and save we will be invited to give the publication a destination and a name. It is saved as a normal publication, while leaving the template untouched in its own folder.

In this book we will be creating 2 templates, one for a business letterhead in this chapter and the other for a newsletter in Chapter 11.

SAVING AS A TEMPLATE FILE

When you save a document as a template file, Publisher saves it in a special folder to make it easily accessible.

To save a document as a template:

1. Click *File* on the Menu Bar.
2. Click *Save As*.

It is not necessary to browse for a destination for the template file. When you decide to save the publication as a template, Publisher automatically saves it in a folder called *Templates*.

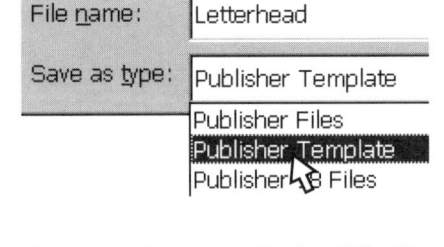

3. Type in a template name in the *File Name* box.
4. Choose *Publisher Template* in the *Save as type* box.
5. Click *Save*.

The publication is now saved in template format in a folder called *Templates* on your hard disk.

OPENING A TEMPLATE FILE

1. Click *File* on the Menu Bar.
2. Click *New*.

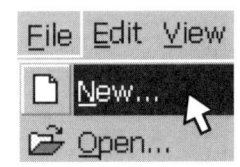

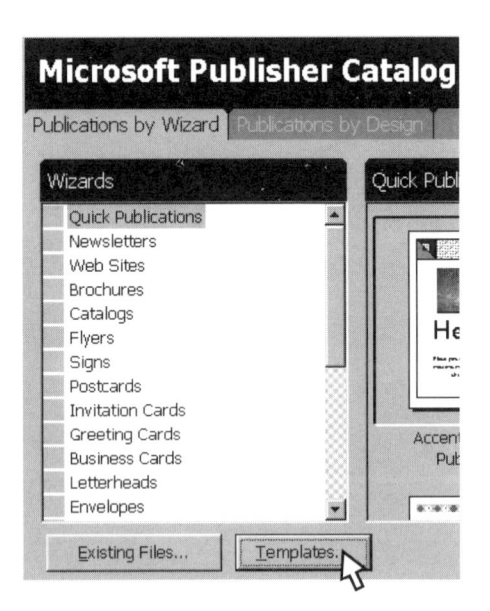

The *Microsoft Publisher Catalog* window opens. This window will also appear every time you start the program unless you changed the settings. See Chapter 2 on setting up Publisher.

3. Click the *Templates* button at the bottom of the window.

Page 60   Desktop Publishing Made Easy

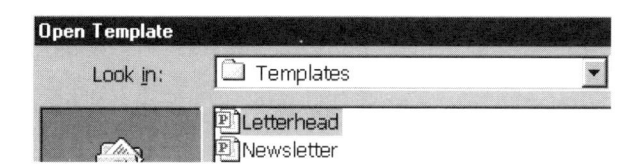

Chapter 5 — Designing a Business Letterhead

Publisher finds the folder **Templates** on the hard disk. You will see the list of templates created.

4. Click the appropriate template file.
5. Click **Open** in the bottom right of the window.

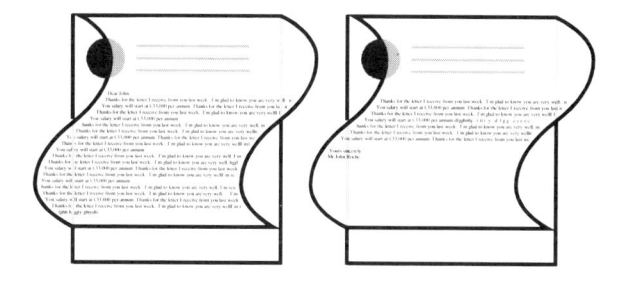

The objects created in the background appear on all pages of the letter.

WHAT IS A BACKGROUND?

When you want to duplicate objects (pictures, text etc.) on every page of a document you put them in the background. In our next exercise, ***Designing a Business Letterhead***, we will create the letterhead objects in the background to make them available on every page of the letter we write. Being created in the background also means that they cannot be accidentally moved or deleted, because the letter is always written in the foreground.

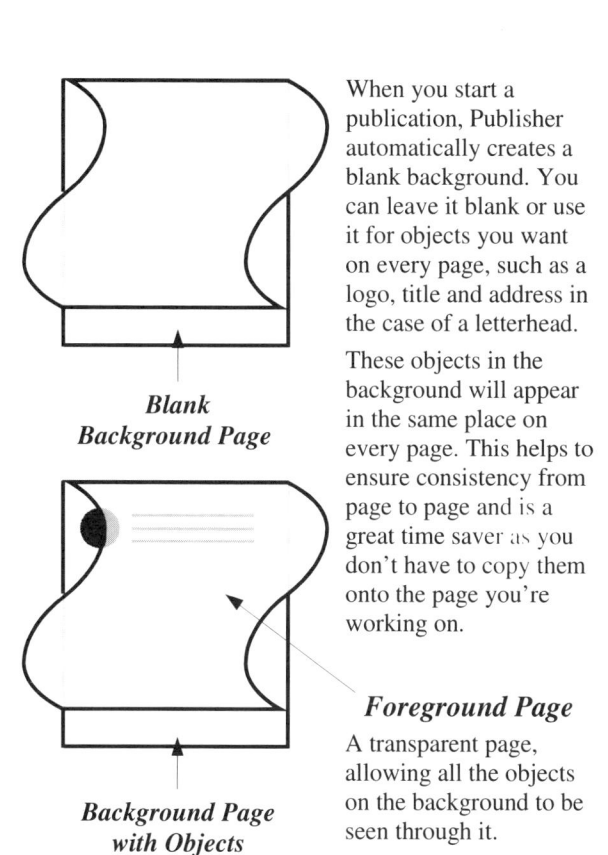

Blank Background Page

Background Page with Objects

When you start a publication, Publisher automatically creates a blank background. You can leave it blank or use it for objects you want on every page, such as a logo, title and address in the case of a letterhead.

These objects in the background will appear in the same place on every page. This helps to ensure consistency from page to page and is a great time saver as you don't have to copy them onto the page you're working on.

Foreground Page
A transparent page, allowing all the objects on the background to be seen through it.

CREATING A BACKGROUND

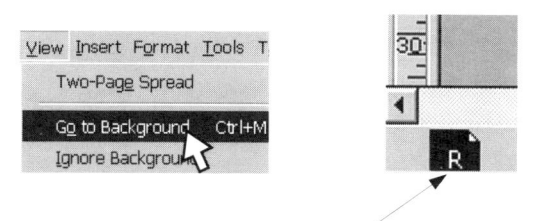

Page Navigation button

1. Click **View** on the Menu Bar.
2. Click **Go to Background**.

You can now create the objects that you want to appear on every page of your publication. You will notice that the **Page Navigation** button changes from the number *1* to the character *R*. We shall see more about this in Chapter 11.

Having created the objects in the background, we go to the foreground to finish the template.

3. Click **View** on the Menu Bar.
4. Click **Go to Foreground**.

Having created the letterhead in the background, we can now set new margins and create the text frame, into which we can type letter.

Designing a Business Letterhead   Chapter 5

COPYING A LOGO FROM ONE FILE TO ANOTHER

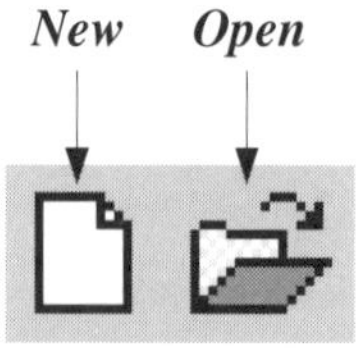

1. Open the *Logo* file and select the logo – the unscaled one.
2. Click *Copy* from the Standard Toolbar.
3. Open the destination file.

New   Open

If the destination file is a new file click the *New* tool on the Standard Toolbar; if an existing file click the *Open* tool.

If you altered the *Logo* file you will be asked at this stage if you want to save it. You probably will not, so click *No*.

4. In the destination file click *Paste* from the Standard Toolbar.

Every time you copy an object it is pasted to the *Clipboard* – the computer's memory. When you exit from Publisher you will sometimes be asked if you want to save the Clipboard – the object in the computer's memory. If you don't need the object anymore – to paste into some other page or other publication – click *No*.

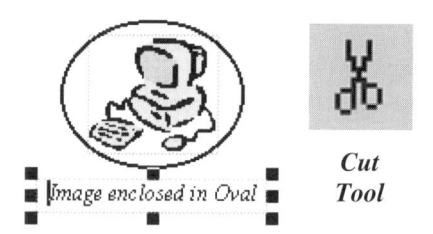

Cut Tool

3. Click the text frame to select it.
4. Click the *Cut* tool on the Standard toolbar.

If the oval and the pixel edited image need to be grouped, group them.

USING WORDART TO CREATE A TEXT DESIGN

1. Click the *WordArt Frame* tool from the Tool Palette.

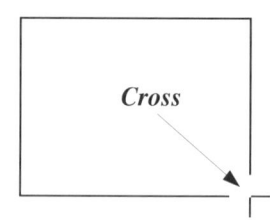

Cross

2. When pointer changes to a cross, drag over and down on the page to create a WordArt frame.

The result is seen below. A WordArt frame is created with a *Text Entry* box underneath it. When you type text into the *Text Entry* box and press the *Update Display* tab, the text appears in the WordArt frame.

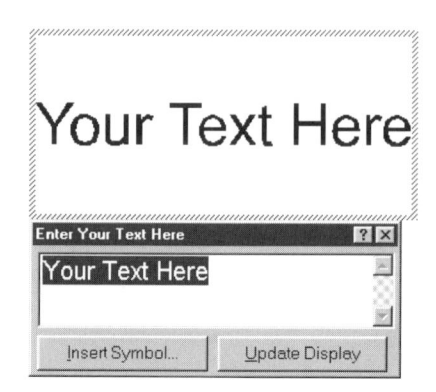

UNGROUPING THE LOGO AND THE TEXT FRAME, DELETING THE TEXT FRAME

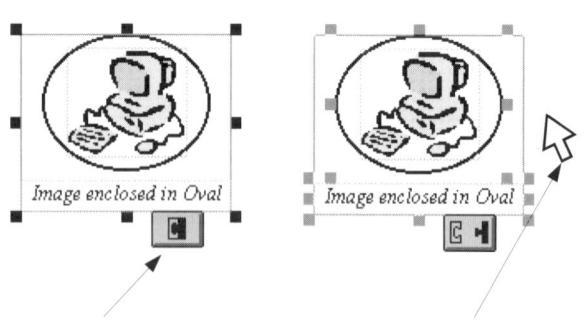

Click here to ungroup   *Click away to deselect*

1. Click the *Ungroup Objects* button to ungroup the text frame from the rest of group.
2. Click away from the ungrouped objects to deselect them.

Page 62   Desktop Publishing Made Easy

Chapter 5 — Designing a Business Letterhead

3. Type text into the **Text Entry** Box.
4. Click the **Update Display** tab.

In the illustration above I pressed the ENTER key on the keyboard twice to enter 3 lines of text.

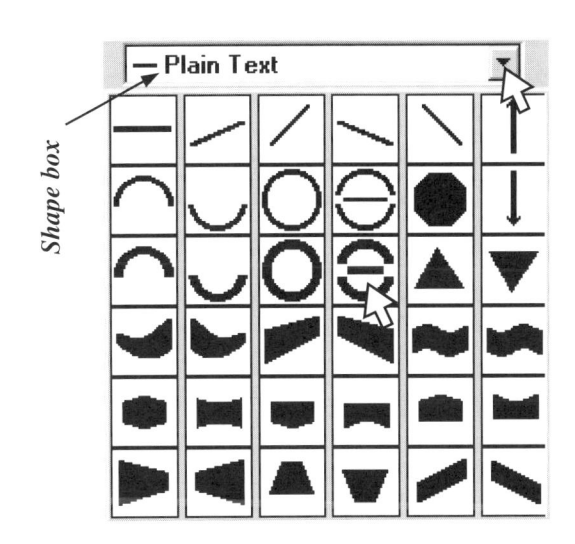

The shape of the text can be altered by clicking a shape in the **Shape** box.

7. Click the arrow to the right of the **Shape** box.
8. Click through all the shapes to see the effects they have on the text.
9. Choose the fourth shape in row 3.

The result is seen below.

Important to note:

- To deselect WordArt click outside of the frame.
- To select WordArt text double-click the frame.
- To select the WordArt frame click the frame.

WordArt must be selected before you can edit the text (change the font, font colour, embolden, make italic, shadow text, stretch text etc).

If only the frame is selected, you can work on the frame but not on the text.

The 5 tools above (**Bold**, *Italic* and the 3 **Special Effects** tools) are from the WordArt Formatting Toolbar. Click them to see what they do. Click them again to undo the formatting.

5. Click the *Italic* tool *I*.
6. Click the **Stretch** tool ←A→.

The text above is now italicised and stretched to fill the full width and depth of the frame.

WordArt is very useful for creating fancy effects in text and while very effective should not be overused. Regular text is often more appropriate.

Using Microsoft Publisher

Designing a Business Letterhead | **Chapter 5**

INSERTING A WORDART OBJECT INSIDE AN OVAL OF THE SAME DIMENSIONS AS THE LOGO

The object of this tutorial is to use WordArt to create a design for a business address and phone number, similar in shape to the logo designed in the previous chapter.

To do this we will copy and paste the logo across to a new file, extract the oval from the pasted logo and change the shape of the WordArt frame to the exact shape of the oval. Finally we will insert the WordArt frame into the oval and group them.

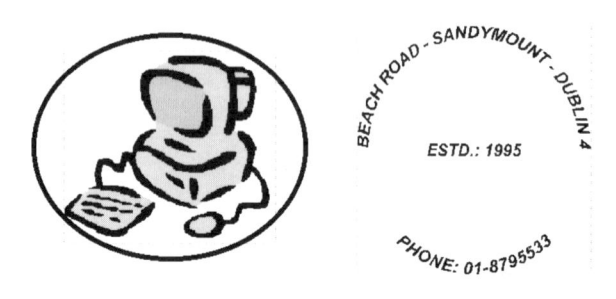

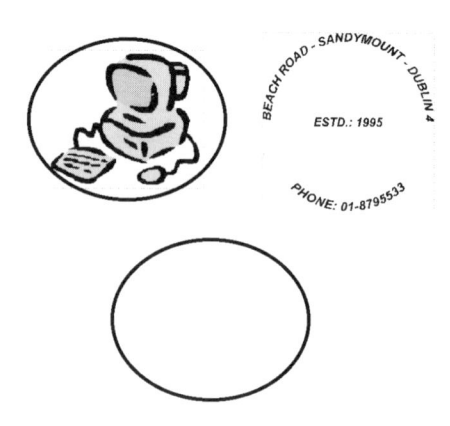

5. Ungroup the pasted logo.
6. Delete the picture and keep the oval.

The oval into which we will insert the WordArt object is therefore the same as the logo's oval.

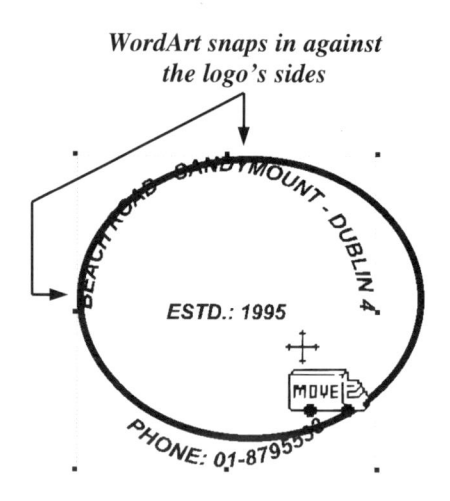

1. Copy the logo across from the *Logo* file.
2. Create a WordArt object like the one done in the last tutorial.

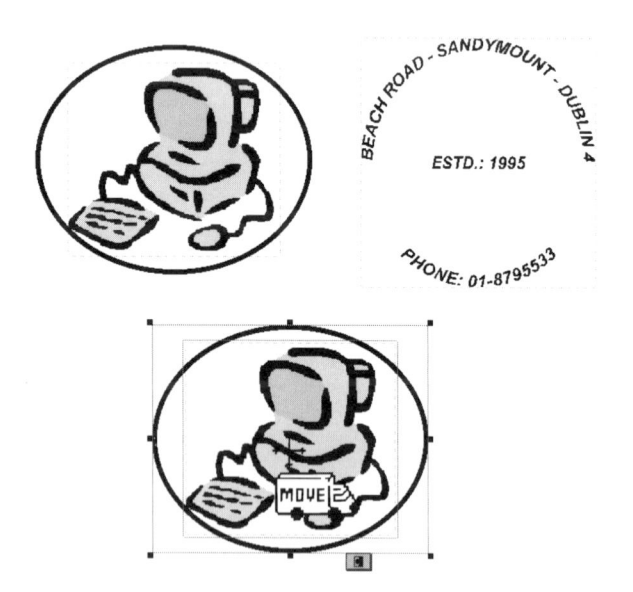

WordArt snaps in against the logo's sides

7. With **Snap to Objects** enabled, move the WordArt object in against the oval until it snaps in against any two sides.

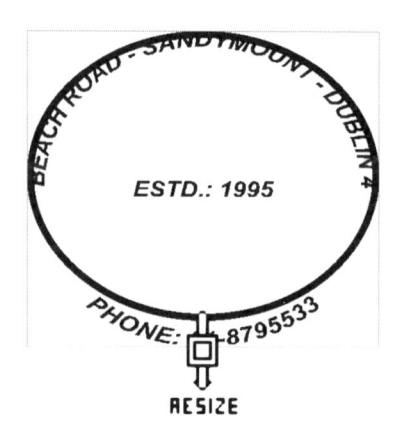

3. Copy and paste the logo.
4. Move the pasted logo away from the other objects.

8. Resize the WordArt frame until all the sides snap in against the sides of the oval.

Desktop Publishing Made Easy

Chapter 5

Designing a Business Letterhead

The WordArt frame and the oval are the same size and the text has the same shape as the oval.

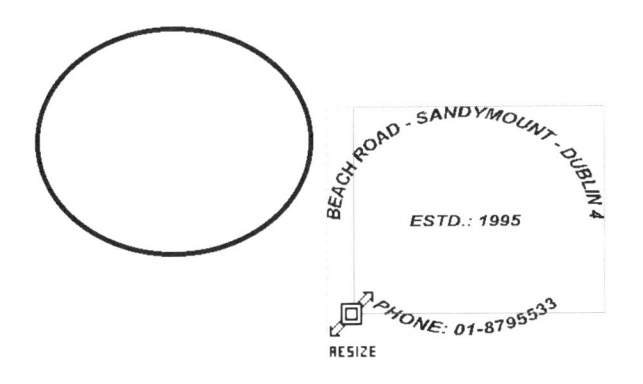

9. Move the WordArt frame and the oval apart.
10. Resize the WordArt frame proportionately from a corner handle to make it slightly smaller than the oval.

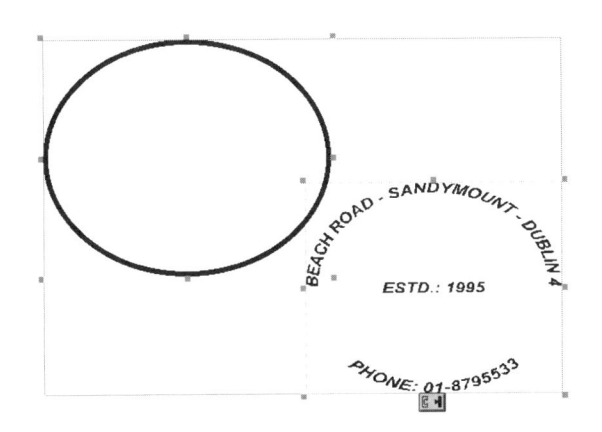

11. Multiple-select the logo and the WordArt.

12. Align the objects centrally both horizontally and vertically in relation to each other.
13. Group the objects.

If you feel you either resized the WordArt frame too much (too big a space between edge of oval and the WordArt text) or too little (WordArt text touching the edge of the oval), then repeat steps 9-12 until you get it right. See above.

REVERSING TEXT ON A TINTED BACKGROUND

Text is normally black on a white background. Publisher can give the background a tint ranging from grey to black or any shade of colour, on which white (reversed) text or black text or any colour text is placed.

This is done for effect and emphasis.

1. Create a text frame.
2. Type in the text.
3. Increase the font size and make it bold.
4. Centre the text horizontally.
5. Centre the text vertically.

Using Microsoft Publisher

Designing a Business Letterhead   Chapter 5

Font Color

We will now reverse the text – make it white – and place it on a black background.

6. Highlight the text.
7. Click the **Font Color** tool from the Formatting Toolbar.

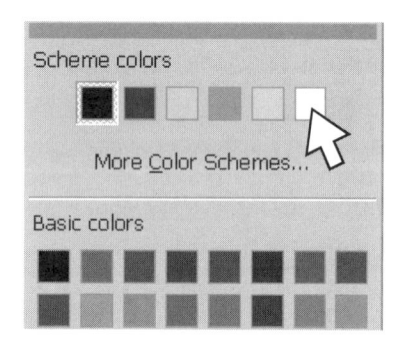

8. In the **Scheme colors** section choose the white colour.
9. Click **OK**.

The colour of the text has changed to white. It is on a white background and is therefore invisible. See the invisible white text highlighted and not highlighted in the illustrations below.

If we change the background colour of the text frame to black, the white text will become visible.

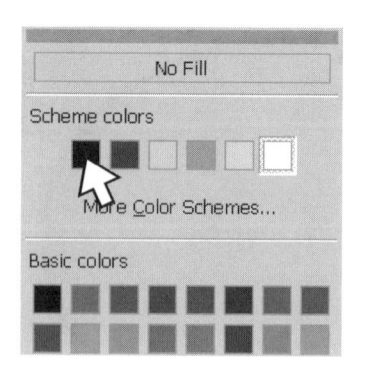

Fill Color

10. To change the background colour to black, click the text frame to select it.
11. Click the **Fill Color** tool on the Formatting Toolbar.
12. In the **Scheme colors** section choose the black colour.

Below is white text on a black background.

In the illustration above are more examples of reversed text on tinted backgrounds. The lighter the tint, the more difficult it is to read the text.

Below is an example of black text on a tinted background. The darker the tint, the more difficult it is to read the text.

Page 66   Desktop Publishing Made Easy

Chapter 5 — Designing a Business Letterhead

CREATING A RECTANGLE

1. Click the *Rectangle Frame* tool from the Tool Palette.

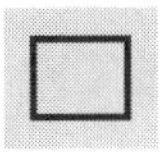

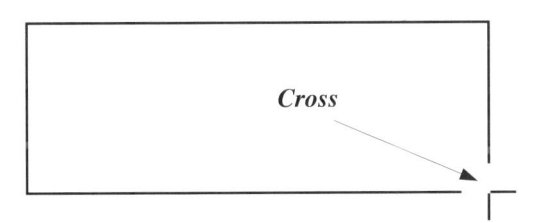

2. When pointer changes to a cross, drag over and down on the page to create a rectangle.

To create a perfect square hold down the SHIFT key on the keyboard as you drag over and down.

USING A CUSTOM SHAPE AS A TINTED BACKGROUND FOR TEXT

We saw how to reverse text on its own tinted background. However, you may like to use a custom shape with a tint as a background for text.

To do this we must create a custom shape and place the text frame over it.

1. Create a custom shape and a text frame in that order.
2. Type text into the text frame and format it.
3. Give the custom shape a 20% fill of black by clicking the *Fill Color* tool on the Formatting Toolbar, choosing *Fill Effects*, clicking the *Tints/Shades* radio button, choosing black in the *Base color* box, scrolling to the left in the *Style* section and clicking the *20%* fill box.
4. Multiple-select the 2 objects. 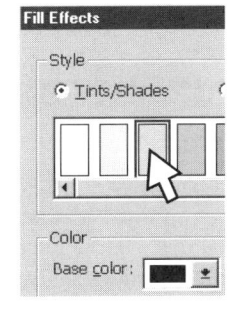
5. Centre align them horizontally and vertically in relation to each other.

The white background of the text frame has to be made transparent to allow the tinted background of the custom shape be seen.

6. Click the text frame to select it.
7. Click *No Fill* in the *Fill Color* window.

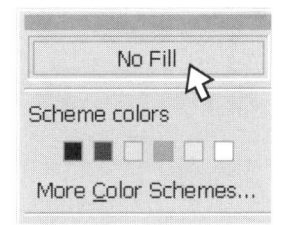

This makes the text frame background transparent to allow the background tint of the custom shape become visible.

8. Group the objects.

You may not like a border to the custom shape. To get rid of it:

9. Click *None* from the *Line/Border Style* tool on the Formatting Toolbar.

Below is an example of reversed text on a custom shape with a black tinted background.

Using Microsoft Publisher

Designing a Business Letterhead — Chapter 5

EXERCISE 5.1

COMPLETION INSTRUCTIONS

Carry out the instructions in numerical order

See the sketch sheet on the next page

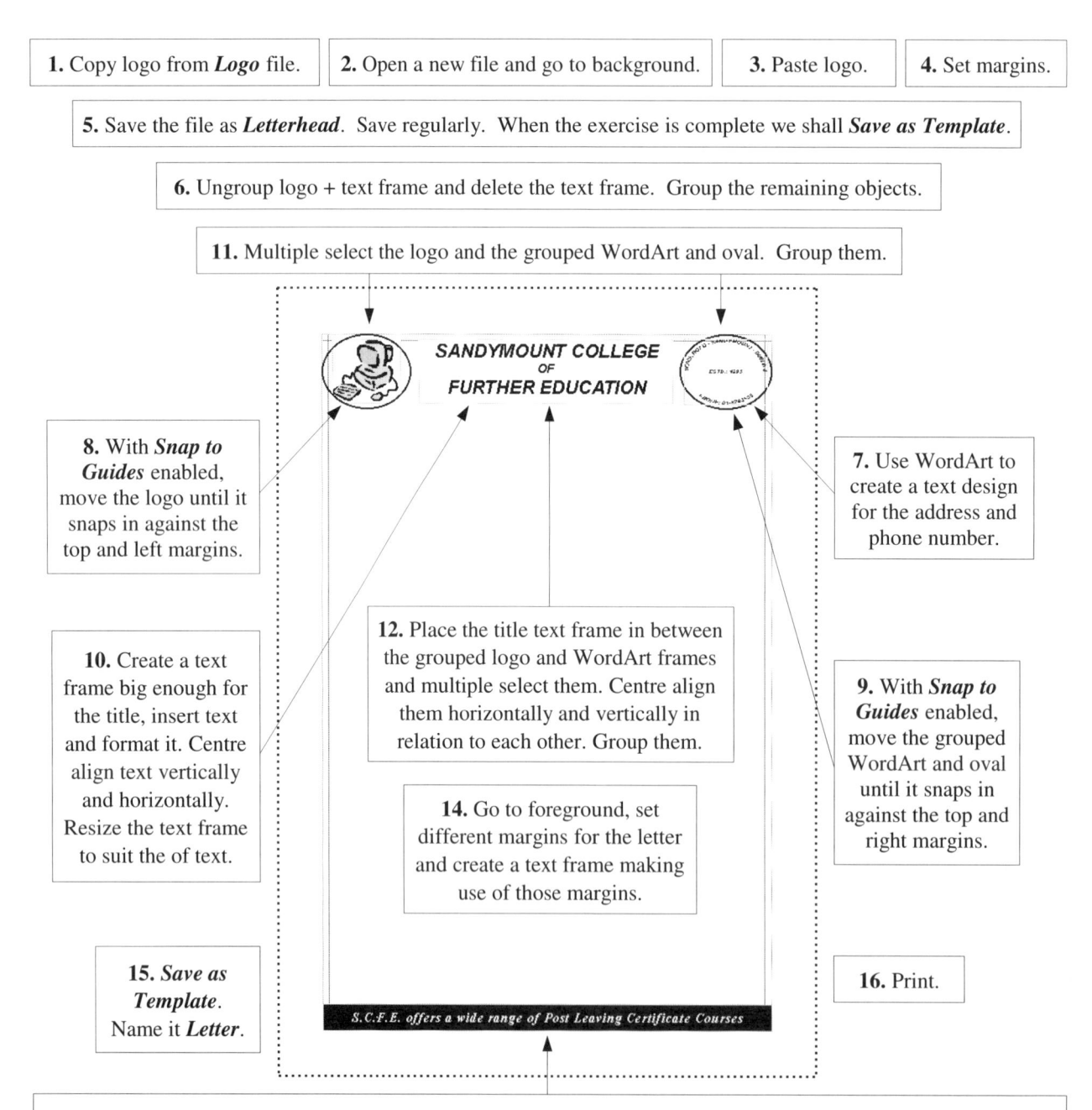

1. Copy logo from *Logo* file.

2. Open a new file and go to background.

3. Paste logo.

4. Set margins.

5. Save the file as *Letterhead*. Save regularly. When the exercise is complete we shall *Save as Template*.

6. Ungroup logo + text frame and delete the text frame. Group the remaining objects.

11. Multiple select the logo and the grouped WordArt and oval. Group them.

8. With *Snap to Guides* enabled, move the logo until it snaps in against the top and left margins.

7. Use WordArt to create a text design for the address and phone number.

10. Create a text frame big enough for the title, insert text and format it. Centre align text vertically and horizontally. Resize the text frame to suit the of text.

12. Place the title text frame in between the grouped logo and WordArt frames and multiple select them. Centre align them horizontally and vertically in relation to each other. Group them.

9. With *Snap to Guides* enabled, move the grouped WordArt and oval until it snaps in against the top and right margins.

14. Go to foreground, set different margins for the letter and create a text frame making use of those margins.

15. *Save as Template*. Name it *Letter*.

16. Print.

13. Create a text frame stretching from the left to the right margin for the bottom of the page. Insert text and format it. Centre align the text vertically and horizontally in the text frame. Resize the text frame to suit the text. Reverse the text on a black background. With *Snap to Guides* enabled, move the text frame in against the bottom margin.

Chapter 5　　　　　　　　　　　　　　　　　Designing a Business Letterhead

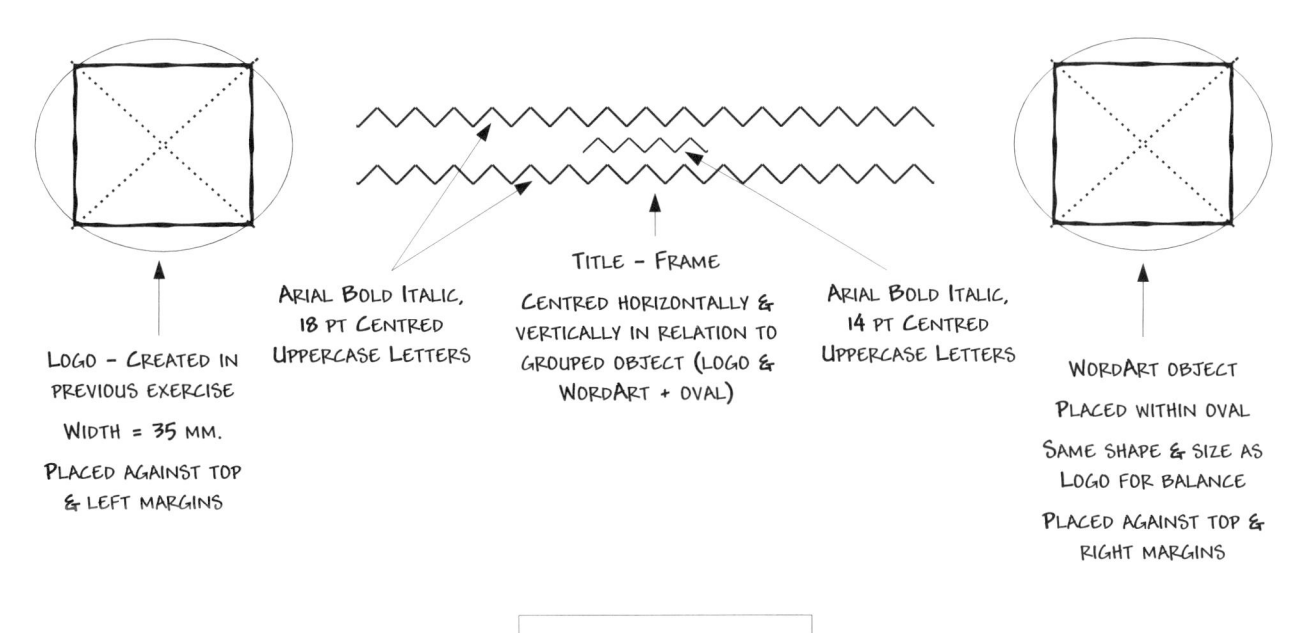

LOGO – CREATED IN PREVIOUS EXERCISE
WIDTH = 35 MM.
PLACED AGAINST TOP & LEFT MARGINS

ARIAL BOLD ITALIC, 18 PT CENTRED UPPERCASE LETTERS

TITLE – FRAME
CENTRED HORIZONTALLY & VERTICALLY IN RELATION TO GROUPED OBJECT (LOGO & WORDART + OVAL)

ARIAL BOLD ITALIC, 14 PT CENTRED UPPERCASE LETTERS

WORDART OBJECT
PLACED WITHIN OVAL
SAME SHAPE & SIZE AS LOGO FOR BALANCE
PLACED AGAINST TOP & RIGHT MARGINS

SKETCH SHEET FOR LETTERHEAD

A4 PAGE

MARGINS: 17.5 MM. ALL AROUND
PORTRAIT

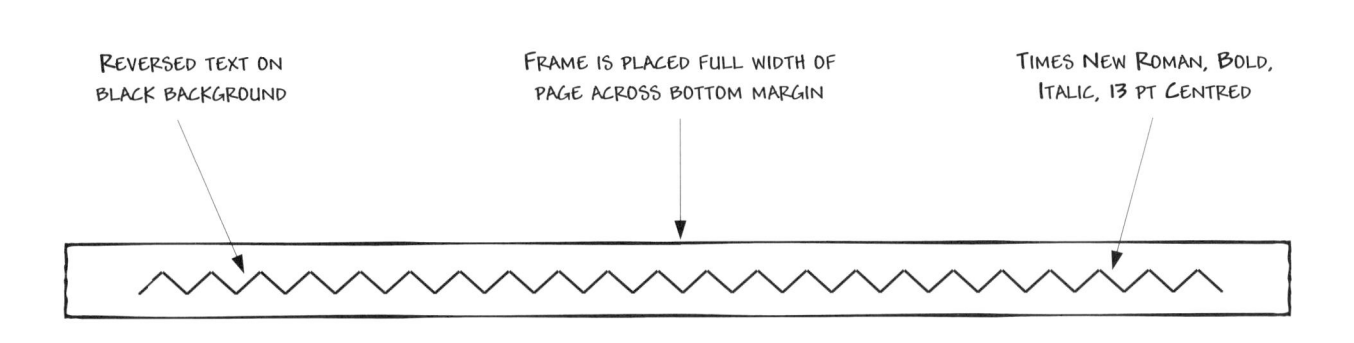

REVERSED TEXT ON BLACK BACKGROUND

FRAME IS PLACED FULL WIDTH OF PAGE ACROSS BOTTOM MARGIN

TIMES NEW ROMAN, BOLD, ITALIC, 13 PT CENTRED

SANDYMOUNT COLLEGE OF FURTHER EDUCATION

BEACH ROAD - SANDYMOUNT - DUBLIN 4
ESTD.: 1995
PHONE: 01-8795533

S.C.F.E. offers a wide range of Post Leaving Certificate Courses

Exercise 5.2

Design a Business Letterhead for a Garage

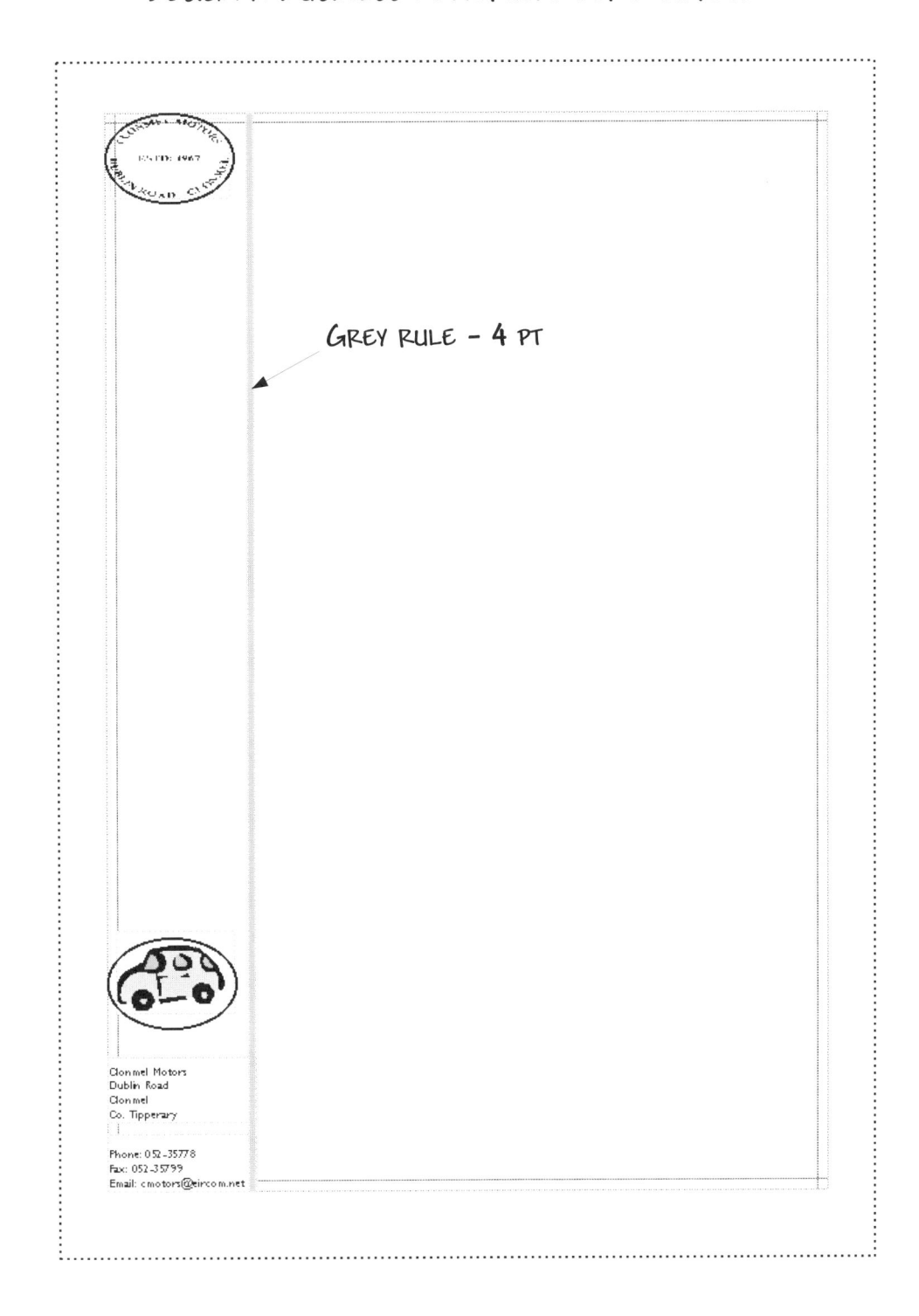

Grey rule – 4 pt

Clonmel Motors
Dublin Road
Clonmel
Co. Tipperary

Phone: 052-35778
Fax: 052-35799
Email: cmotors@eircom.net

Exercise 5.3

Design a Business Letterhead for a Building Contractor

Transparent text frames are placed on custom shape

Foley Construction
Newtown Road
Wexford

Phone
051-44748

Fax
051-44798

Email
foley@sircom.net

10% fill of black

Use ruler guides to place custom shape between objects

CHAPTER 6

DESIGNING A BUSINESS CARD

SANDYMOUNT COLLEGE OF FURTHER EDUCATION

Beach Road, Sandymount, Dublin 4

Mr John Fitzgerald (Principal)

Phone: 01-8795533   Fax: 01-8795673

E-mail: scfe@eircom.net

PAGE SETUP

The default electronic page in Microsoft Publisher is *A4*, the same as the default printer page. You will, however, have set up a smaller electronic page for some publications, e.g. a business card or compliment slip. To do this it is necessary to set up a custom page in Publisher.

To set up a custom page for a Business Card:

1. Click *File* from the Menu Bar.
2. Click *Page Setup*.

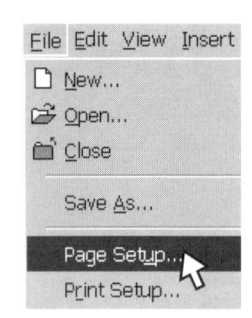

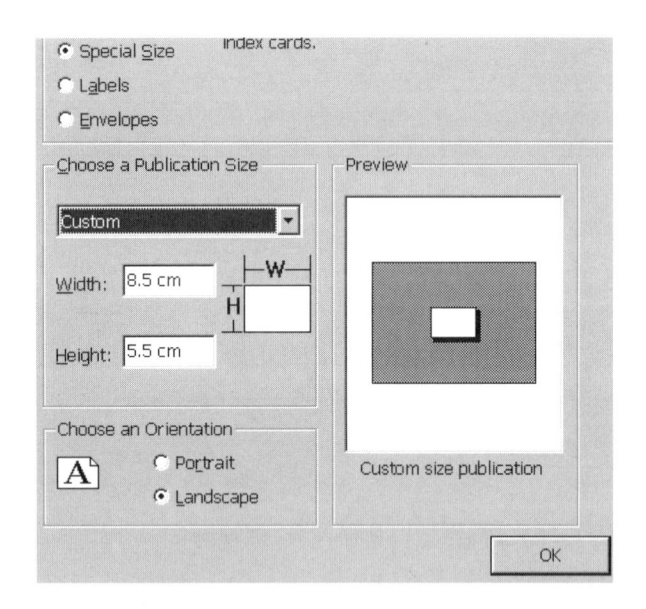

3. Click *Special Size* in the *Choose a Publication Layout* section.
4. Choose *Custom* in the *Choose a Publication Size* box.
5. Type 8.5 cm. in the *Width* box and 5.5 cm. in the *Height* box.
6. Choose *Portrait* or *Landscape* in the *Choose an Orientation* section. In the *Preview* section the white represents the business card and the shaded represents the A4 paper in the printer.
7. Click *OK*.

CREATING RULES

1. Click the *Line* tool from the Tool Palette.

2. Drag in any direction to create a rule.

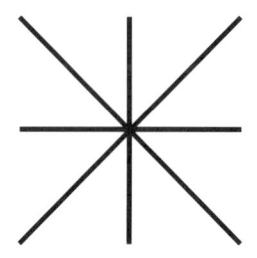

3. Pressing the SHIFT key on the keyboard while dragging ensures that the rules are horizontal, vertical or at an angle of 45°.

ALIGNING RULES WITH TEXT

If text is left aligned and placed directly above or below a horizontal rule, it may look better if it is aligned with the left edge of the rule.

Left edge of the rule and text frame. The space between the 'S' and the edge may not look well.

The default text frame margins in Microsoft Publisher are 1 mm. If the text frame and rule are aligned by use of a ruler guide or margin guide, the text will be 1 mm. to the right of the rule.

Chapter 6 — Designing a Business Card

Sandymount Colle

1. Click *Format* on the Menu Bar.
2. Click *Text Frame Properties*.
3. Change the left margin to 0 cm.
4. Click *OK*.

The alignment of the text with the rule can be more pleasing to the eye.

UNGROUPING LOGO, CHANGING OVAL THICKNESS AND RE-GROUPING

The logo will have to be decreased in size to suit the smaller sizes of the business card and the compliment slip. The oval's 2 pt thickness may then appear too great and can be changed to 1 pt.

Logo with oval of 1 pt thickness

Logo with oval of 2 pt thickness

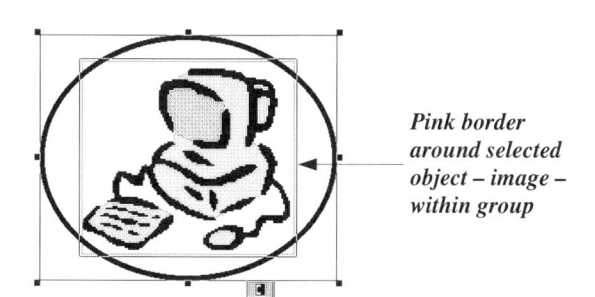

Pink border around selected object – image – within group

An object within a group can be selected. When you click on it a pink border appears around its edges. You can change the border thickness of an object within a group. You cannot delete an object within a group; you must first ungroup the objects.

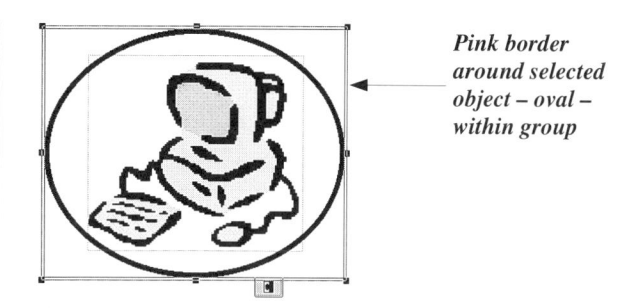

Pink border around selected object – oval – within group

1. To select the oval move the mouse pointer to its edge and click. A pink border appears around its edges. Moving in further will select the image and not the oval.
2. Change the oval's thickness to 1 pt.

See the result below.

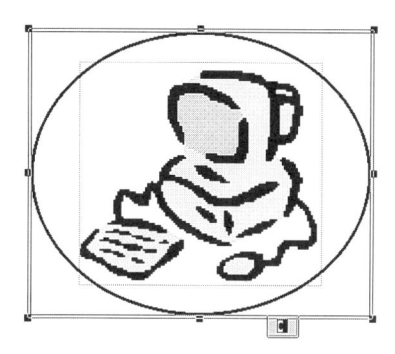

COMPLETION INSTRUCTIONS

See *Exercise 6.1* on page 76

1. Set up a custom page for a business card.
2. Save as *Business Card*. Save regularly.
3. Copy the logo across from the *Letterhead* file.
4. Change the oval's thickness to 1 pt and rescale the logo to suit the business card.
5. Place the logo in a suitable position.
6. Place a ruler guide 2 mm. to the right of the logo. This can be used for aligning some of the rules and text frames.
7. Create text frames, insert text, format text, resize text frames to suit text. See the sketch sheet on page 77 for specifications.
8. Place the text frames in appropriate positions.
9. Draw rules of 1 pt thickness as shown.
10. Place rules in appropriate positions under text frames and along the top and bottom margins. Nudge to ensure consistent space between text and rules. Group each text frame with its appropriate rule for balancing on the page.
11. Balance the objects on the page by nudging.
12. Save and print using crop marks.

Designing a Business Card　　　　　　　　　　　　　　　　　　　　　　Chapter 6

EXERCISE 6.1

COMPLETION INSTRUCTIONS

Carry out the instructions on the previous page in numerical order

See the sketch sheet on the next page

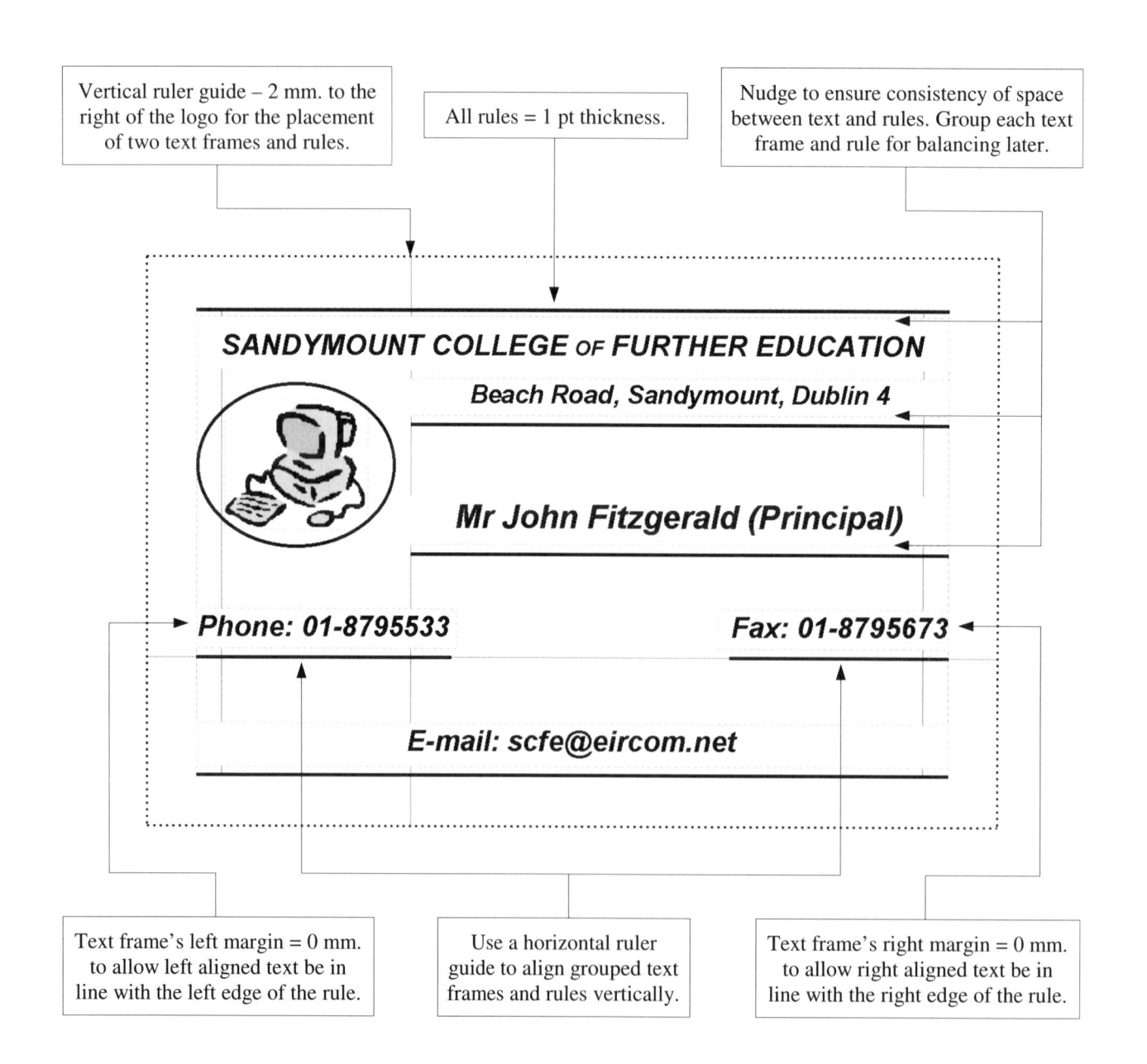

Vertical ruler guide – 2 mm. to the right of the logo for the placement of two text frames and rules.

All rules = 1 pt thickness.

Nudge to ensure consistency of space between text and rules. Group each text frame and rule for balancing later.

SANDYMOUNT COLLEGE OF FURTHER EDUCATION

Beach Road, Sandymount, Dublin 4

Mr John Fitzgerald (Principal)

Phone: 01-8795533　　　　　　　　　　*Fax: 01-8795673*

E-mail: scfe@eircom.net

Text frame's left margin = 0 mm. to allow left aligned text be in line with the left edge of the rule.

Use a horizontal ruler guide to align grouped text frames and rules vertically.

Text frame's right margin = 0 mm. to allow right aligned text be in line with the right edge of the rule.

Page 76　　　　　　　　　　　　　　　　　　　　　　　　Desktop Publishing Made Easy

Chapter 6 *Designing a Business Card*

CUSTOM PAGE (85 MM. X 55 MM.) – LANDSCAPE

MARGINS = 5 MM. ALL AROUND

CROP MARKS

LOGO (20 MM. IN WIDTH & PLACED AGAINST LEFT MARGIN) OVAL THICKNESS CHANGED TO 1 PT TO SUIT RULES

ARIAL BOLD ITALIC, 8 PT CENTRED
UPPERCASE LETTERS
FRAME CENTRED IN RELATION TO RULE

ARIAL BOLD ITALIC, 8 PT CENTRED
FRAME CENTRED IN RELATION TO RULE

ARIAL BOLD ITALIC, 7 PT CENTRED
FRAME CENTRED IN RELATION TO RULE

CROP MARKS

ARIAL BOLD ITALIC, 8 PT LEFT ALIGNED

ARIAL BOLD ITALIC, 8 PT RIGHT ALIGNED

ARIAL BOLD ITALIC, 9 PT CENTRED
FRAME CENTRED IN RELATION TO RULE

ALL RULES ARE 1 PT THICKNESS

SKETCH SHEET FOR BUSINESS CARD

Using Microsoft Publisher Page 77

Designing a Business Card — Chapter 6

[Business card (rotated): SANDYMOUNT COLLEGE OF FURTHER EDUCATION, Beach Road, Sandymount, Dublin 4. Mr John Fitzgerald (Principal). Phone: 01-8795533 Fax: 01-8795673 E-mail: scfe@eircom.net]

Exercise 6.2

Design a Business Card for a Garage

Custom Page (85 mm. x 55 mm.) – Portrait

Set margins of 5 mm. all around

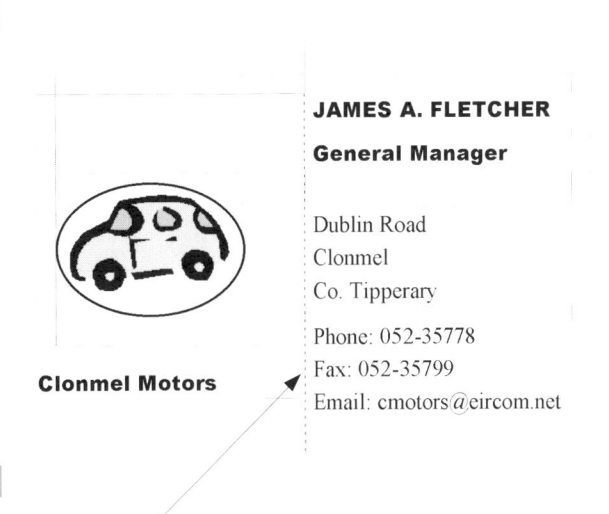

JAMES A. FLETCHER
General Manager

Dublin Road
Clonmel
Co. Tipperary

Phone: 052-35778
Fax: 052-35799
Email: cmotors@eircom.net

Clonmel Motors

Use ruler guide to align these text frames

Designing a Business Card   *Chapter 6*

Exercise 6.3

Design a Business Card for a Building Contractor

Custom Page (85 mm. x 55 mm.) – Portrait   Set margins of 5 mm. all around

Centre the text frame vertically inside the rectangle
Centre the text vertically inside the text frame

FOLEY CONSTRUCTION

Newtown Road
Wexford

Charles J. Foley
Site Manager

Phone: 053-44748
Fax: 053-44798
Email: foleyc@eircom.net

The rectangle above with no border on the left side can be created as follows:

1. Create a rectangle of 1 pt thickness.
2. Click the Line/Border Style tool.
3. Select More Styles.
4. Select the Left border in the Select a Side box.
5. Click None in the Choose a Thickness box.
6. Click OK.

Chapter 6 — Designing a Business Card

IN CHAPTERS 5 AND 6 YOU HAVE DONE THE FOLLOWING:

- Learned about templates.
- Saved files as templates.
- Opened template files.
- Learned about backgrounds.
- Created backgrounds.
- Copied objects from one file to another.
- Ungrouped grouped objects and deleted one element.
- Used WordArt to create text designs.
- Inserted WordArt objects inside ovals, maintaining the shape of the ovals.
- Reversed text on tinted backgrounds.
- Created rectangles.
- Used custom shapes as tinted backgrounds for text.
- Set up custom pages.
- Created rules.
- Aligned text with rules.
- Changed the thickness of objects.

CHAPTER 7

DESIGNING A COMPLIMENT SLIP

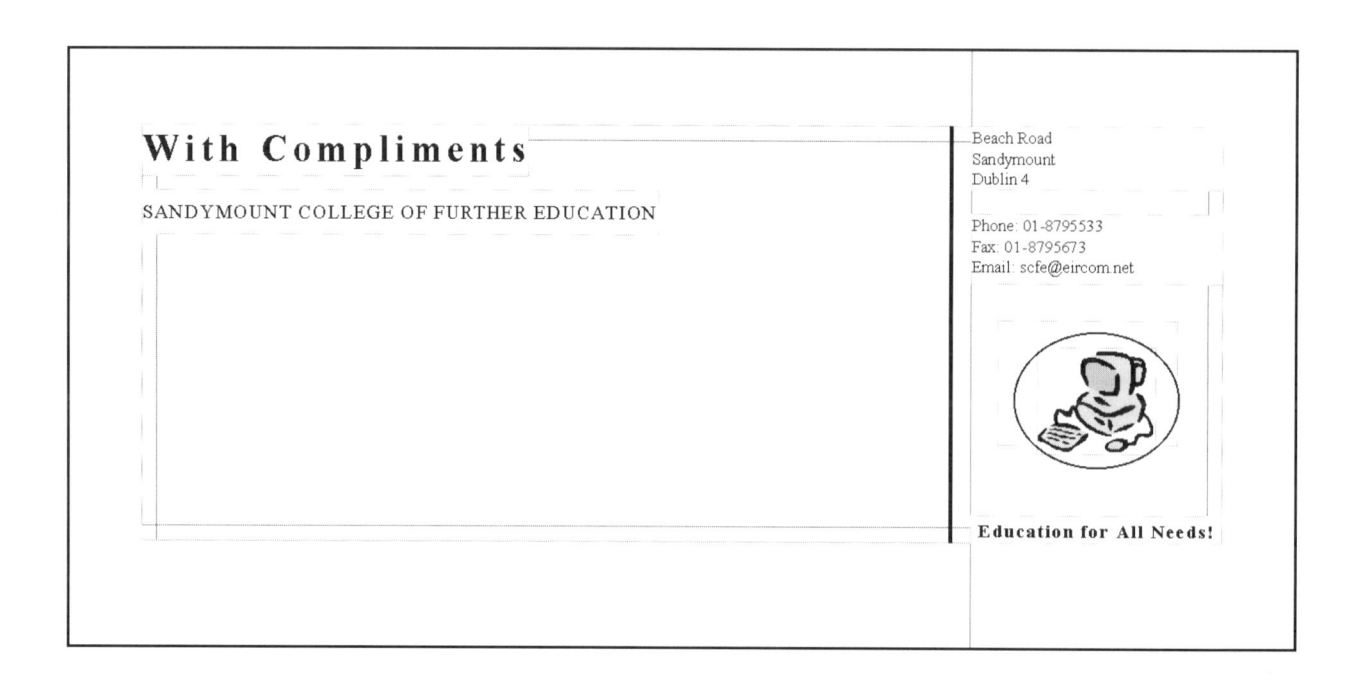

With Compliments

SANDYMOUNT COLLEGE OF FURTHER EDUCATION

Beach Road
Sandymount
Dublin 4

Phone: 01-8795533
Fax: 01-8795673
Email: scfe@eircom.net

Education for All Needs!

Chapter 7 *Designing a Compliment Slip*

TRACKING

Increased spacing between characters (increased *tracking*) can be used to improve readability. It is generally done to make headlines more readable, but can also be done to make a line of text with few words stand out more. It is very rarely if ever used for body text.

To increase tracking:

With Compliments

1. Highlight the text.

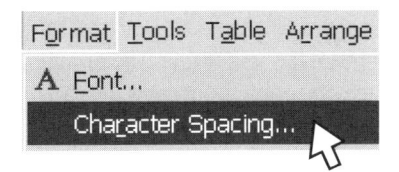

2. Click *Format* from the Menu Bar.
3. Click *Character Spacing*.

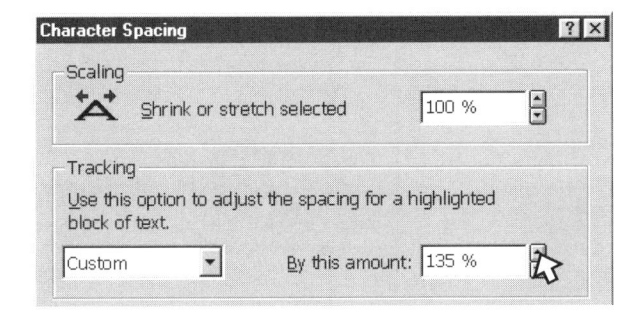

4. In the *Tracking* section choose a percentage value in the *By this amount* box. The tracking has been increased by 35% above.
5. A visual illustration of the tracking increase is shown in the *Sample* section at the bottom of the *Character Spacing* window.
6. Click *Apply* or *OK*.

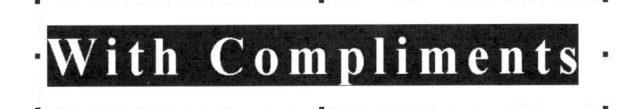

With Compliments

The text above has increased tracking.

KERNING

While tracking is adjusting the space between characters, kerning is adjusting the space between pairs of characters. Some combinations of letters create an unattractively wide space between them, especially in larger point sizes, and this can be rectified by kerning.

World

The uppercase letter '*W*' and the lowercase '*o*' have a larger than average space between them, as have the '*o*' and the '*r*'. We will use kerning to decrease this space.

World

1. Highlight the pair of characters to be kerned.

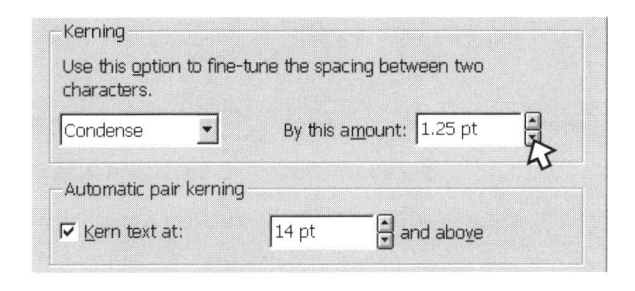

2. Click *Format* from the Menu Bar.
3. Click *Character Spacing*.
4. In the *Kerning* section click the bottom arrow to decrease the space between the pair of characters. The word *Condense* appears in the box opposite to denote a decrease in the space.
5. Click *Apply* or *OK*.

Apply performs the action while retaining the *Character Spacing* window. *OK* performs the action and the window disappears.

In the illustration below both pairs of characters have been kerned.

World

Using Microsoft Publisher

EXERCISE 7.1

COMPLETION INSTRUCTIONS

Carry out the instructions in numerical order

See the sketch sheet on the next page

---

1. Set up a custom page for the compliment slip (210 mm. x 99 mm.).

2. Save as *Compliment Slip*. Save regularly.

3. Copy logo across from the *Business Card* file.

4. Create text frames, type text, format it as shown on the sketch sheet, resize each text frame to suit the text and place the frames in suitable positions on the page, snapping in against the left margin.

6. Create text frames, type up text, format text as shown on the sketch sheet, resize each text frame to suit the text and place the text frames in suitable positions on the page, snapping in against the ruler guide.

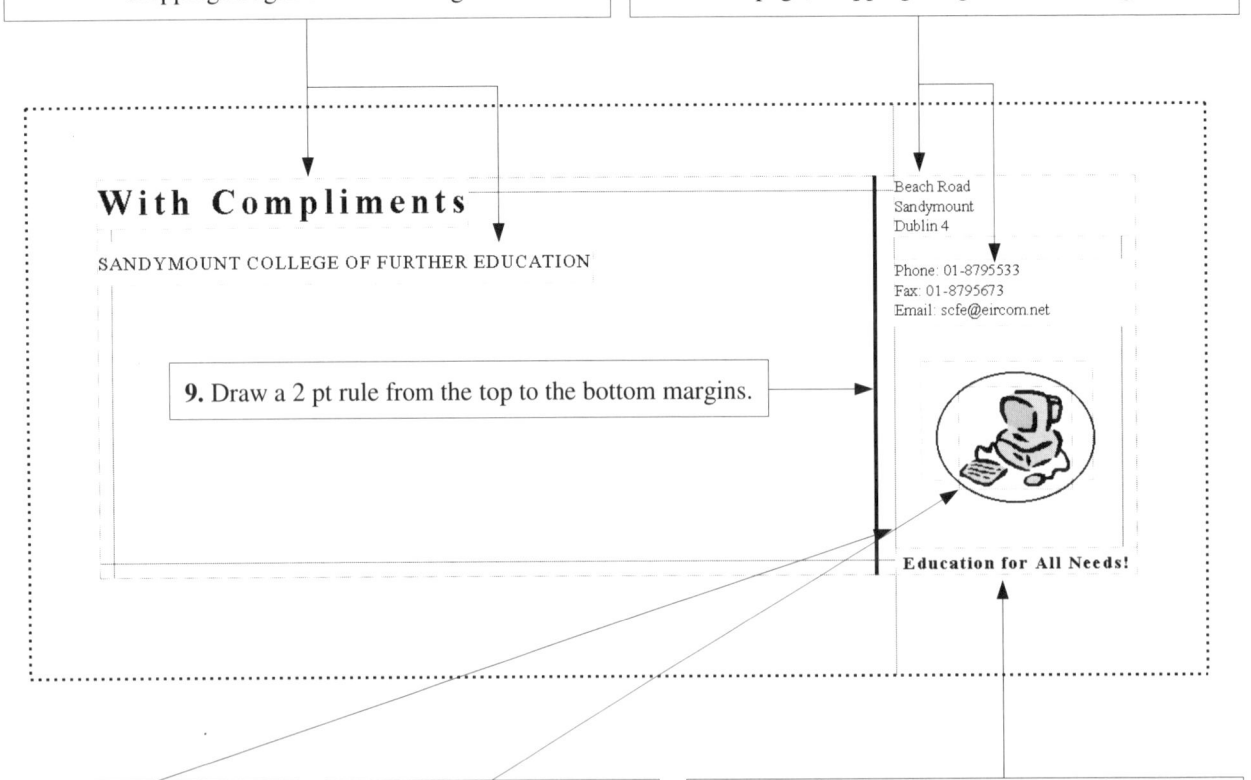

With Compliments

SANDYMOUNT COLLEGE OF FURTHER EDUCATION

Beach Road
Sandymount
Dublin 4

Phone: 01-8795533
Fax: 01-8795673
Email: scfe@eircom.net

9. Draw a 2 pt rule from the top to the bottom margins.

Education for All Needs!

5. Place a vertical ruler guide 155 mm. from the left margin for aligning the two text frames.

8. Place the logo in a suitable position and centre it horizontally between the ruler guide and the right margin.

7. Create a text frame, type up text, format the text as shown on the sketch sheet, resize the text frame to suit the text and place it in a suitable position on the page, snapping in against the bottom margin.

10. Save and print using crop marks.

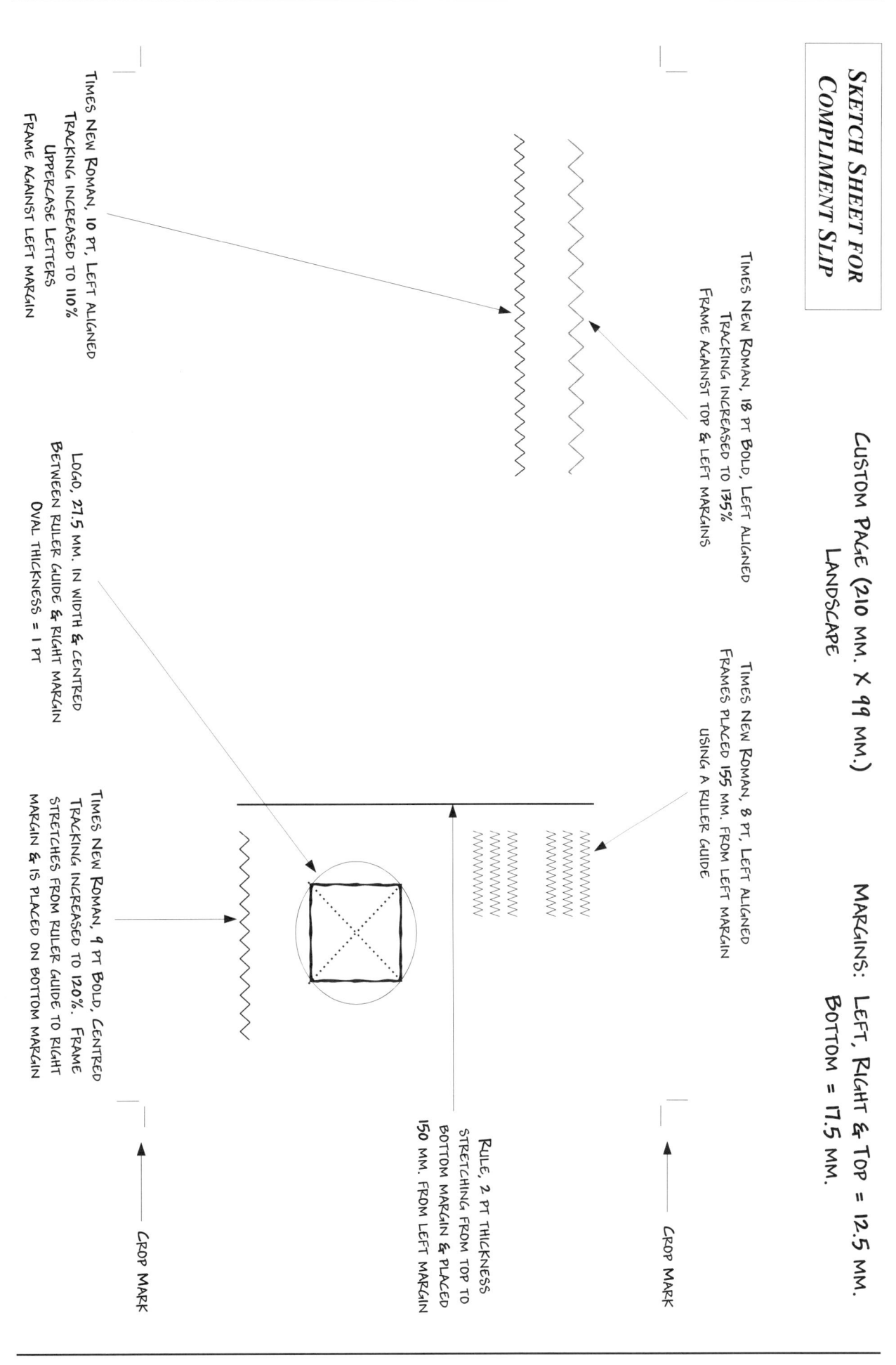

Chapter 7 *Designing a Compliment Slip*

SKETCH SHEET FOR COMPLIMENT SLIP

CUSTOM PAGE (210 MM. X 99 MM.) LANDSCAPE

MARGINS: LEFT, RIGHT & TOP = 12.5 MM. BOTTOM = 17.5 MM.

TIMES NEW ROMAN, 18 PT BOLD, LEFT ALIGNED
TRACKING INCREASED TO 135%
FRAME AGAINST TOP & LEFT MARGINS

TIMES NEW ROMAN, 10 PT, LEFT ALIGNED
TRACKING INCREASED TO 110%
UPPERCASE LETTERS
FRAME AGAINST LEFT MARGIN

TIMES NEW ROMAN, 8 PT, LEFT ALIGNED
FRAMES PLACED 155 MM. FROM LEFT MARGIN
USING A RULER GUIDE

LOGO, 27.5 MM. IN WIDTH & CENTRED
BETWEEN RULER GUIDE & RIGHT MARGIN
OVAL THICKNESS = 1 PT

TIMES NEW ROMAN, 9 PT BOLD, CENTRED
TRACKING INCREASED TO 120%. FRAME
STRETCHES FROM RULER GUIDE TO RIGHT
MARGIN & IS PLACED ON BOTTOM MARGIN

RULE, 2 PT THICKNESS
STRETCHING FROM TOP TO
BOTTOM MARGIN & PLACED
150 MM. FROM LEFT MARGIN

CROP MARK

CROP MARK

Using Microsoft Publisher Page 85

Beach Road
Sandymount
Dublin 4

Phone: 01-8795533
Fax: 01-8795673
Email: scfe@eircom.net

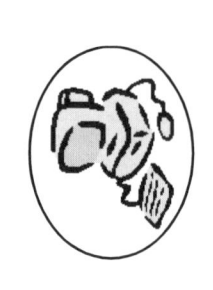

Education for All Needs!

With Compliments

SANDYMOUNT COLLEGE OF FURTHER EDUCATION

Exercise 7.2

Design a Compliment Slip for a Garage

Custom Page (210 mm. x 99 mm.) – Landscape

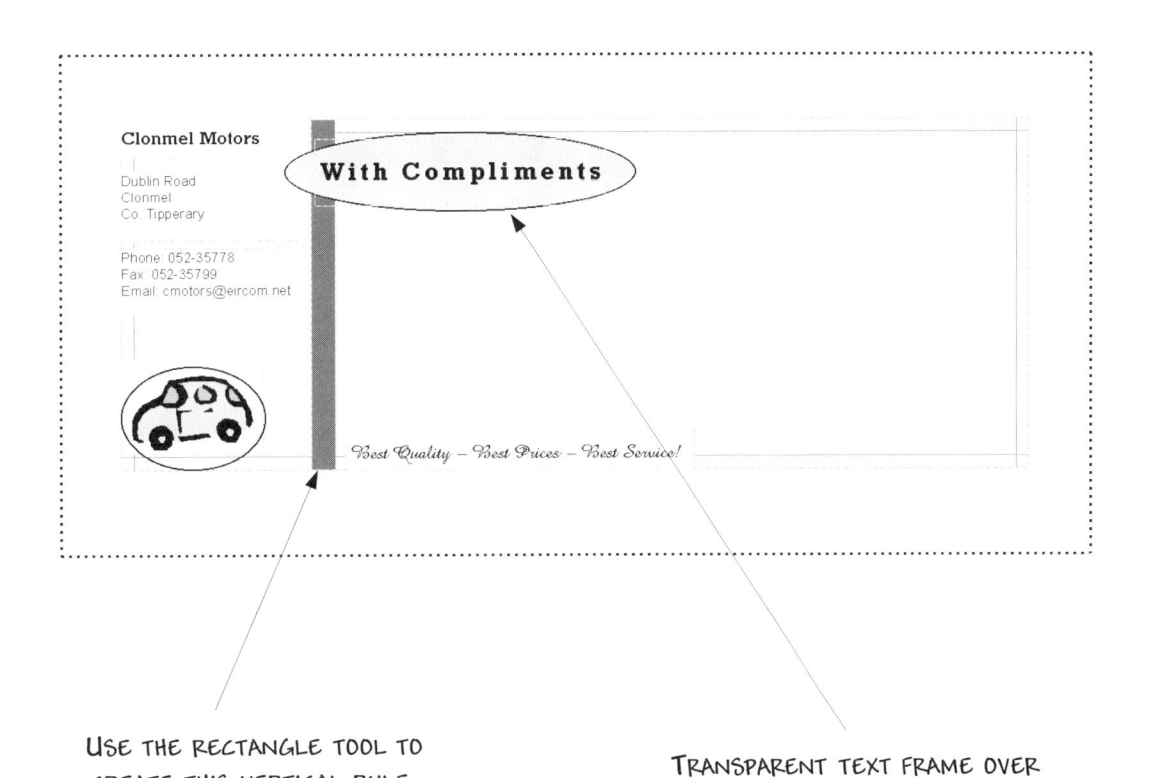

Clonmel Motors

Dublin Road
Clonmel
Co. Tipperary

Phone: 052-35778
Fax: 052-35799
Email: cmotors@eircom.net

With Compliments

Best Quality – Best Prices – Best Service!

Use the rectangle tool to create this vertical rule. Give it a 60% fill of black.

Transparent text frame over custom shape with 20% fill of black

Exercise 7.3

Design a Compliment Slip for a Building Contractor

Custom Page (210 mm. x 99 mm.) – Landscape

Transparent text frames over custom shapes with differents fills

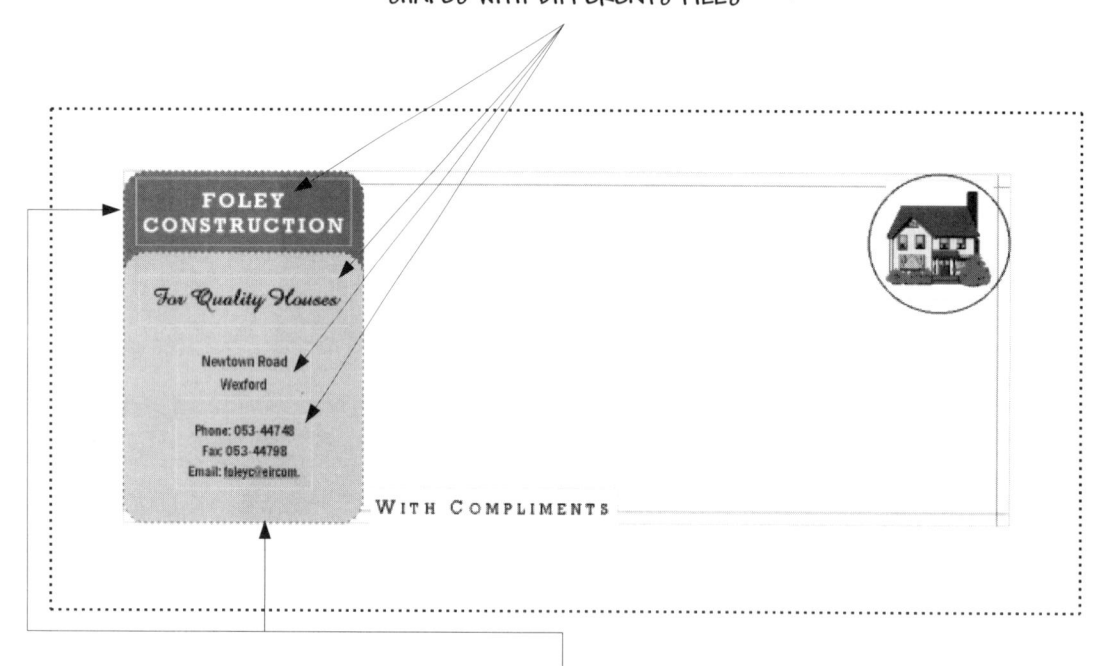

Use the Custom Shape tool to create these two frames. Place the smaller one on top of the larger one. Give them different fills.

CHAPTER 8

DESIGNING A GREETING CARD

(Not part of the FETAC/NCVA DTP Module Descriptor - E20003)

Designing a Greeting Card   Chapter 8

PAPER SIZES

The most popular paper size is *A4*, which is the default electronic page in Publisher. We changed the default A4 page to suit both the business card and the compliment slip.

In the next exercise we will split the *A4* page into 4 sections when we manually set up the 4 pages of the Greeting Card.

Before we do this, a word about paper sizes and their names and measurements: an *A3* page is double an *A4* page, an *A4* is double an *A5* and an *A5* is double an *A6*.

Therefore, each of the pages of the Greeting Card that we will be designing will be of size A6.

The diagram below shows the most common paper sizes used in Desktop Publishing.

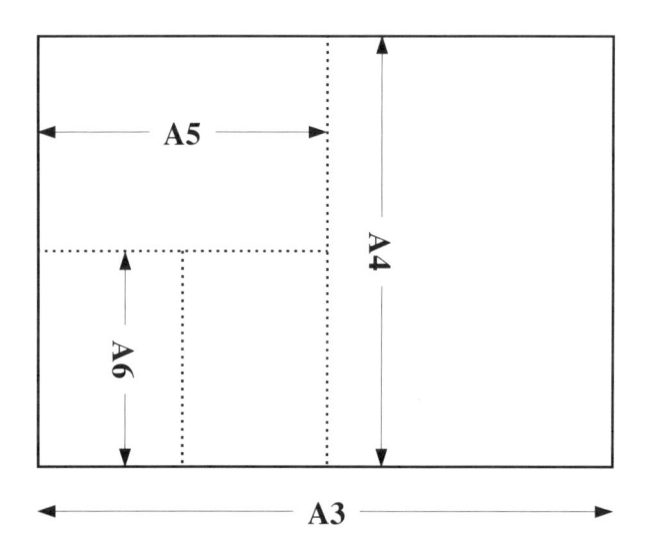

Name	Millimetres
A3	297 x 420
A4	210 x 297
A5	148 x 210
A6	105 x 148

Each size is exactly half the area of the size before it and is geometrically the same.

USING A PRE-DEFINED LAYOUT TO SET UP A GREETING CARD PAGE

Since Sept. 2001 this exercise is no longer part of the Collection of Work on the FETAC/NCVA DTP Module Descriptor. As this book is not written solely for students covering a specific course, I thought it would be a good idea to include an exercise which involves the breaking up of an A4 page into 4 A6 sections.

There are 3 methods of setting up the Greeting Card pages. Two of these methods incorporate pre-defined layouts. I will be concentrating on the third, which is to manually set up the pages, but will briefly show the other two.

The creating and modifying of the objects is the same for all 3 methods. The placement of the objects is simpler in the pre-defined layouts as it is only a matter of centring them on the page or snapping them in against the margins. In the manually set-up Greeting Card we have to centre them within panels in each of the 4 A6 pages.

Let's see the 2 methods of setting up a Greeting Card using pre-defined layouts:

The first method:

If Publisher isn't set up to display the *Microsoft Publisher Catalog* screen at the start up, then:

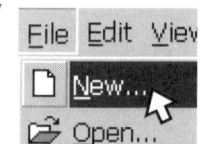

1. Click *File* from the Menu bar.
2. Click *New*.

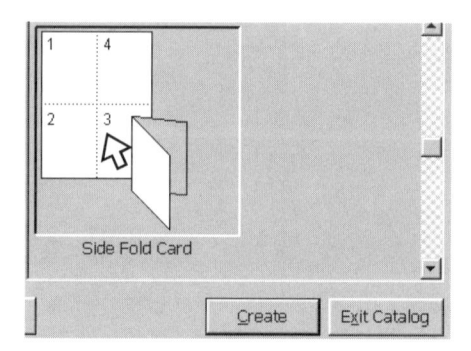

3. Click the *Blank Publications* tab at the top of the screen.
4. Click *Side Fold Card*.
5. Click *Create*.

Page 90   Desktop Publishing Made Easy

Chapter 8 — Designing a Greeting Card

6. **Click Yes** to automatically insert the other 3 pages of the Greeting Card.

The 4 pages of the Greeting Card are 4 A6 pages which make up an A4 page.

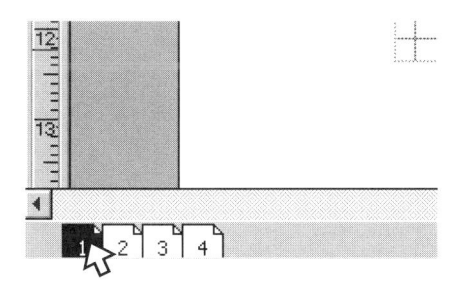

Above is page 1 of the Christmas Card.

7. The other pages can be accessed by clicking the page numbers in the *Page Navigation Control* in the bottom left of the screen.

The second method:

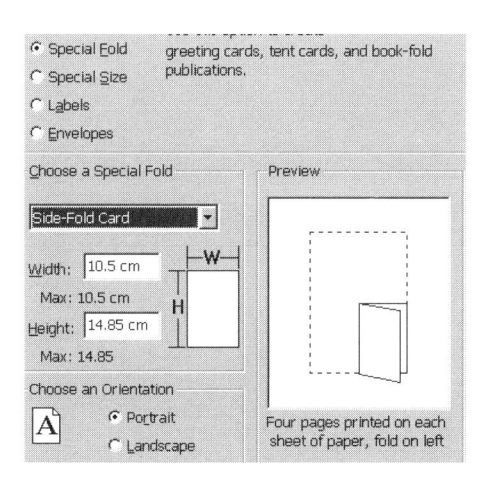

1. Click *File* from the Menu Bar.
2. Click *Page Setup*.
3. In the *Page Setup* window click *Special Fold* in the *Publication Layout* section.
4. Choose *Side-Fold Card* in the *Choose a Publication Size* box.
5. Click *Portrait* in the *Choose an Orientation* section.
6. Click *OK*.

MANUALLY SETTING UP A GREETING CARD PAGE

If you are using a pre-defined layout skip to the *Rotating Objects* tutorial.

Manually setting up the Christmas Card involves dividing an A4 page manually into 4 A6 sections. See the illustration on page 92. If we set the margins to 15 mm. all around in the usual way and set 2 columns and 2 rows in the *Grid Guides* section of the *Layout Guides* window, the image will be centred between the margin grid guides and the central grid guides, but not on the whole A6 section. See A below. It will be centred if ruler guides are used to set the margins on each A6 section. See B below.

We shall therefore set the margins to 0 mm. all around in the usual way and then use ruler guides to set margins of 15 mm. for each section. The space between the ruler guides are the panels into which we will place all objects for the Greeting Card. The illustration on the next page should help you to understand this better.

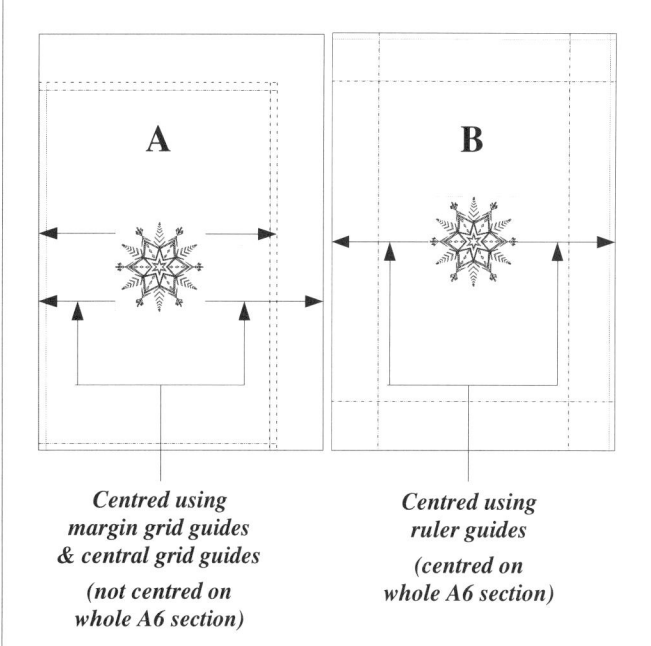

A — Centred using margin grid guides & central grid guides (not centred on whole A6 section)

B — Centred using ruler guides (centred on whole A6 section)

We have to calculate the position of each of the 4 horizontal and vertical ruler guides in setting up the margins of 15 mm. This calculation is done on page 93, but it will be worth your time to study the illustration on the next page in order to understand the calculations more clearly.

Using Microsoft Publisher

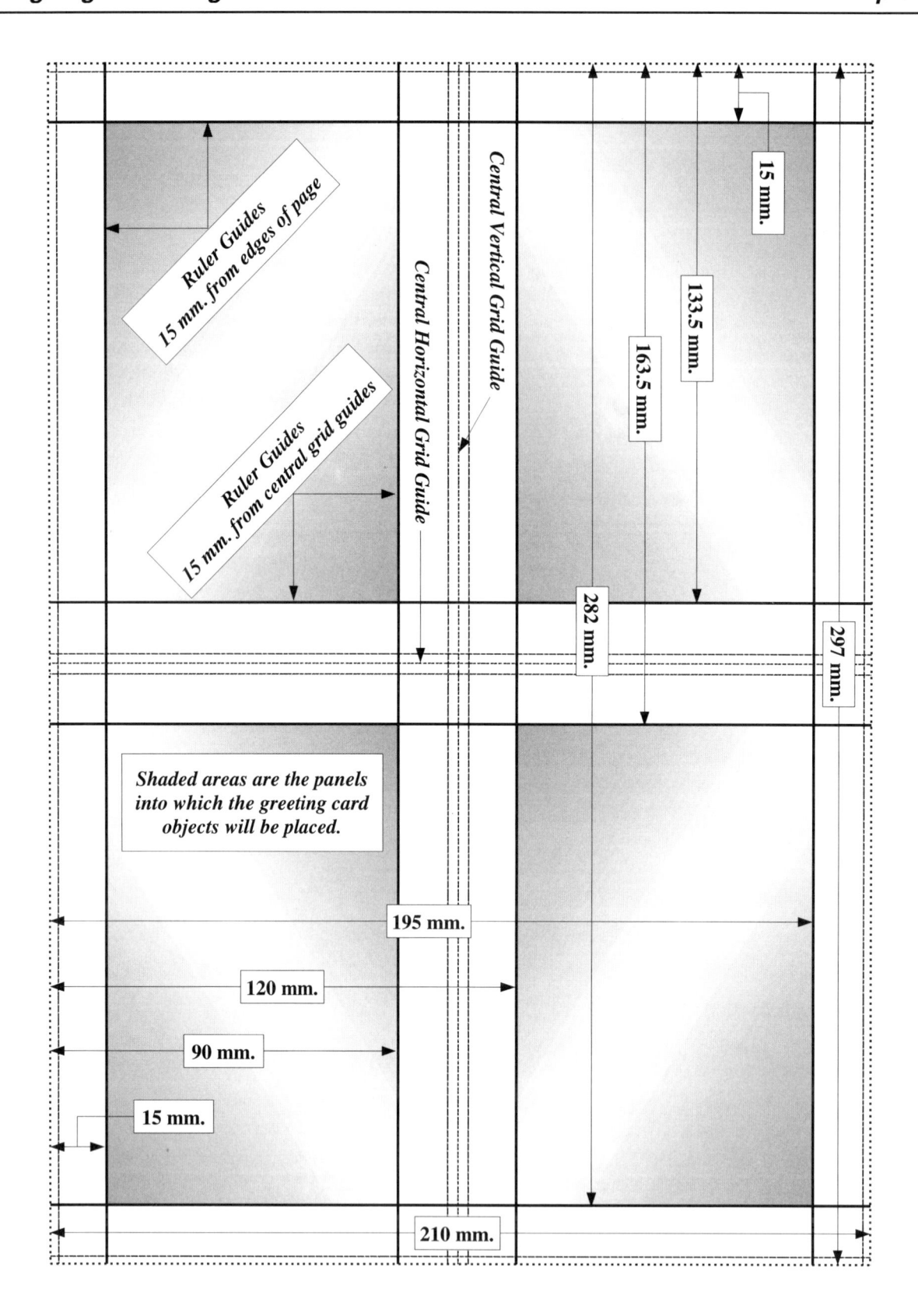

Designing a Greeting Card   *Chapter 8*

[Figure: Diagram showing page layout with ruler guides and measurements]

- *Ruler Guides 15 mm. from edges of page*
- *Ruler Guides 15 mm. from central grid guides*
- *Central Vertical Grid Guide*
- *Central Horizontal Grid Guide*
- 15 mm.
- 133.5 mm.
- 163.5 mm.
- 282 mm.
- 297 mm.
- *Shaded areas are the panels into which the greeting card objects will be placed.*
- 195 mm.
- 120 mm.
- 90 mm.
- 15 mm.
- 210 mm.

MANUALLY SETTING UP A GREETING CARD PAGE

The figure above shows the placement of the 4 horizontal and the 4 vertical ruler guides which set up the margins of 15 mm. for each A6 section. The shaded area (4 panels) is the area inside the manually set up margins into which all the objects (pictures frames, text frames etc.) will be placed. The ruler guides can be placed using the measurements shown above, but you will need a high zoom for accurate placement.

Chapter 8 — Designing a Greeting Card

An A4 Page is 210 mm. x 297 mm. Therefore the central grid guides are at the positions 105 mm. and 148.5 mm. on the ruler.

The position of the 4 vertical ruler guides:

15 mm. = in from the left of the page
90 mm. = (105 mm. – 15 mm.)
120 mm. = (105 mm. + 15 mm.)
195 mm. = (210 mm. – 15 mm.)

The position of the 4 horizontal ruler guides:

15 mm. = down from the top of the page
133.5 mm. = (148.5 mm. – 15 mm.)
163.5 mm. = (148.5 mm. + 15 mm.)
282 mm. = (297 mm. – 15 mm.)

To set up the Greeting Card Page:

1. Open a new file.
2. Set all the margins to 0 mm.
3. Set a value of *2* in the *Columns* and the *Rows* boxes in the *Grid Guides* section.
4. Enable *Snap to Ruler Marks*.
5. Zoom up to increase the number of ruler divisions. This will enable you to be more accurate in placing the ruler guides.
6. Place a ruler guide in each of the positions calculated above.

See the result below. The panels are numbered and shaded to show the pages they represent in the Greeting Card. The objects in panels 1 and 4 have to be rotated by 180° because of the fold.

ALIGNMENT WITHIN PANELS

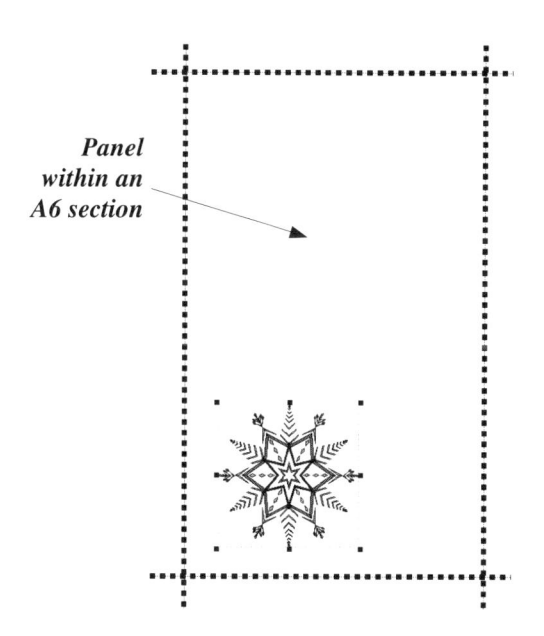

Panel within an A6 section

We saw in Chapter 4 how to align objects. Objects can be aligned in relation to each other or if they are grouped, in relation to the page. How do we align objects on an A6 section of an A4 page?

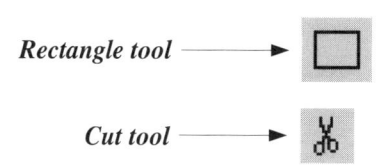

Rectangle tool

Cut tool

The secret is to create another object to fill the panel within the A6 section. In this case we draw a rectangle the full width and depth of the panel.

The illustrations for the instructions below are on the next page.

1. Enable *Snap to Guides*.
2. Draw a rectangle and resize to fill the panel.
3. Multiple-select the object and the rectangle.
4. Click *Align Objects* from *Arrange* on the Menu Bar. Align the 2 objects (rectangle and graphic) horizontally and vertically in relation to each other.
5. Deselect objects by clicking away from them.
6. Select the rectangle and delete it by either pressing the DELETE key on the keyboard or clicking the *Cut* tool on the Standard Toolbar.

Designing a Greeting Card Chapter 8

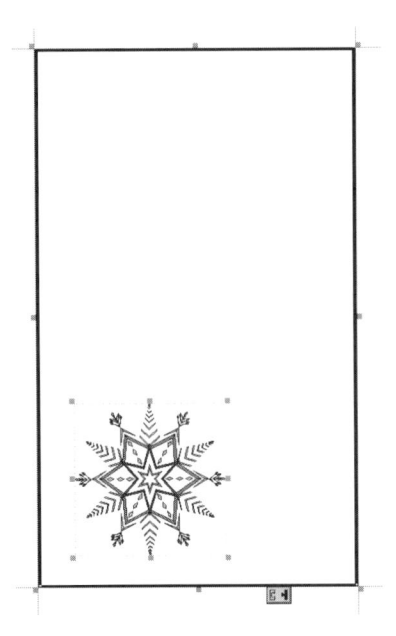

The panel created by the ruler guides has a box (rectangle) drawn around it. The rectangle and the graphic are selected, to be centred vertically and horizontally in relation to each other.

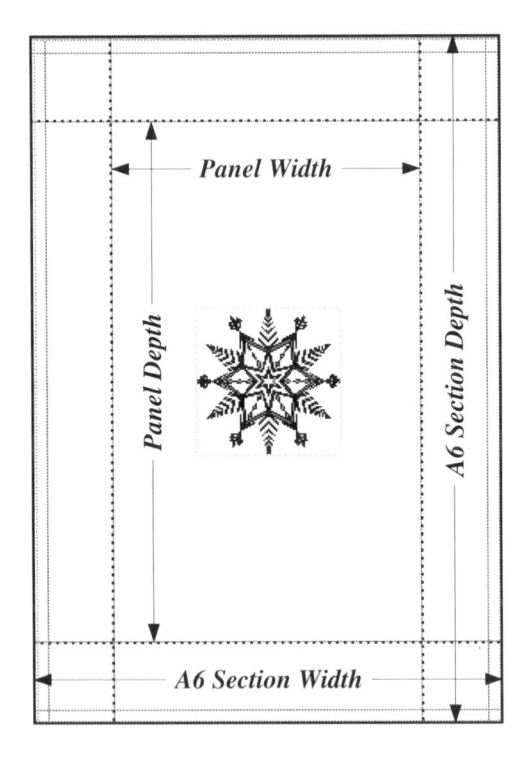

The graphic is centred vertically and horizontally within the panel created by the ruler guides. It is therefore also centred on the A6 section, which makes up a page of the Greeting Card. The box (rectangle) is deleted.

ROTATING OBJECTS

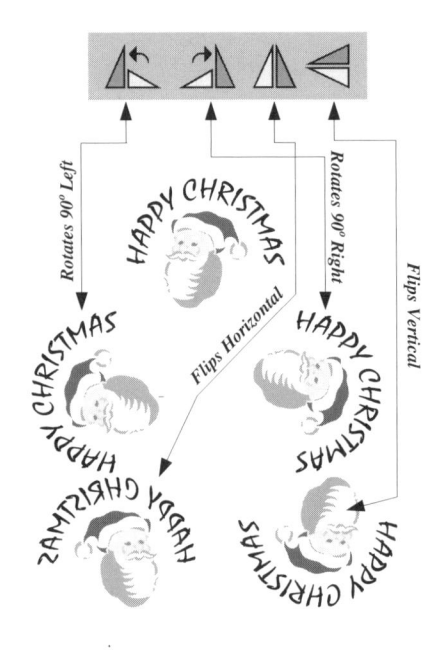

1. Select the object by clicking it.
2. Click any of the rotating tools on the Formatting Toolbar (*Rotate Left*, *Rotate Right*, *Flip Horizontal* and *Flip Vertical*).

Another method:

1. Click the object to select it.
2. Click the *Custom Rotate* tool on the Standard Toolbar.

Custom Rotate

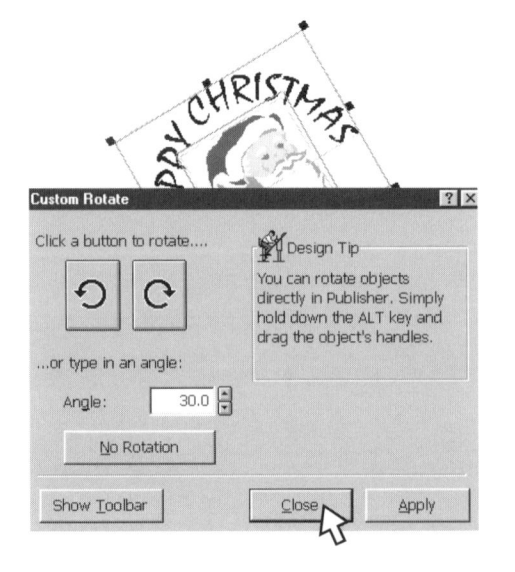

3. Type or click in a value in the *Angle* section.
4. Click *Apply* or *Close*.

Page 94 Desktop Publishing Made Easy

Chapter 8 Designing a Greeting Card

EXERCISE 8.1

COMPLETION INSTRUCTIONS

Carry out the instructions in numerical order

See the sketch sheet on the next page

1. Open a new file.

2. Manually set up the page margins.

3. Save the file as *Greeting Card*. Save regularly.

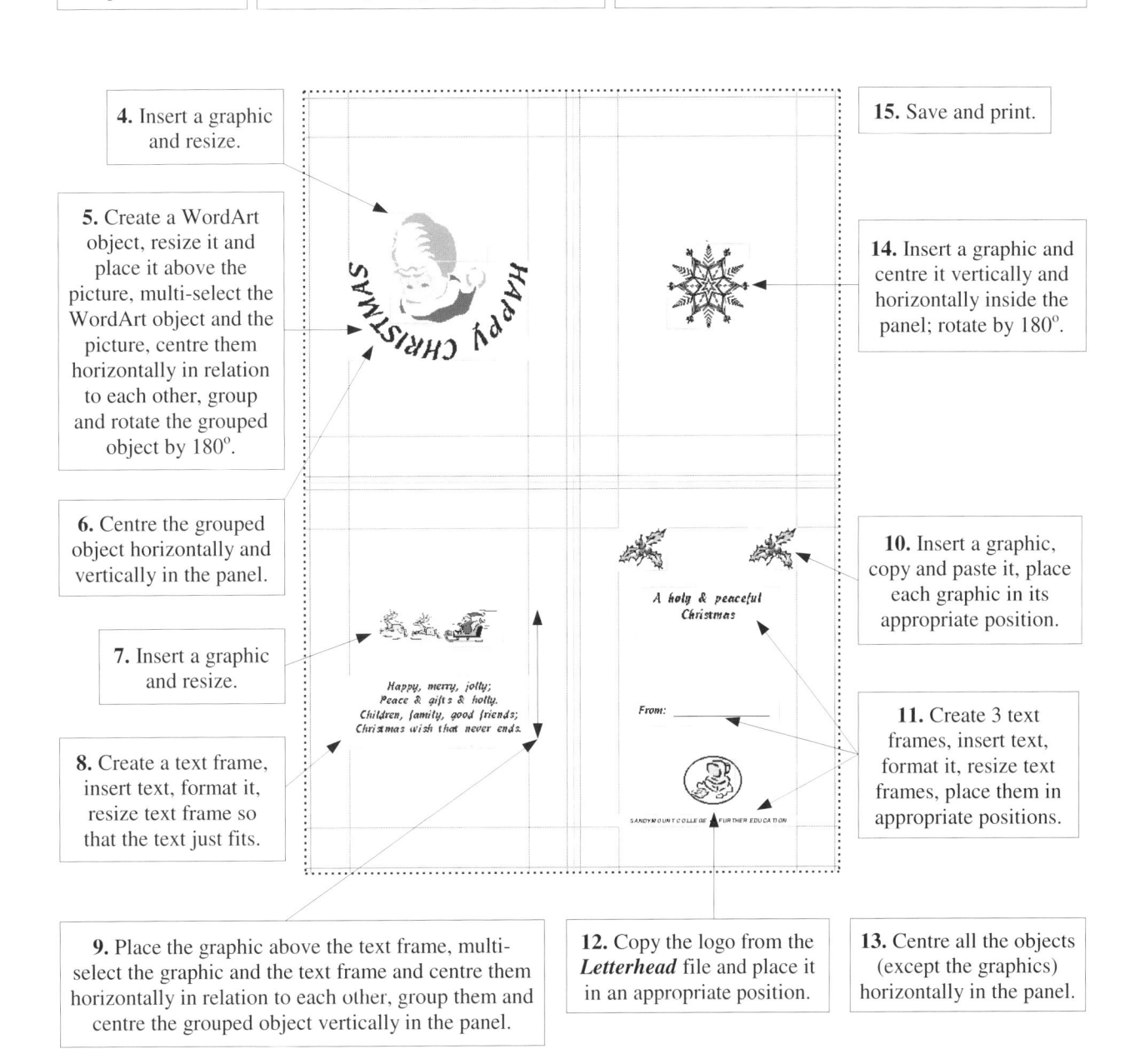

4. Insert a graphic and resize.

5. Create a WordArt object, resize it and place it above the picture, multi-select the WordArt object and the picture, centre them horizontally in relation to each other, group and rotate the grouped object by 180°.

6. Centre the grouped object horizontally and vertically in the panel.

7. Insert a graphic and resize.

8. Create a text frame, insert text, format it, resize text frame so that the text just fits.

9. Place the graphic above the text frame, multi-select the graphic and the text frame and centre them horizontally in relation to each other, group them and centre the grouped object vertically in the panel.

10. Insert a graphic, copy and paste it, place each graphic in its appropriate position.

11. Create 3 text frames, insert text, format it, resize text frames, place them in appropriate positions.

12. Copy the logo from the *Letterhead* file and place it in an appropriate position.

13. Centre all the objects (except the graphics) horizontally in the panel.

14. Insert a graphic and centre it vertically and horizontally inside the panel; rotate by 180°.

15. Save and print.

Using Microsoft Publisher Page 95

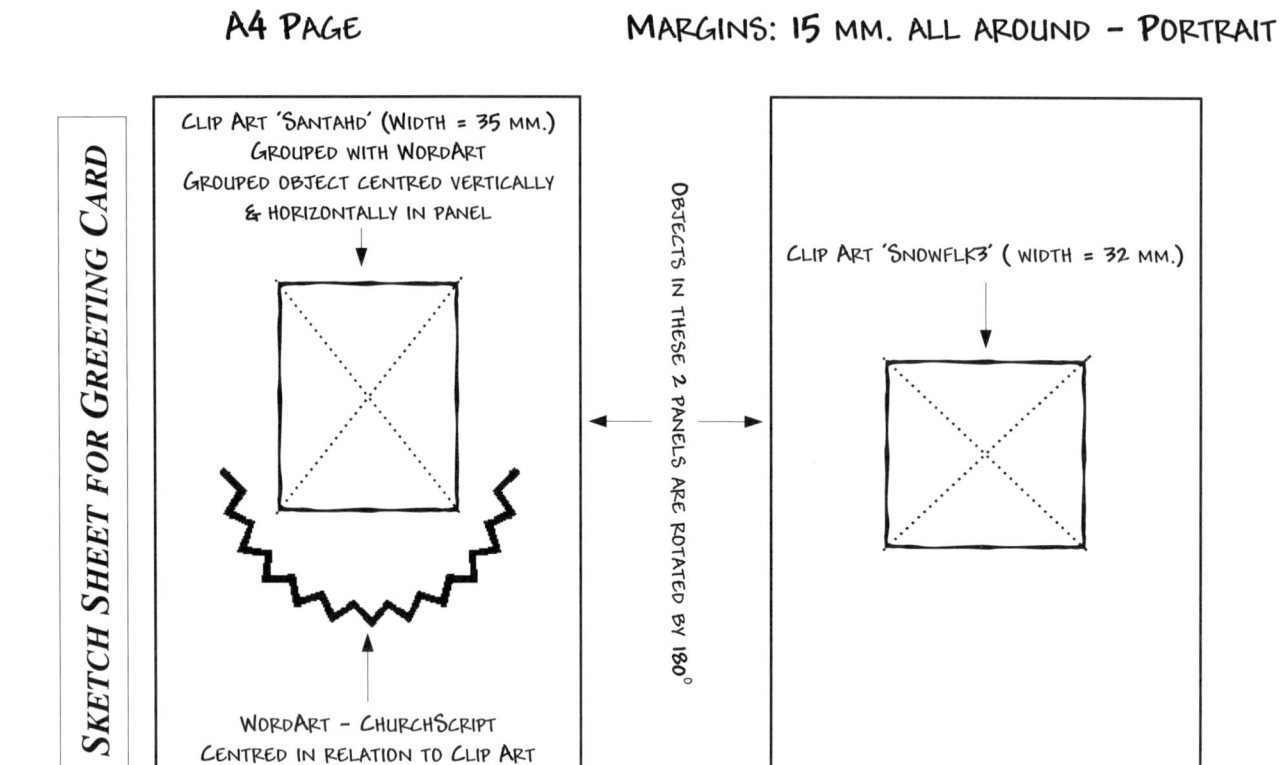

Designing a Greeting Card — Chapter 8

A4 PAGE   MARGINS: 15 MM. ALL AROUND – PORTRAIT

SKETCH SHEET FOR GREETING CARD

CLIP ART 'SANTAHD' (WIDTH = 35 MM.)
GROUPED WITH WORDART
GROUPED OBJECT CENTRED VERTICALLY
& HORIZONTALLY IN PANEL

CLIP ART 'SNOWFLK3' (WIDTH = 32 MM.)

OBJECTS IN THESE 2 PANELS ARE ROTATED BY 180°

WORDART – CHURCHSCRIPT
CENTRED IN RELATION TO CLIP ART

ALL OBJECTS ARE GROUPED INSIDE EACH PANEL.
ALL GROUPED OBJECTS ARE CENTRED VERTICALLY & HORIZONTALLY IN RELATION TO THE PANEL

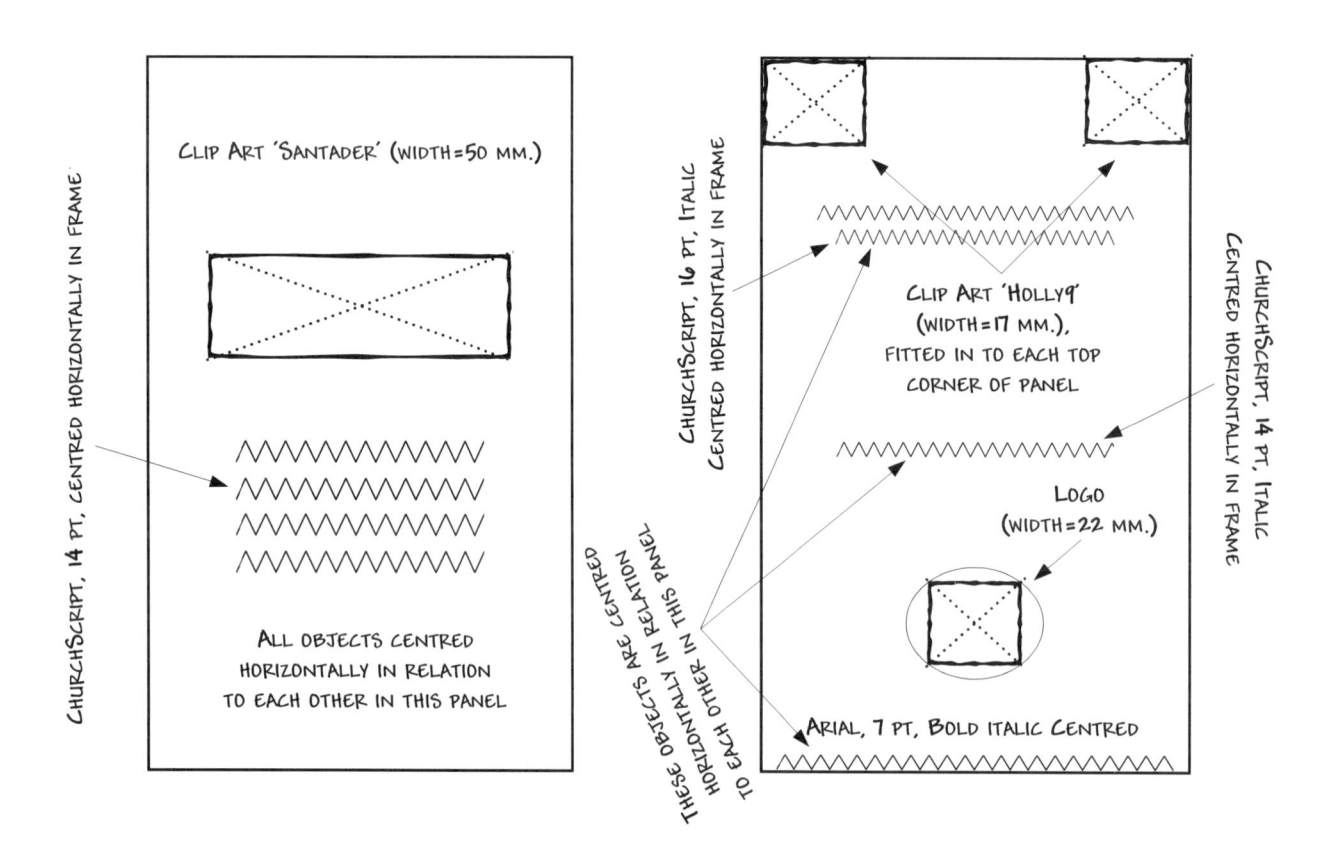

CLIP ART 'SANTADER' (WIDTH=50 MM.)

CHURCHSCRIPT, 14 PT, CENTRED HORIZONTALLY IN FRAME

ALL OBJECTS CENTRED HORIZONTALLY IN RELATION TO EACH OTHER IN THIS PANEL

CHURCHSCRIPT, 16 PT, ITALIC
CENTRED HORIZONTALLY IN FRAME

CLIP ART 'HOLLY9'
(WIDTH=17 MM.),
FITTED IN TO EACH TOP
CORNER OF PANEL

CHURCHSCRIPT, 14 PT, ITALIC
CENTRED HORIZONTALLY IN FRAME

LOGO
(WIDTH=22 MM.)

THESE OBJECTS ARE CENTRED HORIZONTALLY IN RELATION TO EACH OTHER IN THIS PANEL

ARIAL, 7 PT, BOLD ITALIC CENTRED

Chapter 8   Designing a Greeting Card

A holy & peaceful Christmas

Happy, merry, jolly;
Peace & gifts & holly.
Children, family, good friends;
Christmas wish that never ends.

From:_____

SANDYMOUNT COLLEGE OF FURTHER EDUCATION

Using Microsoft Publisher   Page 97

Exercise 8.2

Design a Greeting Card for a Garage informing customers that they've moved premises

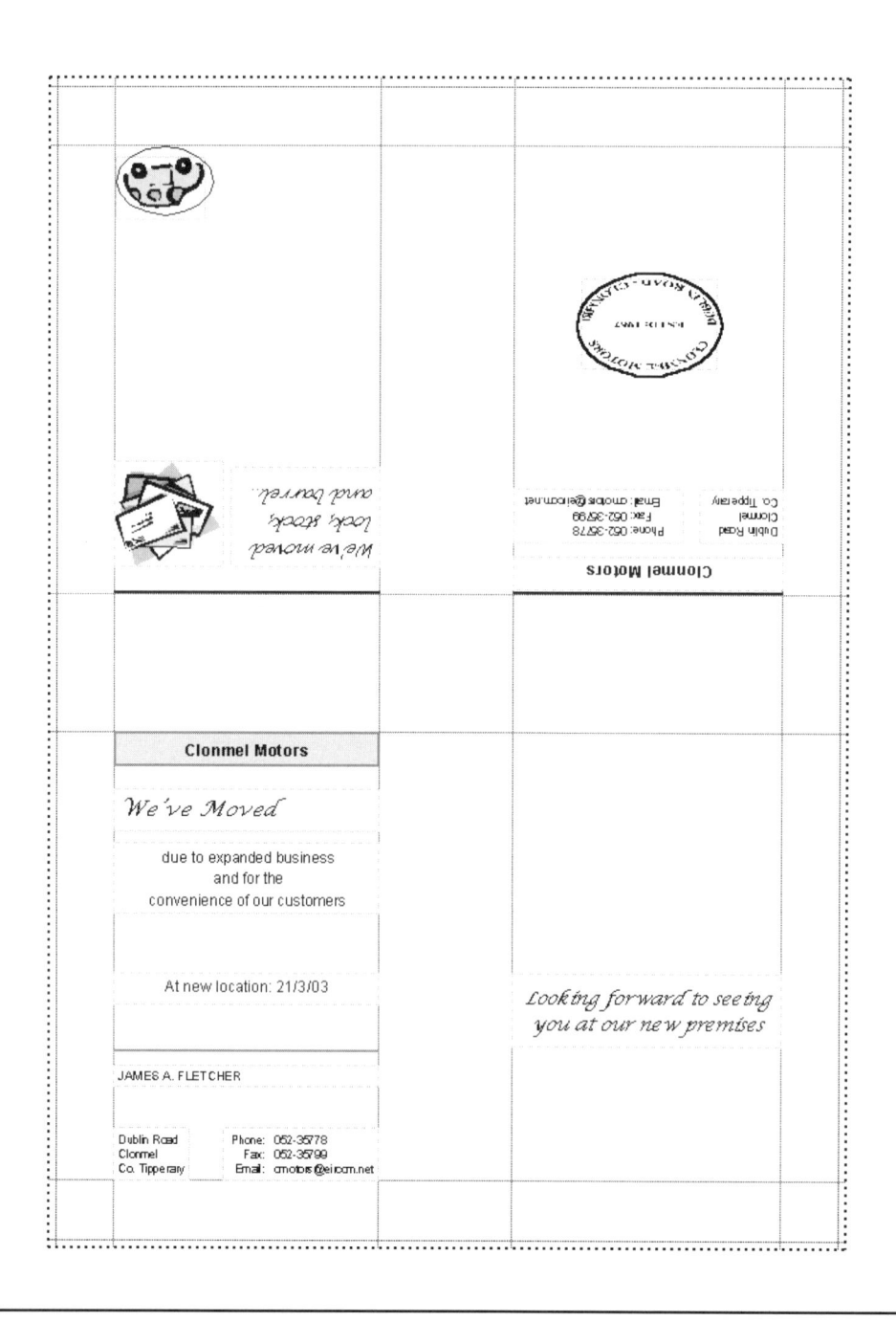

Chapter 8   *Designing a Greeting Card*

EXERCISE 8.3

DESIGN AN INVITATION CARD FOR A BUILDING CONTRACTOR ASKING PROSPECTIVE CUSTOMERS TO VIEW A SHOWHOUSE

Using Microsoft Publisher   *Page 99*

CHAPTER 9

DESIGNING A BROCHURE

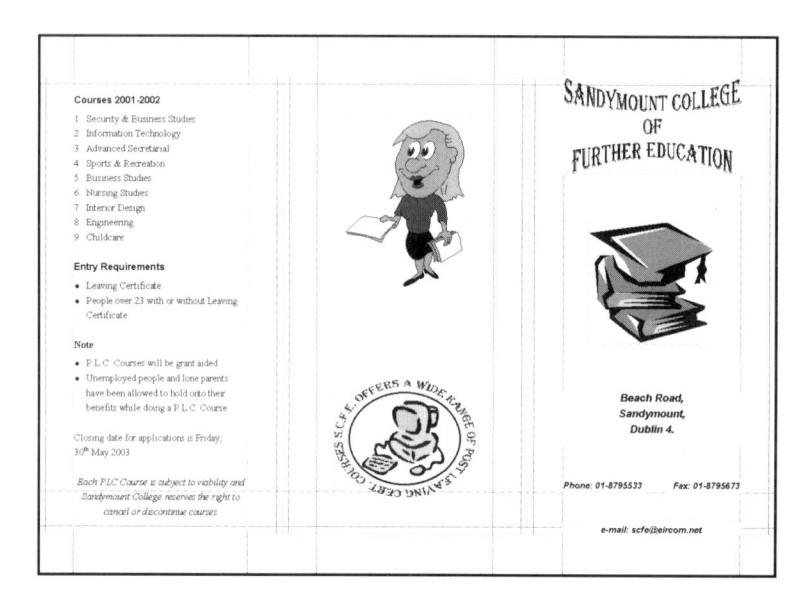

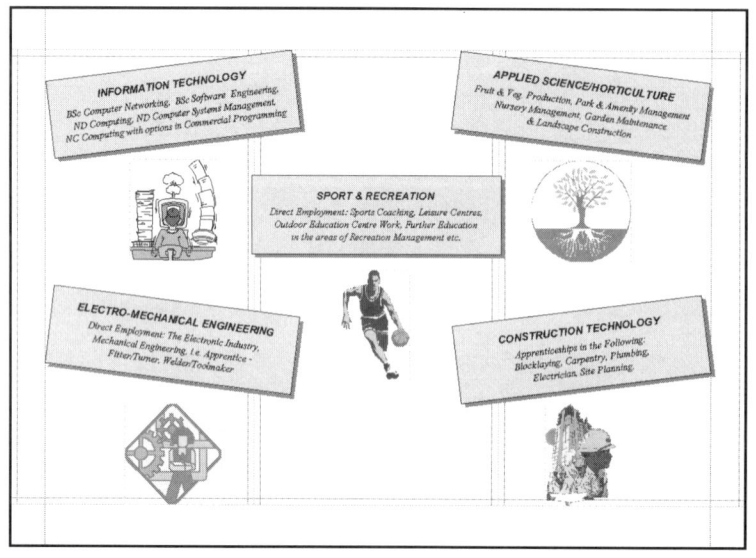

Chapter 9   *Designing a Brochure*

GATEFOLD BROCHURE

Front Side of Brochure

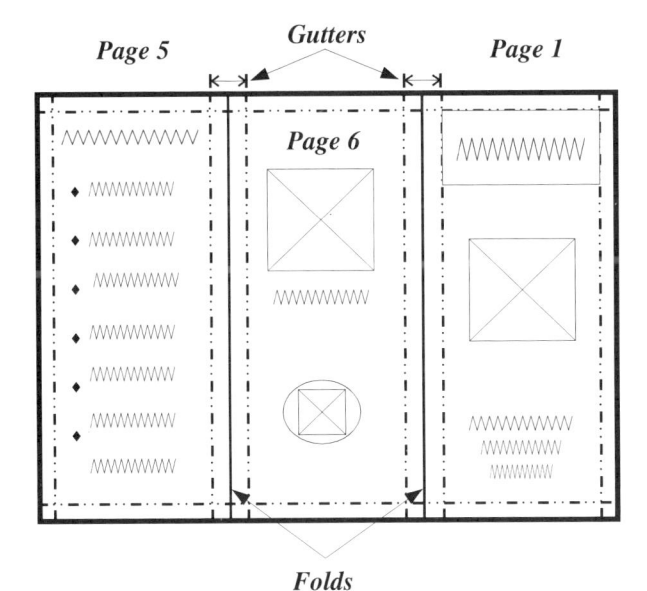

Folds

The illustration above represents a landscape A4 page divided by 2 vertical grid guides into 3 equal columns. These 3 equal columns represent the 3 pages of the front side of the brochure.

It is important that the front side is broken into 3 equal parts, as otherwise the margins will not appear the same for each brochure page when folded and the brochure will not fold properly.

To ensure that the columns will be of equal width, left and right margins of 0 mm. for the A4 page will be set by clicking **Layout Guides** from the **Arrange** menu. The margins for each column and therefore for each page of the front side of the brochure will be set by placing ruler guides in the appropriate positions. An illustration on page 102 shows these positions based on left and right margins of 14 mm.

The illustration to the right is the brochure when folded. The right column of the A4 page becomes the brochure's front page, the left column becomes the brochure's last page and the middle column becomes the brochure's back page.

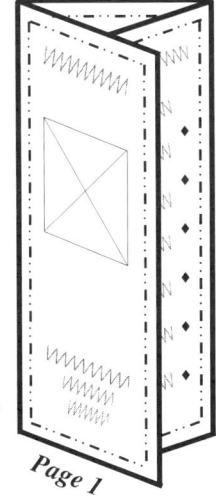

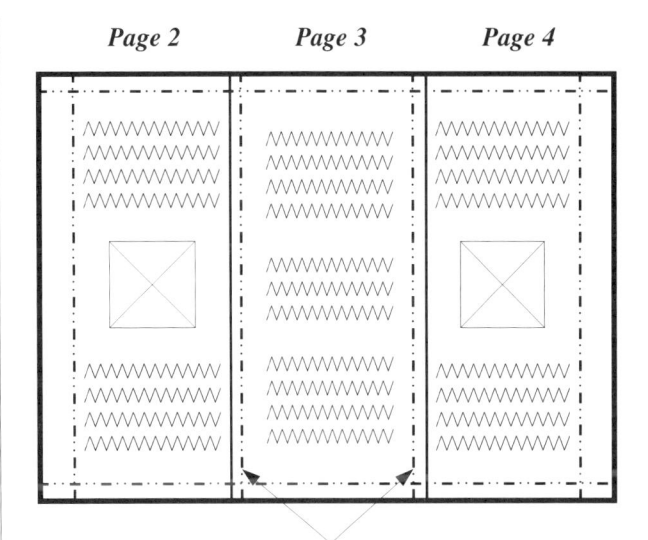

Grid Guides don't have to be where the folds are

Above is the other side of the brochure. The left and right margins can be set by clicking **Layout Guides** from the **Arrange** menu, as it doesn't matter how this side folds. This side does not become apparent until the brochure is opened. However, it is still important to give it a layout so that all the objects can be placed in a pleasing to the eye and balanced manner.

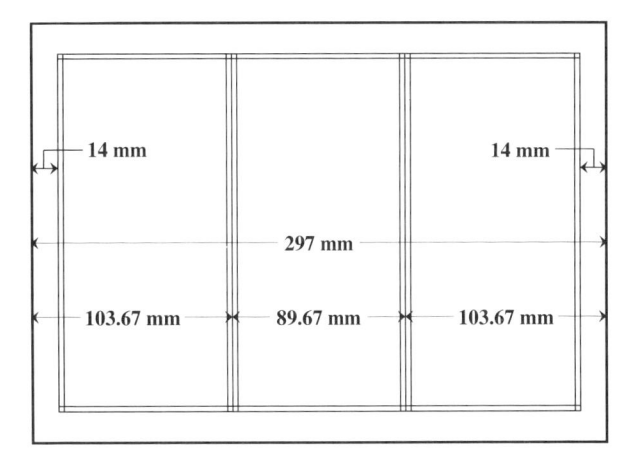

14 mm   14 mm

297 mm

103.67 mm   89.67 mm   103.67 mm

The figure above shows that if the left and right margins are set up from **Layout Guides** in the **Arrange** menu, 2 vertical grid guides will not divide the A4 page into 3 columns of equal width. If left and right margins of 14 mm. are set, the values above represent the width of each column. The brochure will not fold properly, as the left and right columns are too wide for the middle one.

The figure on the top of page 102 shows that by using ruler guides to set margins, the A4 page will divide into 3 columns of equal width.

Using Microsoft Publisher   Page 101

Designing a Brochure   *Chapter 9*

By setting the left and right margins to 0 mm. from *Layout Guides* in the *Arrange* menu, the page will be divided into 3 equal columns by the 2 vertical grid guides. When the brochure is folded at the vertical grid guides, the front, last and back page will fit exactly over each other. See the illustration to the right.

Place the ruler guides an equal distance (14 mm.) from the left and right edges of the A4 page and from each side of the grid guides to create the panels, into which the objects that make up the pages of the front side of the brochure can be placed.

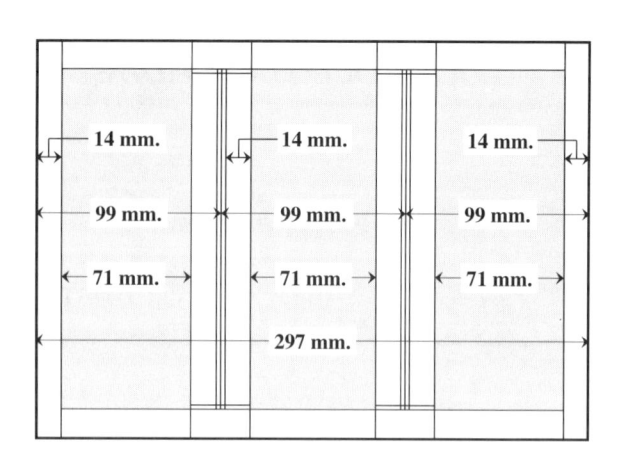

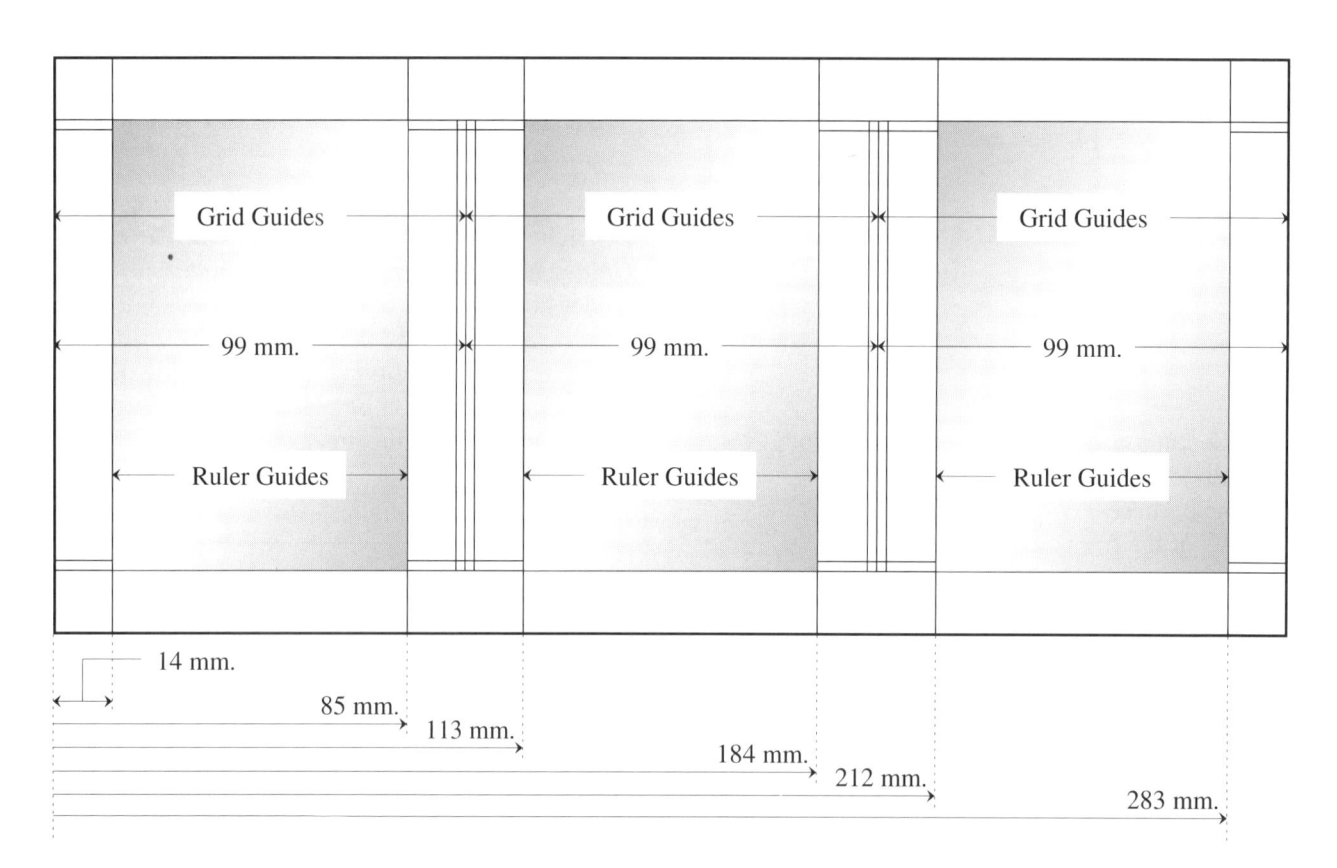

SETTING UP THE FRONT SIDE OF A GATEFOLD BROCHURE

The front side of the gatefold brochure contains 3 equal columns and these 3 columns represent the front, back and last page of the brochure. We shall set the left and right margins of the A4 page to 0 mm., and set each column's left and right margins to 14 mm. by placing ruler guides in the appropriate positions on the A4 page. The figure above with the grid guides breaking up the page into 3 equal columns shows where to place each ruler guide – at 14 mm., 85 mm., 113 mm., 184 mm., 212 mm. and 283 mm. from the left edge of the page. The shaded areas above are the panels, into which all objects (picture frames, text frames etc.) will be placed.

1. Set the top and bottom margins to 16 mm. and the left and right margins to 0 mm. Insert 3 in the *Columns* box in the *Grid Guides* section.
2. Zoom in and use the scroll bars to scroll around the page.
3. Enable *Snap to Ruler Marks*.
4. Place the 6 vertical ruler guides in the positions shown above.

Page 102   *Desktop Publishing Made Easy*

Chapter 9   Designing a Brochure

BULLETING AND NUMBERING

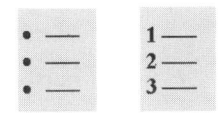

Bullets and Numbering Tools

A list can be most useful when each item in it is marked with a symbol or *bullet* or numbered sequentially to make it stand out more clearly.

To insert bullets or numbers:

1. Highlight the text.
2. Click either the **Bullets** or the **Numbering** tool on the Formatting Toolbar.

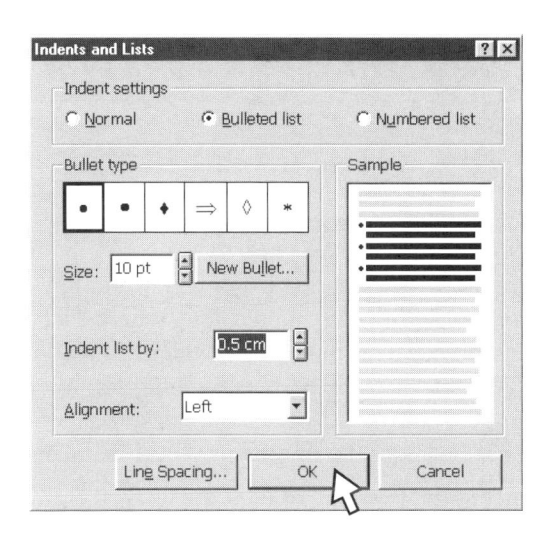

5. Type an indent value in the **Indent list by** box. I've inserted 0.5 cm. above.
6. Click **OK**.

A different bullet can be chosen by clicking a box in the **Bullet type** section.

Courses 2001-2002

- Security & Business Studies
- Information Technology
- Advanced Secretarial
- Sports & Recreation
- Business Studies
- Nursing Studies
- Interior Design
- Engineering
- Childcare

Above is the list using bullets. The space between the bullet and the text can be adjusted. To do this:

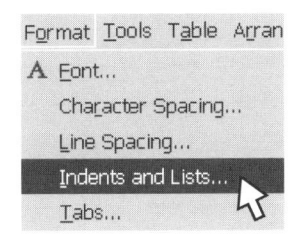

Courses 2001-2002

- Security & Business Studies
- Information Technology
- Advanced Secretarial
- Sports & Recreation
- Business Studies
- Nursing Studies
- Interior Design
- Engineering
- Childcare

The bulleted list above has decreased indents.

Courses 2001-2002

1. Security & Business Studies
2. Information Technology
3. Advanced Secretarial
4. Sports & Recreation
5. Business Studies
6. Nursing Studies
7. Interior Design
8. Engineering
9. Childcare

3. Click **Format** from the Menu Bar.
4. Click **Indents and Lists ...**

7. By clicking the **Numbered list** radio button the list can be numbered as shown above.

Using Microsoft Publisher   Page 103

Designing a Brochure   Chapter 9

INDENTING PARAGRAPHS

The appearance of a paragraph can be changed by *indenting* it. A *first line indent* – moving the first line of each paragraph in from the left margin – lets the reader identify more easily where each paragraph starts. Blocks of text can be moved in from the left or right margins by *indenting* them. A *hanging indent* moves all the lines of a paragraph except the first line in from the margin.

To indent the first line of paragraphs by 0.5 cm.:

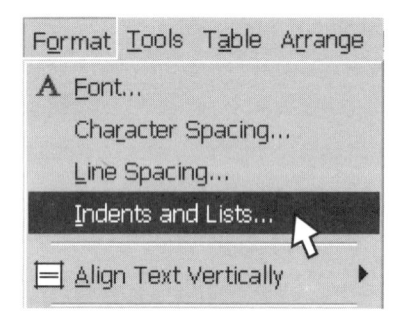

1. Highlight the text to be indented.
2. Click *Format* from the Menu Bar.
3. Click *Indents and Lists...*

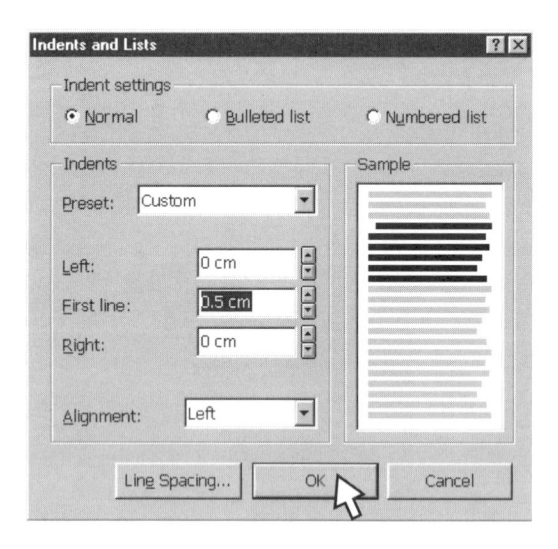

4. In the *Indents* section type a value in the *First line* box. In the illustration above a value of 0.5 cm. has been inserted.

This moves in the first line of every highlighted paragraph by 0.5 cm.

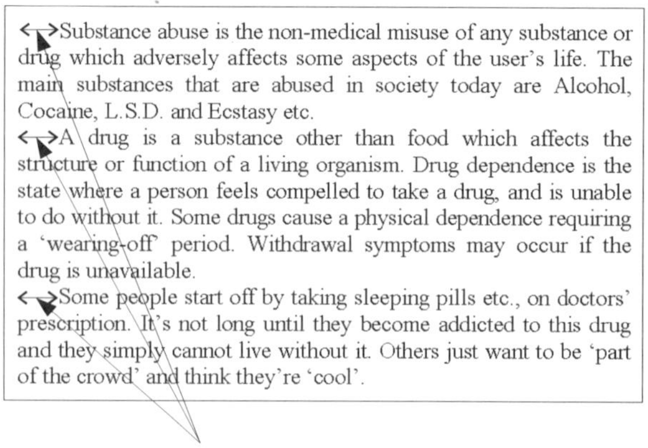

First Line Indents of 0.5 cm.

Indenting can also be done from the top ruler.

First Line Indent marker (triangle)   *Right Indent marker (triangle)*

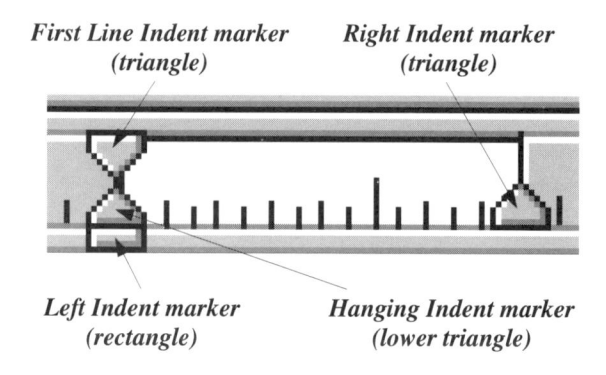

Left Indent marker (rectangle)   *Hanging Indent marker (lower triangle)*

Drag the indent marker across the horizontal ruler

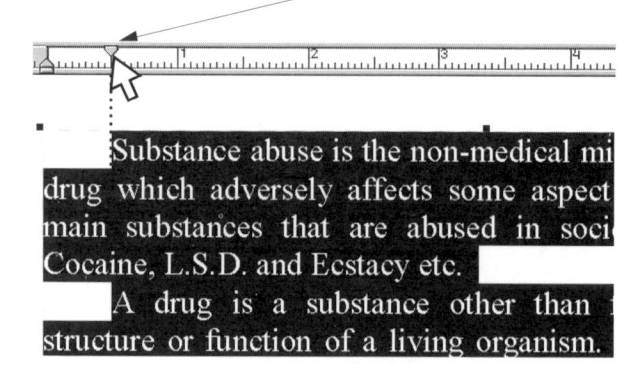

1. Highlight the text to be indented.
2. Drag the *Left Indent*, *First Line Indent*, *Hanging Indent* or *Right Indent* markers across the horizontal ruler.

INSERTING TABS

A *tab* creates an invisible stopping point or tab stop which lets you indent a line of text. Publisher has a preset tab of 0.5 cm. This means that every time you press the TAB key on the keyboard the insertion point moves in 0.5 cm. on the line.

Left, Right, Centre and Decimal Tabs

Tabs can be found where the top and side rulers meet. Click once and the tab changes.

Select tab type by clicking here on the Tab Selector

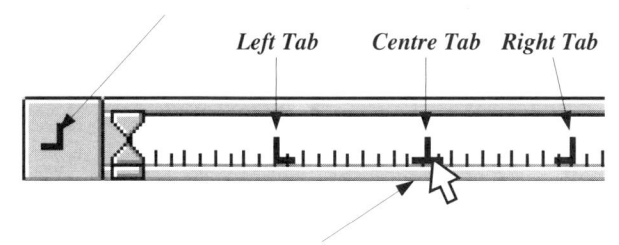

Left Tab Centre Tab Right Tab

Click to position the tab on the horizontal ruler

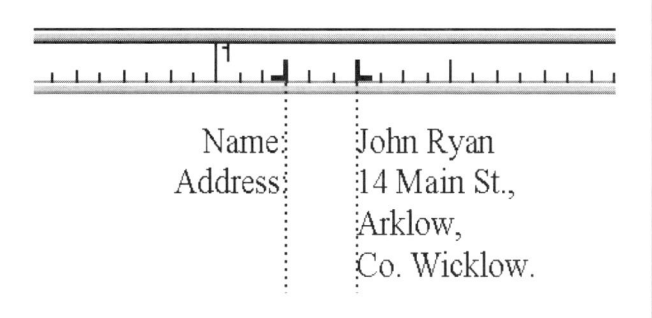

```
Name:    John Ryan
Address: 14 Main St.,
         Arklow,
         Co. Wicklow.
```

1. Click on the tab selector to select the tab type.
2. Click on the ruler to position the tab.

Note:
1. Set the tabs before you type in the text.
2. When you come to the word or words you want to tab press the TAB key on the keyboard and then type.

or

1. Type in all the text.
2. Highlight the text to be tabbed.
3. Set the tabs.
4. Click immediately before word to be tabbed and press the TAB key on the keyboard.

Another way to set tabs:

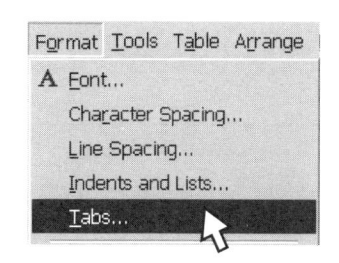

1. Highlight the text to be tabbed.
2. Click **Format** on the Menu Bar.
3. Click **Tabs**.

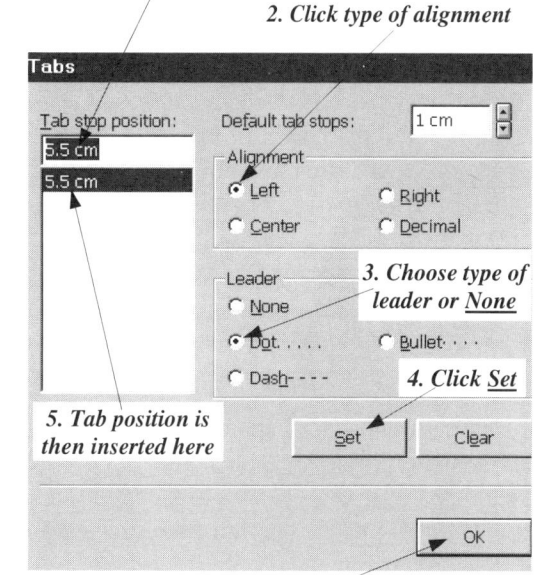

1. Type in tab position here

2. Click type of alignment

3. Choose type of leader or None

4. Click Set

5. Tab position is then inserted here

6. When all tabs have been set click OK

Designing a Brochure — Chapter 9

4. Type a tab value in the **Tab stop position** box.
5. Click one of the **Alignment** buttons.
6. Choose a type of leader in the **Leader** section or choose **None**.
7. Click **Set**. The tab position is then placed in the larger rectangle below where you typed it. All the tabs you set will be placed here.
8. When all the tabs have been set click **OK**.

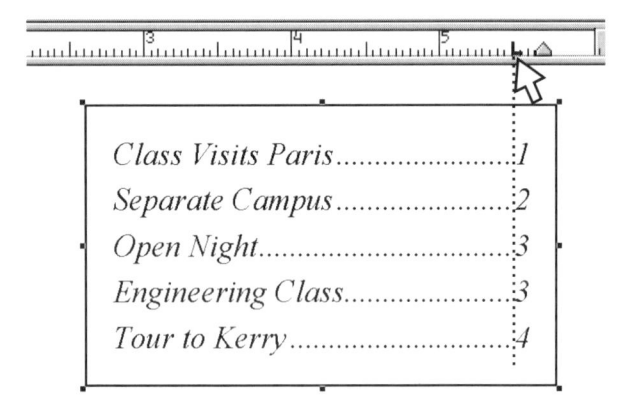

```
Class Visits Paris ................... 1
Separate Campus ................... 2
Open Night ............................ 3
Engineering Class .................. 3
Tour to Kerry ........................ 4
```

A left tab is set at 55 mm. for the page numbers. The tab also has a dot leader.

LINE SPACING (LEADING)

The space between lines of text can be changed. Publisher uses single line spacing, which means that the vertical space between each line of text is proportional to the height of one line of text. Adding more space can make the paragraph more dramatic and is considered good practice in DTP. However, it should not be overdone. Decreasing the line spacing darkens the page.

In the publishing industry the space between lines of text is called *leading* – pronounced 'ledding'. More about *leading* in Chapter 10.

Publisher uses the special spacing measurement, the *sp* measurement. This adjusts the space between lines of text according to the height of the font. 1 *sp* means the height of the font + an extra 20%. Therefore, a 10 point font has a *leading* of: (10 pt + 20% of 10 pt) = 12 pt.

Substance abuse is the non-medical misuse of any substance or drug which adversely affects some aspects of the user's life. The main substances that are abused in society today are Alcohol, Cocaine, L.S.D. and Ecstasy etc.
A drug is a substance other than food which affects the structure or function of a living organism. Drug dependence is the state where a person feels compelled to take a drug, and is unable to do without it. Some drugs cause a physical dependence requiring a 'wearing-off' period. Withdrawal symptoms may occur if the drug is unavailable.
Some people start off by taking sleeping pills etc., on doctors' prescription. It's not long until they become addicted to this drug and they simply cannot live without it. Others just want to be 'part of the crowd' and think they're 'cool'.

The text above is 10 pt size and it has a leading of 1 sp. =10 pt + 2 pt = 12 pt.

To increase its leading:

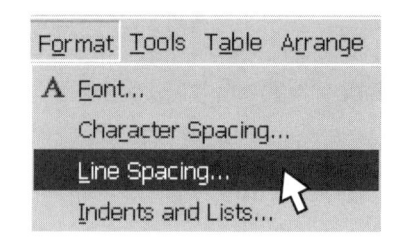

1. Highlight the text.
2. Click **Format** on the Menu Bar.
3. Click **Line Spacing**.

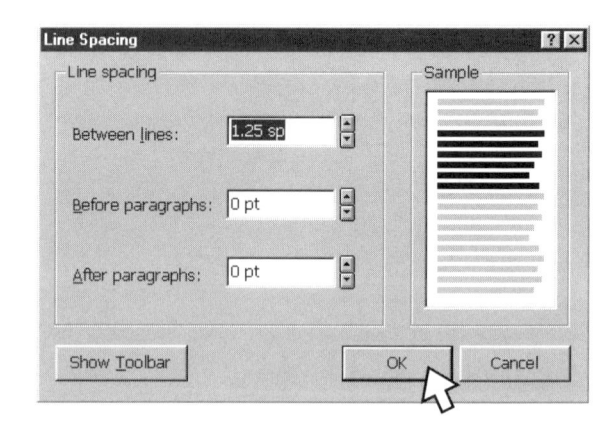

4. Type a value in the **Between lines** box.
5. Click **OK**.

The default setting of 1 space = 120% of font size. The text we used was 10 pt and the line spacing was increased by 25%.

Default leading (sp) = 10 pt x 120% = 12 pt.

12 pt increased by 25% = 15 pt.

Therefore the new leading (line spacing) is 15 pt.

Chapter 9 — Designing a Brochure

> Substance abuse is the non-medical misuse of any substance or drug which adversely affects some aspects of the user's life. The main substances that are abused in society today are Alcohol, Cocaine, L.S.D. and Ecstasy etc.
>
> A drug is a substance other than food which affects the structure or function of a living organism. Drug dependence is the state where a person feels compelled to take a drug, and is unable to do without it. Some drugs cause a physical dependence requiring a 'wearing-off' period. Withdrawal symptoms may occur if the drug is unavailable.
>
> Some people start off by taking sleeping pills etc., on doctors' prescription. It's not long until they become addicted to this drug and they simply cannot live without it. Others just want to be 'part of the crowd' and think they're 'cool'.

The leading of the 10 pt text above has been increased from 12 pt to 15 pt.

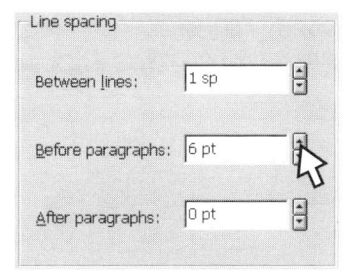

[Line spacing dialog: Between lines: 1 sp; Before paragraphs: 6 pt; After paragraphs: 0 pt]

Being able to quickly identify each paragraph of text improves readability. Indenting the first line of each paragraph facilitates this. However, another way of doing it is to increase the spacing between the paragraphs.

6. Highlight the text, Click **Format** on the Menu Bar and click **Line Spacing**.
7. Insert a value in the **Before paragraphs** box or the **After paragraphs** box.
8. Click **OK**.

An extra spacing of 6 pt between the paragraphs has been set below.

> Substance abuse is the non-medical misuse of any substance or drug which adversely affects some aspects of the user's life. The main substances that are abused in society today are Alcohol, Cocaine, L.S.D. and Ecstasy etc.
>
> A drug is a substance other than food which affects the structure or function of a living organism. Drug dependence is the state where a person feels compelled to take a drug, and is unable to do without it. Some drugs cause a physical dependence requiring a 'wearing-off' period. Withdrawal symptoms may occur if the drug is unavailable.
>
> Some people start off by taking sleeping pills etc., on doctors' prescription. It's not long until they become addicted to this drug and they simply cannot live without it. Others just want to be 'part of the crowd' and think they're 'cool'.

[Line spacing dialog: Between lines: 15 pt; Before paragraphs: 0 pt; After paragraphs: 0 pt]

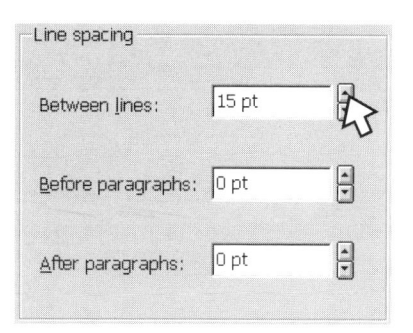

A point size can also be inserted in the **Between lines** box. If for example the font size is 12 pt, then a 15 pt line spacing is 125% of the font size, slightly more than the default leading of 120%. Make sure in this case that you type *'pt'* after the value, otherwise Microsoft Publisher assumes you mean space (*sp*).

In Desktop Publishing it is more usual to stick with the point (*pt*) measurement!

SHADOWING FRAMES

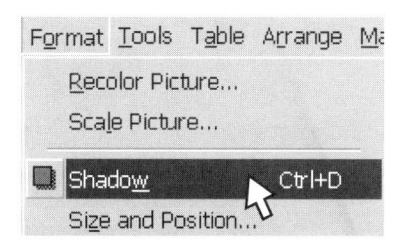

[Format menu showing: Recolor Picture..., Scale Picture..., Shadow Ctrl+D, Size and Position...]

1. Select the frame by clicking it.
2. Click **Format** from the Menu Bar.
3. Click **Shadow**.

See the result below.

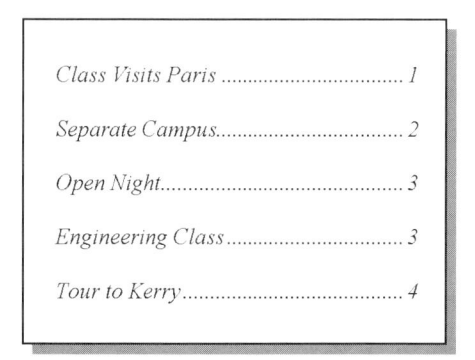

> *Class Visits Paris* 1
>
> *Separate Campus* 2
>
> *Open Night* 3
>
> *Engineering Class* 3
>
> *Tour to Kerry* 4

INSERTING EXTRA PAGES

Extra pages are not automatically inserted when you need them as happens in word processing applications. You have to insert them.

To do this:

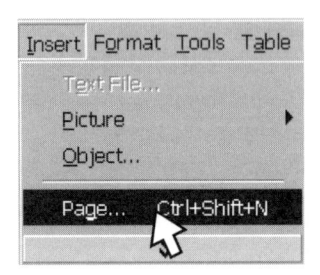

1. Click *Insert* from the Menu Bar.
2. Click *Page*.

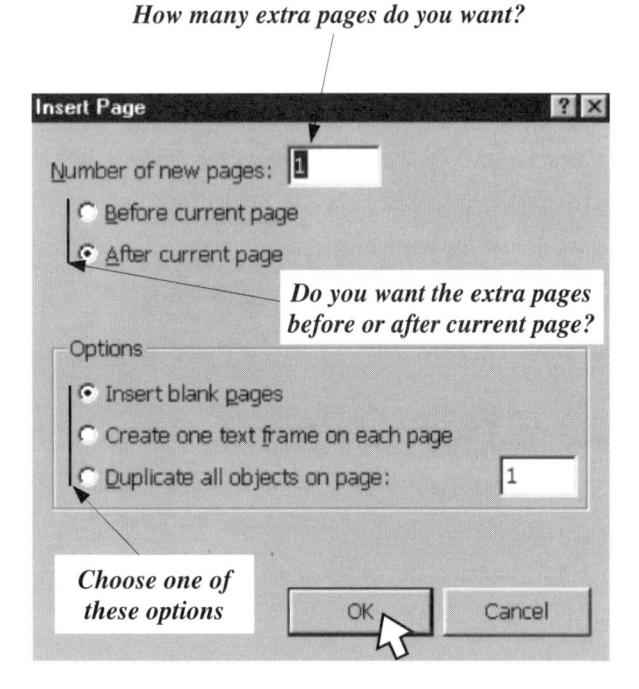

How many extra pages do you want?

Do you want the extra pages before or after current page?

Choose one of these options

3. Choose the number of pages by inserting a value in the *Number of new pages* box.
4. Click either the *Before current page* or the *After current page* button.
5. Choose one of the 3 options by clicking one of the *Option* buttons.
6. Click *OK*.

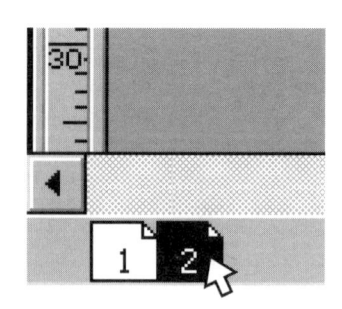

7. Change between pages by clicking the *Page Navigation Control* in the bottom left corner of the Publisher window.

INSERTING WORDART AROUND THE LOGO

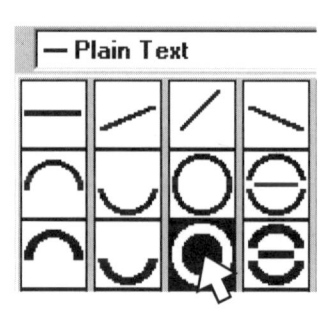

Stretch Tool

1. Create the WordArt object, choosing the oval style from the list of styles, and stretch the text to the frame's edges by using the *Stretch* tool.
2. Copy the logo across from the *Letterhead* file.

Chapter 9   *Designing a Brochure*

Snapping in against 2 of the logo's sides

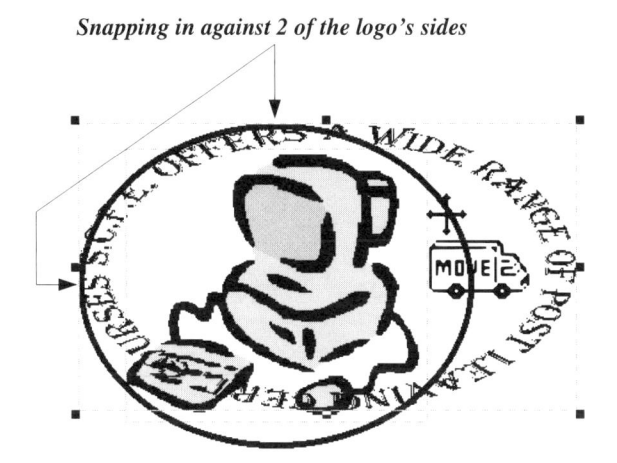

3. Enable *Snap to Objects* if it is not already enabled.
4. Move the WordArt object onto the logo until it snaps in against 2 of the logo's sides.

5. Resize the WordArt object until it snaps in against all the sides of the logo.

The WordArt object has the same shape as the logo. It will now be resized up proportionately from one of the corner handles.

6. Resize the WordArt object proportionately from one of the corner handles, making it larger than the logo. It retains its shape.

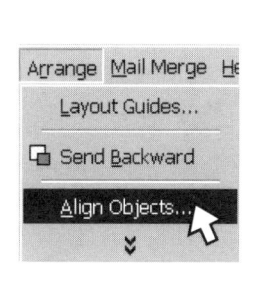

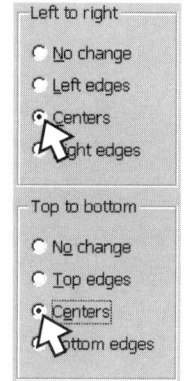

7. Multi-select the logo and the WordArt object.
8. Click *Align Objects* from the *Arrange* menu.
9. In the *Align Objects* window click *Centers* from *Left to right* and from *Top to bottom*.

10. Repeat steps 6 to 9 above until you are happy that the WordArt text fits around the logo, leaving a suitable space between them.
11. Group the objects.

Using Microsoft Publisher   Page 109

Designing a Brochure   Chapter 9

EXERCISE 9.1

COMPLETION INSTRUCTIONS – PAGE 1

Carry out the instructions in numerical order

See the sketch sheet on page 112

1. Open a new file.

2. Change the orientation to Landscape.

3. Set the top and bottom margins to 16 mm. and the left and right margins to 0 mm. Manually place ruler guides to set the left and right panel margins (see sketch sheet).

4. Save as ***Brochure***. Save often.

7. Insert a picture and resize. Position it roughly as shown. Centre horizontally in the panel.

5. Create a WordArt object and insert picture. Resize and place in appropriate positions. WordArt stretches from guide to guide. Centre the picture in the panel.

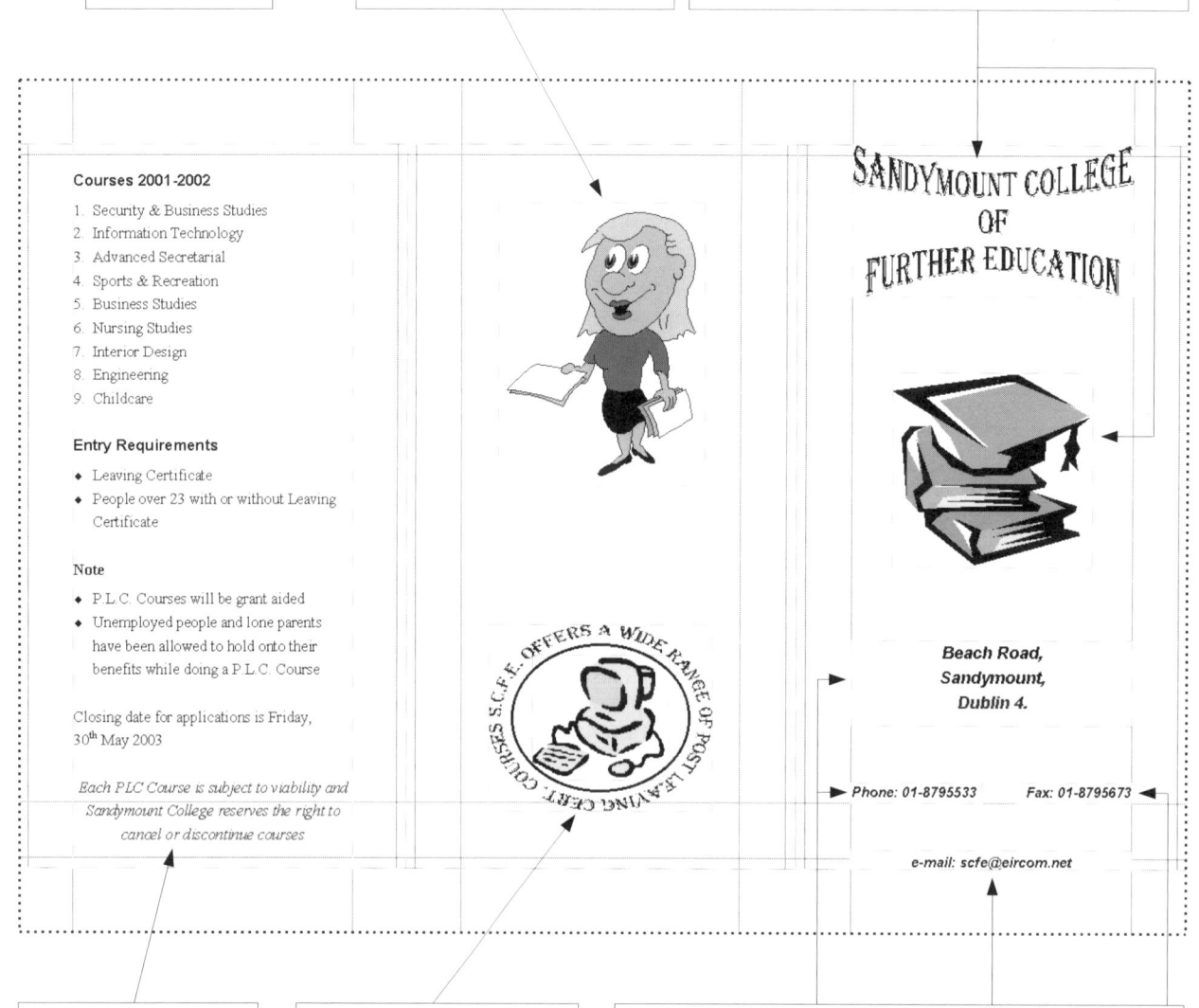

10. Save.

Courses 2001-2002
1. Security & Business Studies
2. Information Technology
3. Advanced Secretarial
4. Sports & Recreation
5. Business Studies
6. Nursing Studies
7. Interior Design
8. Engineering
9. Childcare

Entry Requirements
- Leaving Certificate
- People over 23 with or without Leaving Certificate

Note
- P.L.C. Courses will be grant aided
- Unemployed people and lone parents have been allowed to hold onto their benefits while doing a P.L.C. Course

Closing date for applications is Friday, 30th May 2003

Each PLC Course is subject to viability and Sandymount College reserves the right to cancel or discontinue courses

SANDYMOUNT COLLEGE OF FURTHER EDUCATION

Beach Road,
Sandymount,
Dublin 4.

Phone: 01-8795533   Fax: 01-8795673

e-mail: scfe@eircom.net

9. Create text frame(s). Insert text. Format it. Resize text frame(s).

8. Copy the logo from the ***Letterhead*** file. Resize it. Position it as shown. Centre it horizontally in the panel.

6. Create text frames, insert text, format text, resize text frames, position them in appropriate positions. The address and email text frames can stretch from guide to guide. The other text frames can snap in against the left or right guides.

Chapter 9   *Designing a Brochure*

EXERCISE 9.1

COMPLETION INSTRUCTIONS – PAGE 2

Carry out the instructions in numerical order

See the sketch sheet on page 113

11. Insert one extra page.

12. Insert 5 images from clip art. Resize them.

15. Save and print.

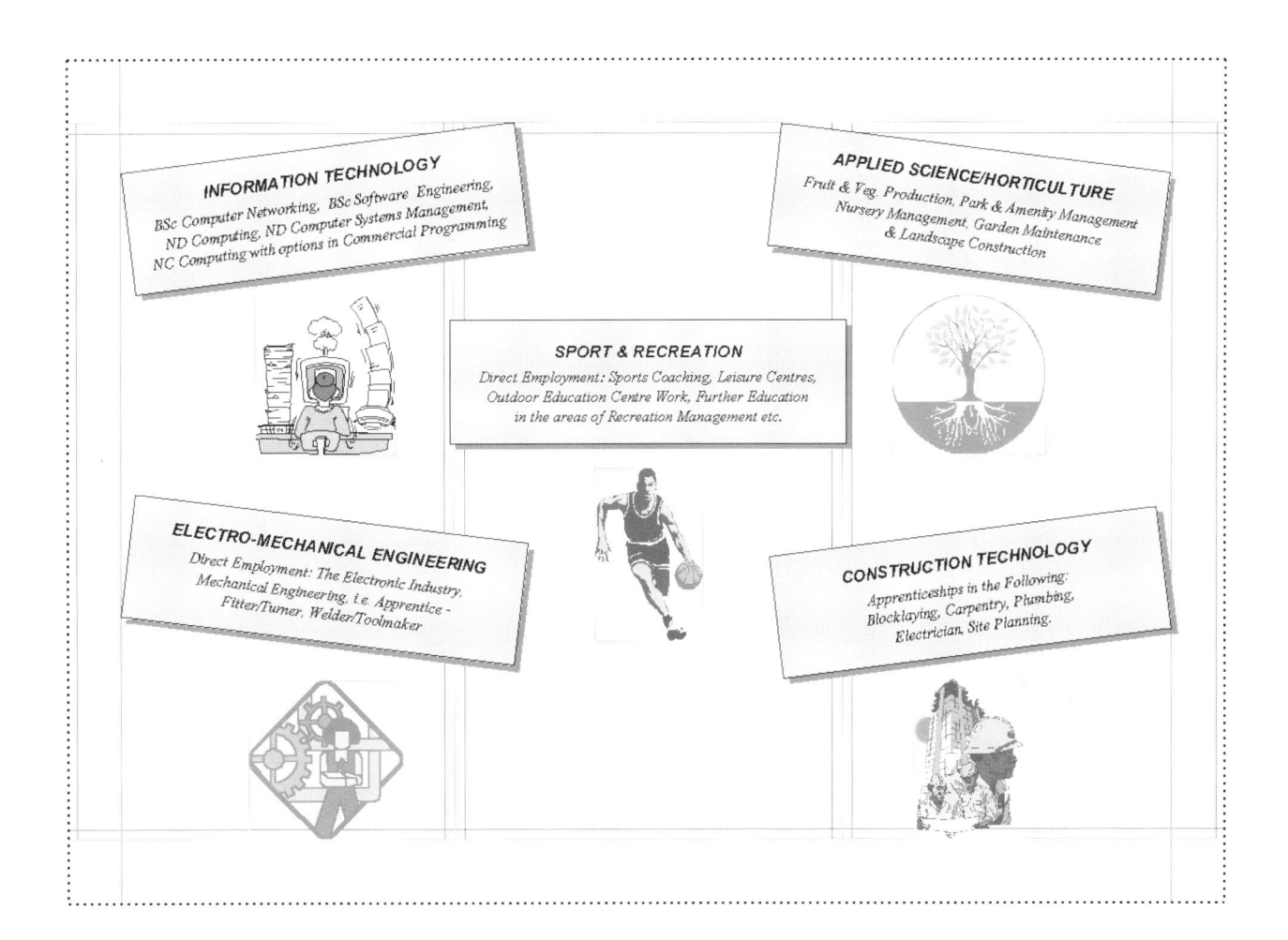

13. Create 5 text frames, insert text, format it, resize text frames, give each a 1 pt border, a 10% fill of black and shadow them. Rotate all text frames (except one) as shown on the sketch sheet.

14. Place each image a consistent distance away from its appropriate text frame and centre it horizontally in relation to the text frame. Group each image with the text frame and place the grouped objects as shown on the sketch sheet.

Using Microsoft Publisher   Page 111

Designing a Brochure — Chapter 9

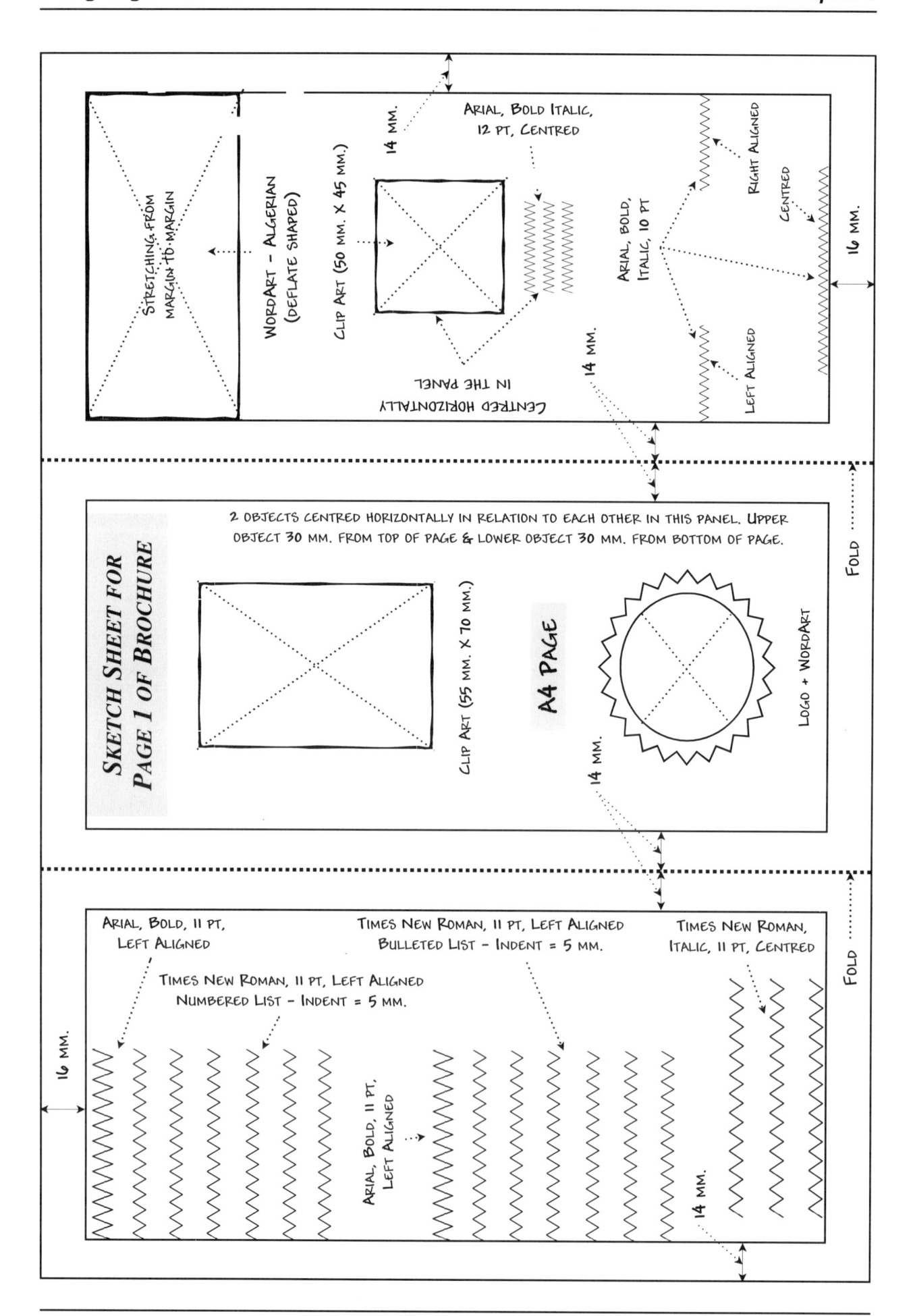

Sketch Sheet for Page 1 of Brochure

Panel 1 (top):
- Stretching from margin to margin
- WordArt – Algerian (Deflate shaped)
- Clip Art (50 mm. x 45 mm.), Centred horizontally in the panel
- 14 mm. (top margin)
- Arial, Bold Italic, 12 pt, Centred
- Arial, Bold, Italic, 10 pt — Right Aligned, Centred, Left Aligned
- 16 mm.
- 14 mm.

Panel 2 (middle) — A4 Page:
- 2 objects centred horizontally in relation to each other in this panel. Upper object 30 mm. from top of page & lower object 30 mm. from bottom of page.
- Clip Art (55 mm. x 70 mm.)
- Logo + WordArt
- 14 mm.
- Fold

Panel 3 (bottom):
- Arial, Bold, 11 pt, Left Aligned
- Times New Roman, 11 pt, Left Aligned — Bulleted List – Indent = 5 mm.
- Times New Roman, Italic, 11 pt, Centred
- Times New Roman, 11 pt, Left Aligned — Numbered List – Indent = 5 mm.
- Arial, Bold, 11 pt, Left Aligned
- 16 mm.
- 14 mm.
- Fold

Chapter 9 — Designing a Brochure

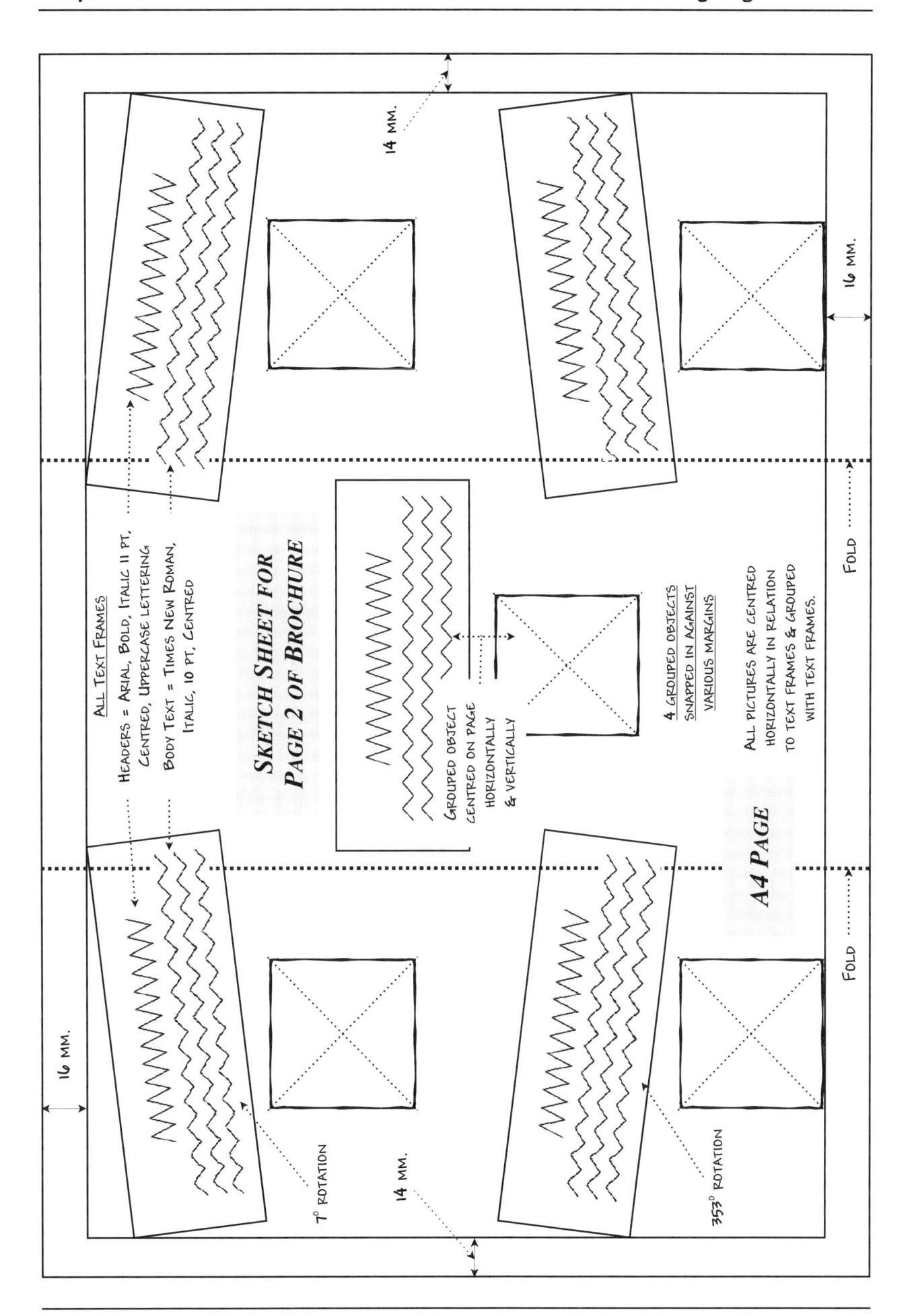

Using Microsoft Publisher — Page 113

Sandymount College of Further Education

**Beach Road,
Sandymount,
Dublin 4.**

Phone: 01-8795533　　　Fax: 01-8795673

e-mail: scfe@eircom.net

S.C.F.E. OFFERS A WIDE RANGE OF POST LEAVING CERT. COURSES

Courses 2001-2002

1. Security & Business Studies
2. Information Technology
3. Advanced Secretarial
4. Sports & Recreation
5. Business Studies
6. Nursing Studies
7. Interior Design
8. Engineering
9. Childcare

Entry Requirements

- Leaving Certificate
- People over 23 with or without Leaving Certificate

Note

- P.L.C. Courses will be grant aided
- Unemployed people and lone parents have been allowed to hold onto their benefits while doing a P.L.C. Course

Closing date for applications is Friday, 30th May 2003

Each PLC Course is subject to viability and Sandymount College reserves the right to cancel or discontinue courses

APPLIED SCIENCE/HORTICULTURE
Fruit & Veg. Production, Park & Amenity Management, Nursery Management, Garden Maintenance & Landscape Construction

CONSTRUCTION TECHNOLOGY
Apprenticeships in the Following: Plumbing, Block-laying, Carpentry, Electrician, Site Planning

SPORT & RECREATION
Direct Employment: Sports Coaching, Leisure Centres, Outdoor Education Centre Work, Further Education in the areas of Recreation Management etc.

INFORMATION TECHNOLOGY
BSc Computer Networking, BSc Software Engineering, ND Computing, ND Computer Systems Management, NC Computing with options in Commercial Programming

ELECTRO-MECHANICAL ENGINEERING
Direct Employment: The Electronic Industry, Mechanical Engineering, i.e. Apprentice - Fitter/Turner, Welder/Toolmaker

Designing a Brochure — Chapter 9

EXERCISE 9.2

DESIGN A BROCHURE FOR A GARAGE

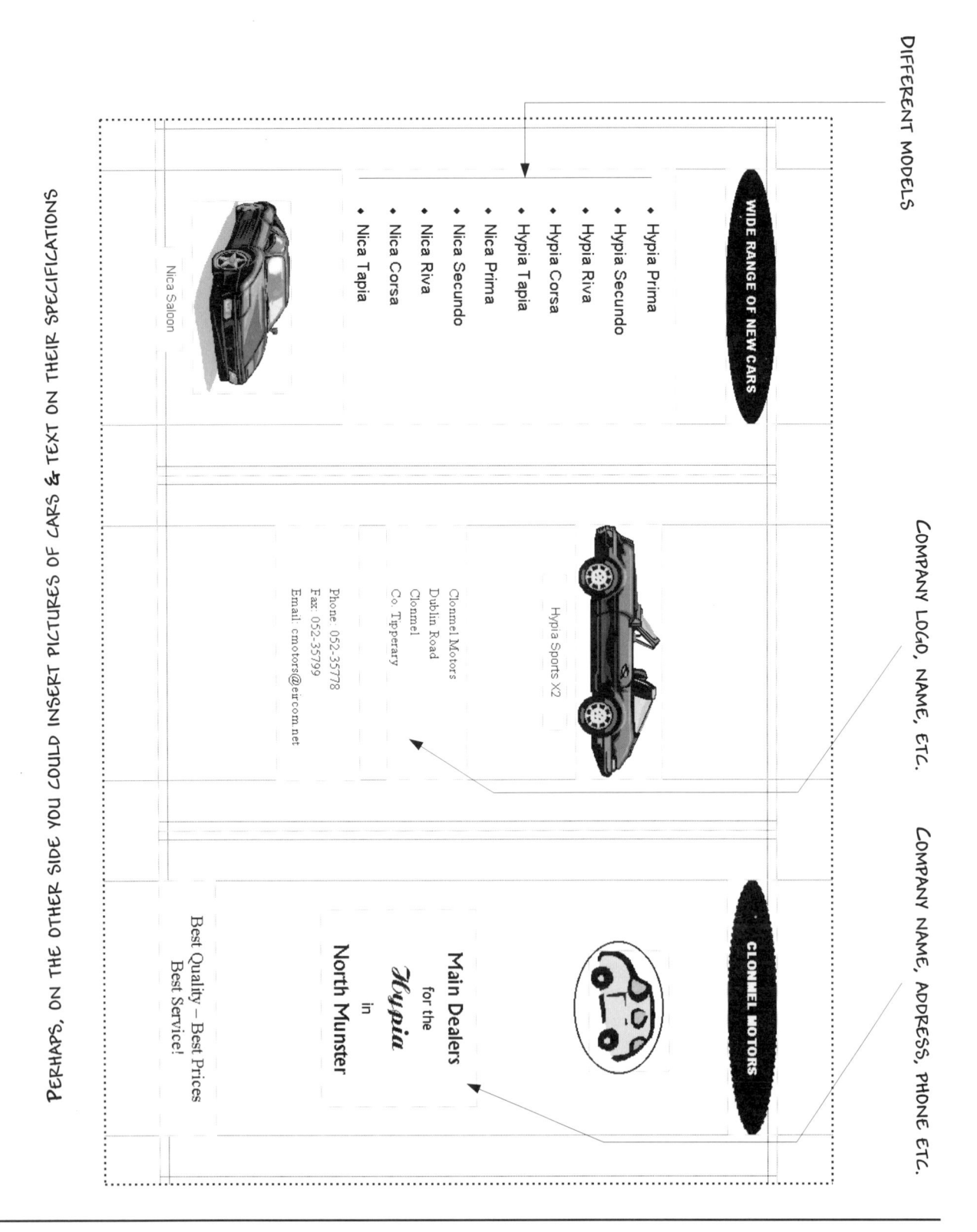

DIFFERENT MODELS

WIDE RANGE OF NEW CARS

- Hypia Prima
- Hypia Secundo
- Hypia Riva
- Hypia Corsa
- Hypia Tapia
- Nica Prima
- Nica Secundo
- Nica Riva
- Nica Corsa
- Nica Tapia

Nica Saloon

Hypia Sports X2

Clonmel Motors
Dublin Road
Clonmel
Co. Tipperary

Phone: 052-35778
Fax: 052-35799
Email: cmotors@eircom.net

COMPANY LOGO, NAME, ETC.

CLONMEL MOTORS

Main Dealers
for the
Hypia
in
North Munster

Best Quality – Best Prices
Best Service!

COMPANY NAME, ADDRESS, PHONE ETC.

PERHAPS, ON THE OTHER SIDE YOU COULD INSERT PICTURES OF CARS & TEXT ON THEIR SPECIFICATIONS

Page 116 — Desktop Publishing Made Easy

EXERCISE 9.3

DESIGN A BROCHURE FOR A BUILDING CONTRACTOR

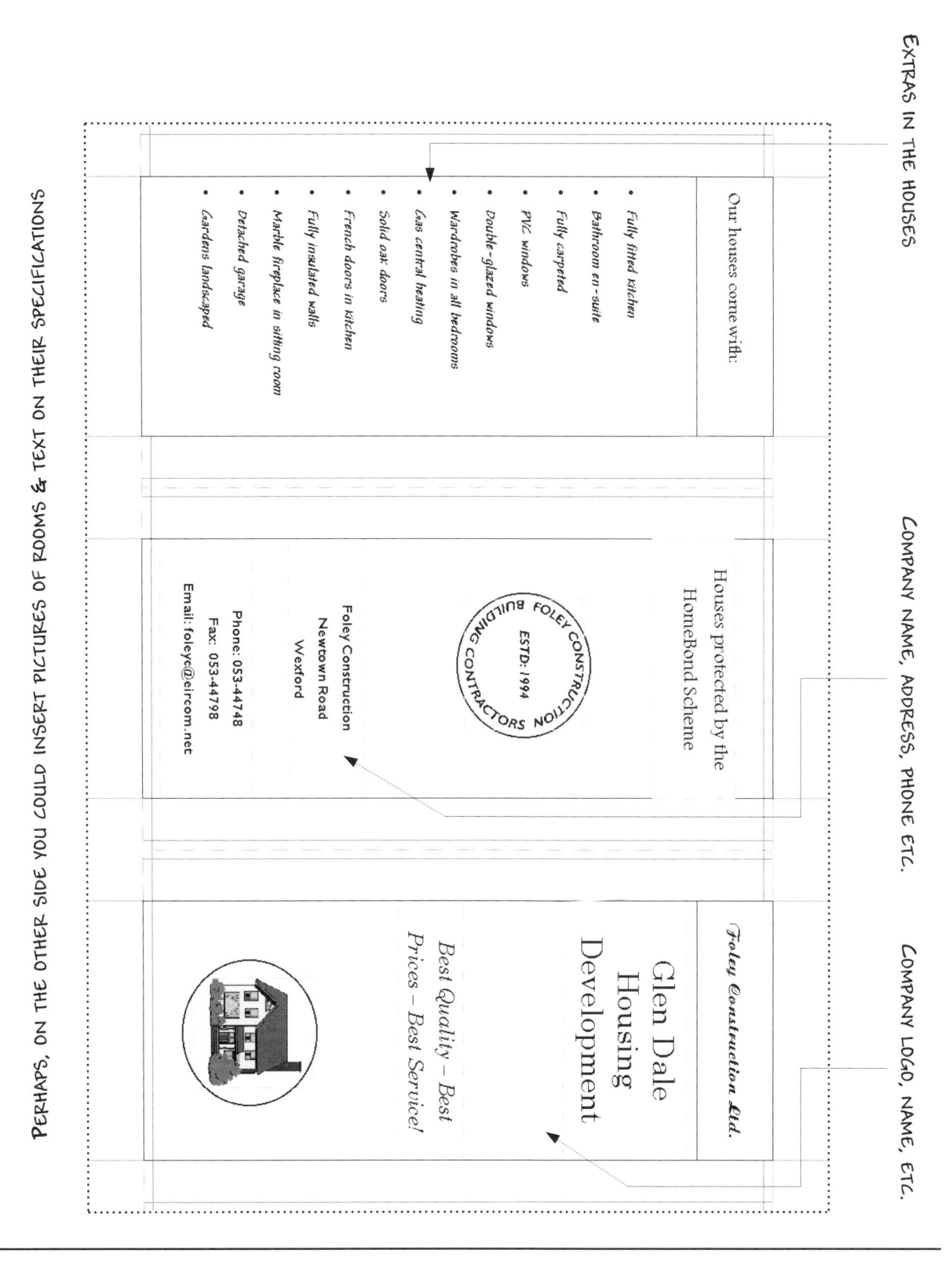

EXTRAS IN THE HOUSES

Our houses come with:

- Fully fitted kitchen
- Bathroom en-suite
- Fully carpeted
- PVC windows
- Double-glazed windows
- Wardrobes in all bedrooms
- Gas central heating
- Solid oak doors
- French doors in kitchen
- Fully insulated walls
- Marble fireplace in sitting room
- Detached garage
- Gardens landscaped

PERHAPS, ON THE OTHER SIDE YOU COULD INSERT PICTURES OF ROOMS & TEXT ON THEIR SPECIFICATIONS

Houses protected by the HomeBond Scheme

FOLEY CONSTRUCTION BUILDING CONTRACTORS ESTD: 1994

Foley Construction
Newtown Road
Wexford

Phone: 053-44748
Fax: 053-44798
Email: foleyc@eircom.net

COMPANY NAME, ADDRESS, PHONE ETC.

Foley Construction Ltd.

Glen Dale Housing Development

Best Quality – Best Prices – Best Service!

COMPANY LOGO, NAME, ETC.

IN CHAPTERS 7-9 YOU HAVE DONE THE FOLLOWING:

- Increased tracking on lines of text.
- Used kerning on pairs of characters.
- Learned about paper sizes.
- Used pre-defined layouts to set up greeting card page.
- Manually set up a greeting card page by breaking up an A4 page into 4 A6 sections.
- Aligned objects within panels.
- Rotated objects.
- Set up a gatefold brochure.
- Marked lists by bulleting and numbering.
- Indented paragraphs.
- Inserted tabs.
- Changed line spacing (leading).
- Shadowed frames.
- Inserted extra pages.
- Inserted WordArt around an object, maintaining the same shape as the object.

Chapter 10

Document Analysis

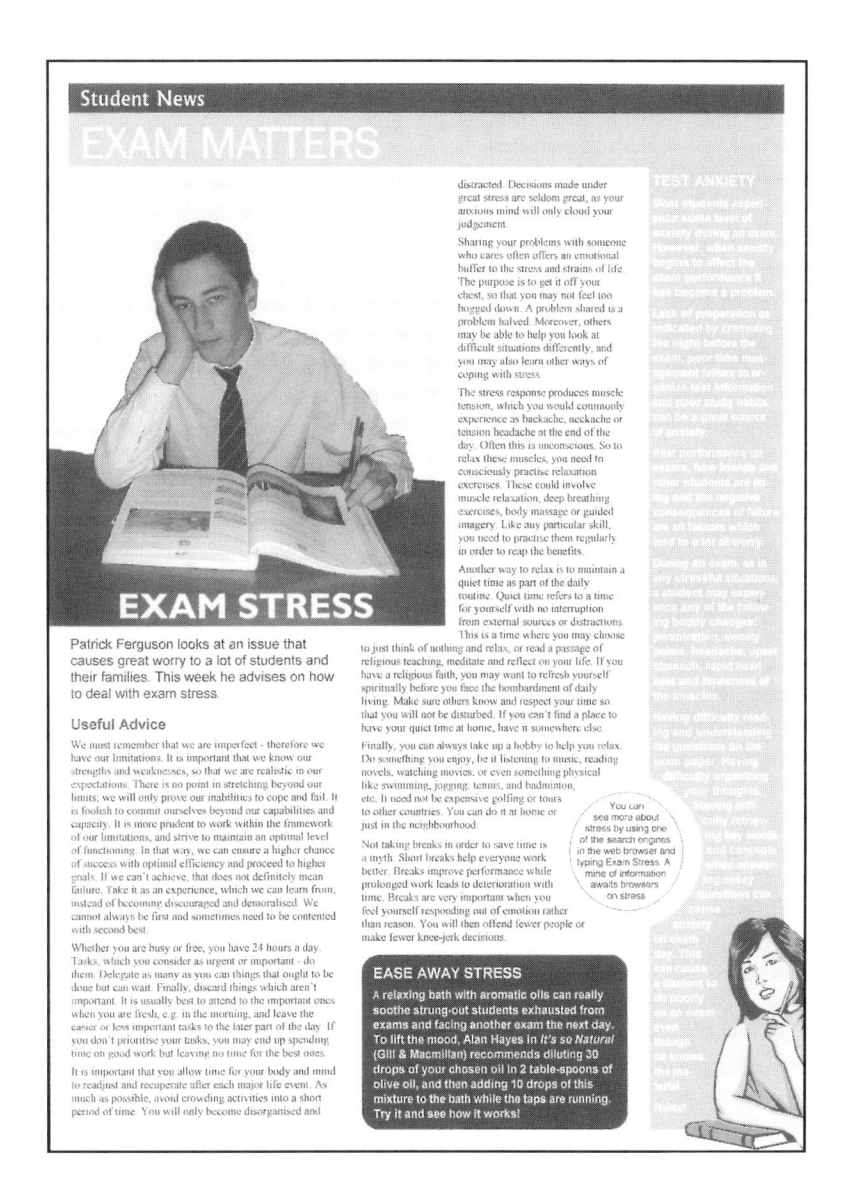

Document Analysis   Chapter 10

TECHNICAL ANALYSIS

Paper Size

1. A poster or magazine page will likely be:
   - A4 size (210 mm. x 297 mm.), or
   - Letter size (216 mm. x 279 mm.), or
   - Legal size (216 mm. x 356 mm.), or
   - Executive size (184 mm. x 267 mm.), or
   - Custom size.

Margins:

Get the ruler and measure!

Column Widths

Drugs don't have to be out on the street for young people to abuse them. An average household has up to 30 items that could be abused, e.g. solvents such as spray-cans, lighter fluid, cleaners and camping gas. Young people start experimenting at home. Solvent abuse is the deliberate inhalation of gases, chemical

fumes and vapours in order to get a *high*, similar to the intoxication produced by alcohol. It is inhaled deeply into the lungs through the nose and mouth. Usually a plastic or paper bag is used. The most dangerous of all is the spraying of aerosols or gas lighter fluids directly into the mouth. It is widely known that some abusers

The column is a little wider than the longest line

If the text has a left alignment as above, it will not stretch the full length of each column. If a character or a word cannot fit fully on the line, it will go on to the next line, leaving the part character or part word space behind on the previous line. When measuring the column width you should always add a little to longest line of text. If the text is justified as below, then each line of text can be measured accurately.

Drugs don't have to be out on the street for young people to abuse them. An average household has up to 30 items that could be abused, e.g. solvents such as spray-cans, lighter fluid, cleaners and camping gas. Young people start experimenting at home. Solvent abuse is the deliberate inhalation of gases, chemical

fumes and vapours in order to get a *high*, similar to the intoxication produced by alcohol. It is inhaled deeply into the lungs through the nose and mouth. Usually a plastic or paper bag is used. The most dangerous of all is the spraying of aerosols or gas lighter fluids directly into the mouth. It is widely known that some abusers

The column is the same length as the line

Gutters

Drugs don't have to be out on the street for young people to abuse them. An average household has up to 30 items that could be abused, e.g. solvents such as spray-cans, lighter fluid, cleaners and camping gas. Young people start experimenting at home. Solvent abuse is the deliberate inhalation of gases, chemical

fumes and vapours in order to get a *high*, similar to the intoxication produced by alcohol. It is inhaled deeply into the lungs through the nose and mouth. Usually a plastic or paper bag is used. The most dangerous of all is the spraying of aerosols or gas lighter fluids directly into the mouth. It is widely known that some abusers

The gutter is a little less than the space

If the text has a left alignment as shown above, the gutter or gutters will be slightly less than the space between the longest line of text on one column and the adjoining column. If the text is justified as shown below, then each column's width can be measured accurately.

Drugs don't have to be out on the street for young people to abuse them. An average household has up to 30 items that could be abused, e.g. solvents such as spray-cans, lighter fluid, cleaners and camping gas. Young people start experimenting at home. Solvent abuse is the deliberate inhalation of

gases, chemical fumes and vapours in order to get a *high*, similar to the intoxication produced by alcohol. It is inhaled deeply into the lungs through the nose and mouth. Usually a plastic or paper bag is used. The most dangerous of all is the spraying of aerosols or gas lighter fluids directly into the

The gutter is the same width as the space

Rules

Hairline: ―――――――――
1 pt: ―――――――――
2 pt: ―――――――――
3 pt: ▬▬▬▬▬▬▬▬▬
4 pt: ▬▬▬▬▬▬▬▬▬
5 pt: ▬▬▬▬▬▬▬▬▬
6 pt: ▬▬▬▬▬▬▬▬▬
7 pt: ▬▬▬▬▬▬▬▬▬
8 pt: ▬▬▬▬▬▬▬▬▬
9 pt: ▬▬▬▬▬▬▬▬▬

The rule thickness is something you should be able to determine from the experience of seeing rules during your course.

Chapter 10 — Document Analysis

Text Alignment

> Drugs don't have to be out on the street for young people to abuse them. An average household has up to 30 items that could be abused, e.g. solvents such as spraycans, lighter fluid, cleaners and camping gas. Young

Left aligned
(flush left, ragged right)

> Drugs don't have to be out on the street for young people to abuse them. An average household has up to 30 items that could be abused, e.g. solvents such as spraycans, lighter fluid, cleaners and camping gas. Young

Right aligned
(flush right, ragged left)

> Drugs don't have to be out on the street for young people to abuse them. An average household has up to 30 items that could be abused, e.g. solvents such as spraycans, lighter fluid, cleaners and camping gas. Young

Centre aligned

> Drugs don't have to be out on the street for young people to abuse them. An average household has up to 30 items that could be abused, e.g. solvents such as spray-cans, lighter fluid, cleaners and camping gas. Young

Justified aligned

Left aligned text is used when you want to create an informal publication. Each word is separated by the same amount of white space. The irregular line endings create extra white space which lightens a publication and makes it easier to read. It is generally used for body text.

Centre aligned text is used for short headlines which span more than one column of body text. You should never use long centre aligned blocks of text as the eye is trained not to have to search for the beginning of each line of text.

Right aligned text should be used very rarely and never for body text as the reader will have to slow down to identify the beginning of each line.

Justified aligned text darkens a publication as it cuts down on the white space either at the beginning or end of a line. It is used for body text, but will create *rivers of white* and unusual *tracking*, especially if the columns are very narrow. This makes text harder to read but can be eliminated by controlled hyphenation. See below how to solve problems related to justified aligned text.

> Drugs don't have to be out on the street for young people to abuse them. ◄ An a v e r a g e household has up to 30 items that

River of White

Unusual Tracking

Controlled Hyphenation

> Drugs don't have to be out on the street for young people to abuse them. An average household has up to 30 items that could

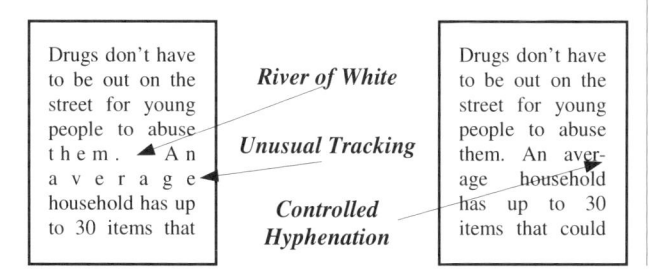

Font Classification

A *font* is a set of all characters, all of one size or style. The term *typeface* refers to a specific style or design of letters.

Most typefaces fall into one of two major categories: *serif* or *sans serif*.

Serif type is characterised by tiny *'strokes'* or *'feet'* attached to the edges of each letter. This helps guide the reader's eye from letter to letter. Usually *serif* type is used for body text. It helps the reader to see the message as groups of words rather than as individual letters.

Here are some examples of *serif* typefaces:

Times New Roman
Rockwell
Bookman Old Style
<code>Courier New</code>

Sans serif (without the little strokes) is used for small amounts of text in order to add impact. Designers use it for headings because it contrasts well with the *serif* body text. However, *serif* type of larger size can also be used for headings.

Here are some examples of *sans serif* typefaces:

Arial
Albertus Medium
Antique Olive
Basic Sans SF

In Desktop Publishing *'font'* means the complete collection of all characters, numbers and symbols of one size and one design of type. All uppercase and lowercase letters, numbers, punctuation marks and symbols in Arial 12 pt make up one font.

Here is an example of the Rockwell 10 pt font:

ABCDEFGHIJKLMNOPQRSTUVWXYZ
abcdefghijklmnopqrstuvwxyz
1234567890()*&^%$£"!?/\|:;@'{}[]_-+=.,><#~

Here is an example of the Arial 11 pt font:

ABCDEFGHIJKLMNOPQRSTUVWXYZ
abcdefghijklmnopqrstuvwxyz
1234567890()*&^%$£"!?/\|:;@'{}[]_-+=.,><#~

Here is an example of the Andy 11 pt font:

ABCDEFGHIJKLMNOPQRSTUVWXYZ
abcdefghijklmnopqrstuvwxyz
1234567890()*&^%$£"!?/\|:;@'{}[]__-+=.,><#~

Using Microsoft Publisher

Font Sizes

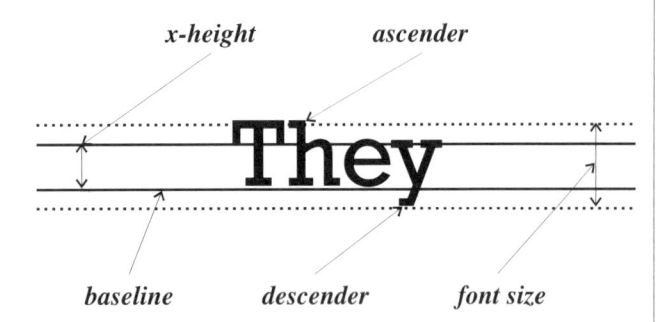

x-height   *ascender*

They

baseline   *descender*   *font size*

Type

72 pt = 1 inch

Type

36 pt = ¹/₂ inch

Type

18 pt = ¹/₄ inch

The *x-height* is an important feature of all fonts. It measures the size of those characters or parts of characters which rest on the baseline, but neither go above or below the height of an *x*. The *ascender* is that part which rises above the *x-height* and the *descender* that part which goes below the *x-height*.

Type is measured by its vertical height from an ascender to a descender. The size of characters is referred to in *point* sizes. 1 pt size = ¹/₇₂ inch. A size of 72 pt is therefore 1 inch in height. This example gives you something to relate to when calculating the size of fonts in documents. See the three examples above.

Leading (pronounced 'ledding') is the term which describes the space between each line of text. Leading always has to be of a greater size than the text itself to allow for a space between the descender of one line and the ascender of the next. If this were not the case the ascenders of one line would overlap with the descenders of the previous one. Below is an example of 10 pt text with an 8 pt leading – written 10/8 pt (minus leading).

> Drugs don't have to be out on the street for young people to abuse them. An average household has up to 30 items that could be abused, e.g. solvents such as spray-cans, lighter fluid, cleaners and camping gas. Young people start experimenting at home. Solvent abuse is the de-

Leading is measured from baseline to baseline of text. The leading in Publisher is by default 120% of the font size. It can however be increased to create more white space for the reader.

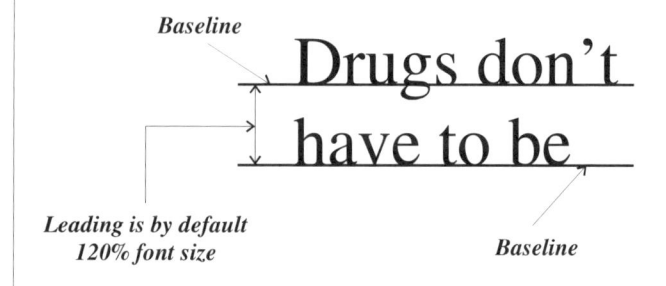

Baseline

Drugs don't have to be

Leading is by default 120% font size   *Baseline*

Below are examples of text with different amounts of leading:

> Drugs don't have to be out on the street for young people to abuse them. A household has up to 30 items that could be abused, e.g. solvents such as spray-cans, lighter fluid, cleaners and camping gas. Young people start experimenting at home.

Font size =10 on 12 pt leading (written 10/12 pt)

> Drugs don't have to be out on the street for young people to abuse them. A household has up to 30 items that could be abused, e.g. solvents such as spray-cans, lighter fluid, cleaners and camping gas. Young people start experimenting at home.

Font size = 10 on 14 pt leading (written 10/14 pt)

Measuring font size is easy.

It's easy to measure type even if you don't have the special plastic ruler for doing it.

For headings there's nothing to it except using the ruler. Measure the vertical height from ascender to descender. If the measurement you get is ⅜ inch, then the point size is 72 x ⅜ = 27 pt or 28 pt.

There is no descender with uppercase letters. As a descender is about ⅓ (the x-height + the ascender), you can multiply your ruler measurement by ⁴⁄₃. If the calculated size of uppercase letters is ⅜ inch, then the real font size is ⅜ x ⁴⁄₃ = ½ inch = 36 pt.

For body text it is different. For one thing a line of text will be too small to measure accurately and for another the leading has to be taken into account. It's important that you get used to what is and what is not a default leading of 120% of the font size.

See the example below.

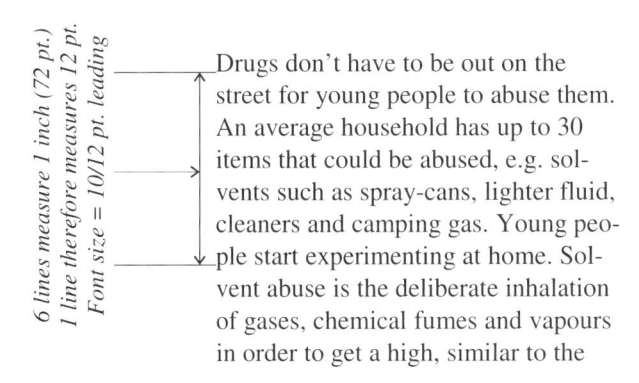

6 lines measure 1 inch (72 pt.)
1 line therefore measures 12 pt.
Font size = 10/12 pt. leading

Drugs don't have to be out on the street for young people to abuse them. An average household has up to 30 items that could be abused, e.g. solvents such as spray-cans, lighter fluid, cleaners and camping gas. Young people start experimenting at home. Solvent abuse is the deliberate inhalation of gases, chemical fumes and vapours in order to get a high, similar to the

From experience you'll know that the text above has a default leading. Let's measure how many lines of text fit into 1 vertical inch. We'll measure from baseline to baseline. Six lines measure 1 inch (72 pt). One line measures ⁷²⁄₆= 12 pt. Therefore the leading is 12 pt. If the leading is 12 pt, the font size must be 10 pt. Remember the leading = 120% of the font size! The font size = 10/12 pt leading.

Now let's say there's an extra space between the descender of one line and the ascender of the next, and again 6 lines measure 1 inch (72 pt). One line measures ⁷²⁄₆= 12 pt. Therefore the leading is 12 pt. Because of the extra space between the descender of one line and the ascender of the next the font size must be slightly less – probably 9 pt. Therefore the font size = 9/12 pt leading.

Font Styles

Here are several different type styles:

Typography	Normal
Typography	Bold
Typography	Italic
Typography	Bold Italic
Typography	Underlined
Typography	Outline
25° C	Superscript
H₂O	Subscript

**VISUAL IMPACT
GOOD DESIGN FEATURES**

Effective design is very important in order to make a publication more readable. People can argue the merits and demerits of a publication as regards design. Nevertheless there are certain principles of good design that cannot be contradicted.

The four most common features of a publication are ***text***, ***illustrations***, ***graphics using the drawing tools*** and ***white space***. I intend discussing the white space feature with each of the other three.

Most of what follow are good design features.

Text – Headlines

1 Headlines should be differentiated from body text. This can be done in two ways:

(a) Use a contrasting typeface. As the body text is in a serif typeface you could use sans serif for the headline. See below.

Headline

The rain in Spain falls mainly on the plain. The rain in Spain falls mainly on the plain. The rain in Spain falls mainly on the plain. The rain in Spain falls mainly on the plain. The rain in Spain falls mainly on the plain. The rain in Spain falls mainly on the plain. The rain in Spain falls mainly on the plain. The rain in Spain falls mainly on the plain. The rain in Spain

(b) Emphasise the headline by using the same typeface but in a larger size. Both therefore will be in a serif typeface. See below.

Headline

The rain in Spain falls mainly on the plain. The rain in Spain falls mainly on the plain. The rain in Spain falls mainly on the plain. The rain in Spain falls mainly on the plain. The rain in Spain falls mainly on the plain. The rain in Spain falls mainly on the plain. The rain in Spain falls mainly on the plain. The rain in Spain falls mainly on the plain. The rain in Spain

---

2 Increased spacing between headlines and body text adds more white space. Increased white space can make documents more readable, which is a very good feature. To do this in Publisher, click anywhere on the headline, click the **Line Spacing** submenu from **Format** on the Menu Bar and insert a value in the **After paragraphs** box.

3 Increased tracking on a short heading can make it stand out more. See below.

Without Increased Tracking

With Increased Tracking

Rain

The rain in Spain falls mainly on the plain. The rain in Spain falls mainly on the plain. The rain in Spain falls mainly on the plain. The rain in Spain falls mainly on the plain. The rain in Spain falls

---

R a i n

The rain in Spain falls mainly on the plain. The rain in Spain falls mainly on the plain. The rain in Spain falls mainly on the plain. The rain in Spain falls mainly on the plain. The rain in Spain falls

---

4 Headlines are usually centred over more than one column. The centred headline with the left aligned body text adds to the contrast. See below.

Headline

The rain in Spain falls mainly on the plain. The rain in Spain falls mainly on the plain. The rain in Spain falls mainly on the plain. The rain in Spain

falls mainly on the plain. The rain in Spain falls mainly on the plain. The rain in Spain falls mainly on the plain. The rain in Spain falls mainly on the

---

5 Reversed text on a tinted background adds emphasis and creates interest in headlines or in advertisements as in the illustration below. It can also distract the eye if there isn't sufficient white space between it and the body text.

Halloween Horror

HERITAGE FESTIVAL

6 In multipage publications consistency of headline style is essential – a good design feature.

Text – Body Text

1 Use a serif typeface for large amounts of body text. A serif typeface is easier to read as the tiny strokes at the edge of the letters help guide the reader's eyes from letter to letter. See below.

Body Text in Serif Typeface

The rain in Spain falls mainly on the plain. The rain in Spain falls mainly on the plain. The rain in Spain falls mainly on the plain. The rain in Spain falls mainly on the plain. The rain in Spain falls mainly on the plain. The rain in Spain falls mainly on the plain. The rain in Spain falls mainly on the plain. The rain in Spain falls mainly on the plain. The rain in Spain falls mainly on the plain. The rain in Spain falls mainly on the

Body Text in Sans Serif Typeface

The rain in Spain falls mainly on the plain. The rain in Spain falls mainly on the plain. The rain in Spain falls mainly on the plain. The rain in Spain falls mainly on the plain. The rain in Spain falls mainly on the plain. The rain in Spain falls mainly on the plain. The rain in Spain falls mainly on the plain. The rain in Spain falls mainly on the plain. The rain in Spain falls mainly on the plain. The rain in Spain falls mainly on the plain. The rain in

Chapter 10　　　　　　　　　　　　　　　　　　　　　Document Analysis

2 The reading line length should be kept to a maximum of 10-13 words (< 60 characters) depending on the size of the text. Break up the text into more than one column if necessary.

3 Breaking up text into columns also increases the white space, which makes the text more readable. See below.

> The rain in Spain falls mainly on the plain. The rain in Spain falls mainly on the plain. The rain in Spain falls mainly on the plain. The rain in Spain falls mainly on the plain. The rain in Spain falls mainly on the plain. The rain in Spain falls mainly on the plain. The rain in Spain falls mainly on the plain. The
>
> rain in Spain falls mainly on the plain. The rain in Spain falls mainly on the plain. The rain in Spain falls mainly on the plain. The rain in Spain falls mainly on the plain. The rain in Spain falls mainly on the plain. The rain in Spain falls mainly on the plain. The rain in

4 If text is left aligned rather than justified more white space is evident at the ragged right edge of the columns. This is a good design feature. White space means improved readability. See below.

Left Aligned Text

> The rain in Spain falls mainly on the plain. The rain in Spain falls mainly on the plain. The rain in Spain falls mainly on the plain. The rain in Spain falls mainly on the plain. The rain in Spain falls mainly on the plain. The rain in Spain falls mainly on the plain. The rain in Spain falls mainly on the plain. The
>
> rain in Spain falls mainly on the plain. The rain in Spain falls mainly on the plain. The rain in Spain falls mainly on the plain. The rain in Spain falls mainly on the plain. The rain in Spain falls mainly on the plain. The rain in Spain falls mainly on the plain. The rain in

Justified Text

> The rain in Spain falls mainly on the plain. The rain in Spain falls mainly on the plain. The rain in Spain falls mainly on the plain. The rain in Spain falls mainly on the plain. The rain in Spain falls mainly on the plain. The rain in Spain falls mainly on the plain. The rain in Spain falls mainly on the plain. The
>
> rain in Spain falls mainly on the plain. The rain in Spain falls mainly on the plain. The rain in Spain falls mainly on the plain. The rain in Spain falls mainly on the plain. The rain in Spain falls mainly on the plain. The rain in Spain falls mainly on the plain. The rain in

5 If the text in narrow columns is justified, rivers of white and unusual spacing of characters (tracking) are often apparent. In such cases controlled hyphenation can solve the problem. In this context controlled hyphenation is a good design feature.

Rivers of White

> Procrastination is the thief of time. Procrastination is the thief of time. Procrastination is the thief of time. Procrastination is the thief of time. Procrastination is the thief of time. Procrastination is the thief of time.
>
> Procrastination is the thief of time. Procrastination is the thief of time. Procrastination is the thief of time. Procrastination is the thief of time. Procrastination is the thief of time. thief of time.

No Rivers of White

> Procrastination is the thief of time. Procrastination is the thief of time. Procrastination is the thief of time. Procrastination is the thief of time. Procrastination is the thief of time.
>
> Procrastination is the thief of time. Procrastination is the thief of time. Procrastination is the thief of time. Procrastination is the thief of time. Procrastination is the thief of time.

6 Increased leading is another way of improving readability. This is a very effective method of increasing white space. See the default leading below and the increased leading on the top of page 126.

Default Leading

> The rain in Spain falls mainly on the plain. The rain in Spain falls mainly on the plain. The rain in Spain falls mainly on the plain. The rain in Spain falls mainly on the plain. The rain in Spain falls mainly on the plain. The rain in Spain falls mainly on the plain. The rain in Spain
>
> falls mainly on the plain. The rain in Spain falls mainly on the plain. The rain in Spain falls mainly on the plain. The rain in Spain falls mainly on the plain. The rain in Spain falls mainly on the plain. The rain in Spain falls mainly on the plain. The rain in Spain falls mainly on the

Document Analysis — Chapter 10

Increased Leading

The rain in Spain falls mainly on the plain. The rain in Spain falls mainly on the plain. The rain in Spain falls mainly on the plain. The rain in Spain falls mainly on the plain. The rain in Spain falls mainly on the plain.

The rain in Spain falls mainly on the plain. The rain in Spain falls mainly on the plain. The rain in Spain falls mainly on the plain. The rain in Spain falls mainly on the plain. The rain in Spain falls mainly on the plain.

Mark Nolan was overjoyed at winning the annual tennis competition held in the local tennis courts over two days last week. His achievement was all the more noteworthy as he had been in a serious accident the previous week injuring his wrist and four toes on his left foot.

In the final he came up against his fiercest rival, Tom O'Brien, who gave him the fright of his life. It was one of the best finals in recent years, featuring some of the most fascinating rallies ever seen at the venue. He now goes on to represent Wexford in the

7 *Widows* and *Orphans* should always be avoided. A widow is when the last line of text in a paragraph appears at the top of the next column or page. An orphan is when the first line of text in a paragraph appears at the bottom of a column or page. See the examples below.

8 The use of bullets or numbering for lists is a good design feature as it helps the reader to identify the list more easily. It also adds white space. It is important however that the indents are not exaggerated. See below.

Widow

Mark Nolan was overjoyed at winning the annual tennis competition held in the local tennis courts over two days last week. His achievement was all the more noteworthy as he had been involved in a serious accident the previous week injuring his wrist and four toes on his left foot.

In the final he came up against his fiercest rival, Tom O'Brien, who gave him the fright of his life. It was one of the best finals in recent years, featuring some of the most fascinating rallies ever seen at the venue.

The following are the courses available:

- Security & Business Studies
- Information Technology
- Advanced Secretarial
- Sport & Recreation
- Business Studies
- Nursing Studies
- Interior Design

Mark Nolan was overjoyed at winning the annual tennis competition held in the local tennis courts over two days last week. His achievement was all the more noteworthy as he had been involved in a serious accident the previous week injuring his wrist and four toes on his left foot.
In the final he came up

against his fiercest rival, Tom O'Brien, who gave him the fright of his life. It was one of the best finals in recent years, featuring some of the most fascinating rallies ever seen at the venue.
He now goes on to represent Wexford in the Community Games which will be held in Mosney in August. Everyone in

9 Pull Quotes add contrast and white space to a publication. See below.

Text Passage with a Pull Quote

Orphan

Widows and Orphans can be avoided by:

- editing the text – either increasing the volume of text or deleting unnecessary words
- decreased tracking in the paragraph, if there are only a few characters to be worked on
- either increasing or decreasing the leading.

The top of next column shows the ***widow*** above removed by deleting the word 'involved'.

Alcohol is probably the most abused drug in civilisation. It is a sedative drug and it can lead to physical, social and psychological addiction. Underage drinking is a major problem to this day. It is illegal to serve anyone under 18 years of age. It is also illegal for a person under 18 to buy alcohol. Anyone who starts to drink at an early age might end up with a bad drinking problem. Drinking to excess should not be tolerated. Alcohol slows down the brain and this makes the drinker become relaxed and uninhibited. The damage that prolonged excessive drinking does to various organs in the body is great. Drinking too much can cause nausea, embarrassment, loss of control, rejection and accidents. Long-term alcohol abuse can lead to physical and mental damage, serious accidents, addiction, even death. Accept that other people have as much right to their decision as you have to yours. Don't ridicule them or try to persuade them to drink. Remember, for them as for you, it's OK to say no. If you choose to drink know the limit, space your drinks, limit their number and take your time. You should also eat while you're drinking. Don't drink to show off or to escape from problems. It's an offence to allow people under fifteen years of age in a bar during business hours, unless accompanied by a parent or guardian. In Ireland, the present

'It is illegal for a person under 18 to buy alcohol'

10 Excessive underlining causes the reader's eyes to become confused. It becomes difficult to separate the text from the horizontal lines because the eyes fluctuate between the underlining and the words. The text becomes difficult to read as the descenders are crossed by the horizontal lines. See below.

A paragraph that is completely underlined is very difficult to read. Your eyes get very tired of reading line after line of underscoring. A paragraph that is completely underlined is very difficult to read. Your eyes get very tired of reading line after line of underscoring. A paragraph that is completely underlined is very difficult to read. Your eyes get very tired of reading line after line of underscoring.

11 Extra spacing between paragraphs is a good design feature as it creates more white space and makes it easier for the reader to distinguish between the paragraphs. It therefore improves readability. See below.

Extra Spacing between Paragraphs

Alcohol is probably the most abused drug in civilisation. It is a sedative drug and it can lead to physical, social and psychological addiction. Underage drinking is a major problem to this day. It is illegal to serve anyone under 18 years of age. It is also illegal for a person under 18 to buy alcohol.

Anyone who starts to drink at an early age might end up with a bad drinking problem. Drinking to excess should not be tolerated. Alcohol slows down the brain and this makes the drinker become relaxed and uninhibited.

The damage that prolonged excessive drinking does to various organs in the body is great. Drinking too much can cause nausea, embarrassment, loss of control, rejection and accidents. Long-term alcohol abuse can lead to physical and mental damage, serious accidents, addiction, even death.

Accept that other people have as much right to their decision as you have to yours. Don't ridicule them or try to persuade them to drink. Remember, for them as for you, it's OK to say no.

If you choose to drink know the limit, space your drinks, limit their number and take your time. You should also eat while you're drinking. Don't drink to show off or to escape from problems. It's an offence to allow people under fifteen years of age in a bar during business hours, unless accompanied by a

12 Another way to make it easier for the reader to distinguish between paragraphs is to indent each paragraph. The size of the indent should depend on the width of the column. Indented paragraphs improve readability.

Indented Paragraphs

Alcohol is probably the most abused drug in civilisation. It is a sedative drug and it can lead to physical, social and psychological addiction. Underage drinking is a major problem to this day. It is illegal to serve anyone under 18 years of age. It is also illegal for a person under 18 to buy alcohol. Anyone who starts to drink at an early age might end up with a bad drinking problem.

Drinking to excess should not be tolerated. Alcohol slows down the brain and this makes the drinker become relaxed and uninhibited. The damage that prolonged excessive drinking does to various organs in the body is great. Drinking too much can cause nausea, embarrassment, loss of control, rejection and accidents. Long-term alcohol abuse can lead to physical and mental damage, serious accidents, addiction, even death.

Accept that other people have as much right to their decision as you have to yours. Don't ridicule them or try to persuade them to drink. Remember, for them as for you, it's OK to say no.

If you choose to drink know the limit, space your drinks, limit their number and take your time. You

Other good body text features of a publication are:

13 Spelling and grammatical errors should be eliminated.

14 Typeface changes should be kept to a minimum. Two or three typefaces are enough per page.

15 Body text should not be written in very small fonts. Less than 8 pt size is difficult to read.

Text – Subheads

1 Subheadings add to contrast and increase the white space in a publication.

2 They should be of a consistent style in each article.

3 Spacing between subheads and body text should also be consistent.

See below.

Alcohol Abuse

Alcohol is probably the most abused drug in civilisation. It is a sedative drug and it can lead to physical, social and psychological addiction. Underage drinking is a major problem to this day. It is illegal to serve anyone under 18 years of age. It is also illegal for a person under 18 to buy alcohol. Anyone who starts to drink at an early age might end up with a bad drinking problem.

Excess Drinking

Drinking to excess should not be tolerated. Alcohol slows down the brain and this makes the drinker become relaxed and uninhibited. The damage that prolonged excessive drinking does to various organs in the body is great. Drinking too much can cause nausea, embarrassment, loss of control, rejection and accidents. Long-term alcohol abuse can lead to physical and mental damage, serious accidents, addiction, even death.

Respect Others

Accept that other people have as much right to their decision as you have to yours. Don't ridicule them or try to persuade them to drink. Remember, for them as for you, it's OK to say no. If you choose to drink know the limit, space your drinks, limit their number and take your time. You should also eat while you're drinking. Don't drink to show off or to escape from problems. It's an offence to allow people under fifteen years of age in a bar during

Document Analysis   **Chapter 10**

Text – Captions

Captions help to relate the illustrations to the rest of the publication. They help to increase readability. They can be placed either above or below the artwork they describe. They should be consistent in style and should be spaced consistently away from the artwork. See below.

Most Abused Drug

Alcohol is probably the most abused drug in civilisation. It is a sedative drug and it can lead to physical, social and psychological addiction. Underage drinking is a major problem to this day. It is illegal to serve anyone under 18 years of age. It is also illegal for a person under 18 to buy alcohol. Anyone who starts to drink at an early age might end up with a bad drinking problem.

Drinking to excess should not be tolerated. Alcohol slows down the brain and this makes the drinker become relaxed and uninhibited. The damage that prolonged excessive drinking does to various organs in the body is great.

Drinking too much can cause nausea, embarrassment, loss of control, rejection and accidents. Long-term alcohol abuse can lead to physical and mental damage, serious accidents, addiction, even death.

Accept that other people have as much right to their decision as you have to yours. Don't ridicule them or try to persuade them to drink. Remember, for them as for you, it's OK to say no. If you choose to drink know the limit, space your drinks, limit their number and take your time. You should also eat while you're drinking. Don't drink to show off or to escape from problems. It's an offence to allow people under fifteen years of age in a bar during business hours, unless accompanied by a parent or guardian. In Ireland, the present legal limit for driving is one pint per man and less for a woman.

Graphics – Using Drawing Tools

1. Rules are lines used to separate parts of a document. They can be horizontal or vertical, thick or thin. Vertical rules are used to separate columns when text is not justified. If you need rules, use thin ones for dense text and thicker ones for sparse text. When used properly they add contrast to a publication. See below.

Alcohol is probably the most abused drug in civilisation. It is a sedative drug and it can lead to physical, social and psychological addiction. Underage drinking is a major problem to this day. It is illegal to serve anyone under 18 years of age. It is also illegal for a person under 18 to buy alcohol. Anyone who starts to drink at an early age might end up with a bad drinking problem.

Drinking to excess should not be tolerated. Alcohol slows down the brain and this makes the drinker become relaxed and uninhibited. The damage that prolonged excessive drinking does to various organs in the body is great. Drinking too much can cause nausea, embarrassment, loss of control, rejection and accidents. Long-term alcohol abuse can lead to physical and mental damage, serious accidents, addiction, even death.

Accept that other people have as much right to their decision as you have to yours. Don't ridicule them or try to persuade them to drink. Remember, for them as for you, it's OK to say no. If you choose to drink know the limit, space your drinks, limit their number and take your time. You should also eat while you're drinking. Don't drink to show off or to escape from problems. It's an offence to allow people under fifteen years of age in a bar during business hours, unless accompanied by a parent or guardian. In Ireland, the present legal limit for driving is one pint per man and less for a woman.

2. Thick vertical rules darken a page unnecessarily when used with justified text. They also create a boxed effect. See below.

Alcohol is probably the most abused drug in civilisation. It is a sedative drug and it can lead to physical, social and psychological addiction. Underage drinking is a major problem to this day. It is illegal to serve anyone under 18 years of age. It is also illegal for a person under 18 to buy alcohol. Anyone who starts to drink at an early age might end up with a bad drinking problem.

Drinking to excess should not be tolerated. Alcohol slows down the brain and this makes the drinker become relaxed and uninhibited. The damage that prolonged excessive drinking does to various organs in the body is great. Drinking too much can cause nausea, embarrassment, loss of control, rejection and accidents. Long-term alcohol abuse can lead to physical and mental damage, serious accidents, addiction, even death.

Accept that other people have as much right to their decision as you have to yours. Don't ridicule them or try to persuade them to drink. Remember, for them as for you, it's OK to say no. If you choose to drink know the limit, space your drinks, limit their number and take your time. You should also eat while you're drinking. Don't drink to show off or to escape from problems. It's an offence to allow people under fifteen years of age in a bar during business hours, unless accompanied by a parent or guardian. In Ireland, the present legal limit for driving is one pint per man and less for a woman.

3. Horizontal rules are used to separate topics within a column. They can be used also for pull quotes. When used properly they also add contrast to a publication. See below.

Alcohol is probably the most abused drug in civilisation. It is a sedative drug and it can lead to physical, social and psychological addiction. Underage drinking is a major problem to this day. It is illegal to serve anyone under 18 years of age. It is also illegal for a person under 18 to buy alcohol. Anyone who starts to drink at an early age might end up with a bad drinking problem. Drinking to excess should not be tolerated. Alcohol slows down the brain and this makes the drinker become relaxed and uninhibited. The damage that prolonged excessive drinking does to various organs in the body is great. Drinking too much can cause nausea, embarrassment, loss of control, rejection and accidents. Long-term alcohol abuse can lead to physical and mental damage, serious accidents, addiction, even death. Accept that other people have as much right to their decision as you have to yours. Don't ridicule them or try to persuade them to drink. Remember, for them as for you, it's OK to say no. If you choose to drink know the limit, space your drinks, limit their number and take your time. You should also eat while you're drinking. Don't drink to show off or to escape from problems. It's an offence to allow people under fifteen years of age in a bar during business hours, unless accompanied by a parent or guardian. In Ireland, the present

'It is illegal for a person under 18 to buy alcohol'

4. Use boxes to separate or highlight parts of a document. They can be used to enclose an advertisement, a coupon etc., or to isolate names or addresses or phone numbers etc.

5. Borders isolate a page or part of a page from the rest of the document. They work with text to create contrast. The basic border consists of a large box drawn around all sides of the publication.

Page 128   *Desktop Publishing Made Easy*

Chapter 10 — Document Analysis

Graphics – Using Illustrations

1 Illustrations should be appropriate to the publication and of such a size as not to deflect from the message. They can add colour to the publication, but should not be overused.

2 It is important to insert illustrations properly in the publication. See the following examples:

Alcohol is probably the most abused drug in civilisation. It is a sedative drug and it can lead to physical, social and psychological addiction. Underage drinking is a major problem to this day. It is illegal to serve anyone under 18 years of age. It is also illegal for a person under 18 to buy alcohol. Anyone who starts to drink at an early age might end up with a bad drinking problem.

Drinking to excess should not be tolerated. Alcohol slows down the brain and this makes the drinker become relaxed and uninhibited. The damage that prolonged excessive drinking does to various organs in the body is great. Drinking too much can cause nausea, embarrassment, loss of control, rejection and accidents. Long-term alcohol abuse can lead to physical and mental damage, serious accidents, addiction, even death.

Accept that other people have as much right to their decision as you have to yours. Don't ridicule them or try to persuade them to drink. Remember, for them as for you, it's OK to say no. If you choose to drink know the limit, space your drinks, limit their number and take your time. You should also eat while you're drinking. Don't drink to show off or to escape from problems. It's an offence to allow people under fifteen years of age in a bar during business hours, unless accompanied by a parent or guardian. In

The text above is justified, but is kept away from the frame around the illustration by setting an offset on the top, bottom and right of the frame. The text on the left is aligned with the left of the frame.

Alcohol is probably the most abused drug in civilisation. It is a sedative drug and it can lead to physical, social and psychological addiction. Underage drinking is a major problem to this day. It is illegal to serve anyone under 18 years of age. It is also illegal for a person under 18 to buy alcohol. Anyone who starts to drink at an early age might end up with a bad drinking problem.

Drinking to excess should not be tolerated. Alcohol slows down the brain and this makes the drinker become relaxed and uninhibited. The damage that prolonged excessive drinking does to various organs in the body is great.

Drinking too much can cause nausea, embarrassment, loss of control, rejection and accidents. Long-term alcohol abuse can lead to physical and mental damage, serious accidents, addiction, even death.

Accept that other people have as much right to their decision as you have to yours. Don't ridicule them or try to persuade them to drink. Remember, for them as for you, it's OK to say no. If you choose to drink to drink know the limit, space your drinks, limit their number and take

The text above is justified and closely follows the left outline of the illustration without touching it. This is achieved by using the manual text wrap, which is available in Microsoft Publisher. The right side of the illustration is aligned with the right edge of the text. This manual run-around is a very good design feature as it integrates the text more cleverly with the artwork.

Alcohol is probably the most abused drug in civilisation. It is a sedative drug and it can lead to physical, social and psychological addiction. Underage drinking is a major problem to this day. It is illegal to serve anyone under 18 years of age. It is also illegal for a person under 18 to buy alcohol. Anyone who starts to drink at an early age might end up with a bad drinking problem. Drinking to excess should not be tolerated. Alcohol slows down the brain and this makes the drinker become relaxed and uninhibited. The damage that prolonged excessive drinking does to various organs in the body is great. Drinking too much can cause nausea, embarrassment, loss of control, rejection and accidents. Long-term alcohol abuse can lead to physical and mental damage, serious accidents, addiction, even death. Accept that other people have as much right to their decision as you have to yours. Don't ridicule them or try to persuade them to drink. Remember, for them as for you, it's OK to say no. If you choose to drink know the limit, space your drinks, limit their number and take your time. You should also eat while you're

If a picture is centred horizontally inside a text frame that has only one column of text, your eyes assume that when the text reaches the left edge of the picture it is the end of the line. This is not the case as the text continues on the same line to the right of the picture. This is a very bad design flaw and should always be avoided. It is best to create two columns of text. See how this is done below.

The picture above is centred horizontally in a text frame with two columns of text. This is a good design feature as your eyes can do what they are trained to do – read from the end of one line to the beginning of the next.

Student News

EXAM MATTERS

EXAM STRESS

Patrick Ferguson looks at an issue that causes great worry to a lot of students and their families. This week he advises on how to deal with exam stress.

A

Useful Advice

We must remember that we are imperfect – therefore we have our limitations. It is important that we know our strengths and weaknesses, so that we are realistic in our expectations. There is no point in stretching beyond our limits; we will only prove our inabilities to cope and fail. It is foolish to commit ourselves beyond our capabilities and capacity. It is more prudent to work within the framework of our limitations, and strive to maintain an optimal level of functioning. In that way, we can ensure a higher chance of success with optimal efficiency and proceed to higher goals. If we can't achieve, that does not definitely mean failure. Take it as an experience, which we can learn from, instead of becoming discouraged and demoralised. We cannot always be first and sometimes need to be contented with second best.

Whether you are busy or free, you have 24 hours a day. Tasks, which you consider as urgent or important – do them. Delegate as many as you can things that ought to be done but can wait. Finally, discard things which aren't important. It is usually best to attend to the important ones when you are fresh, e.g. in the morning, and leave the easier or less important tasks to the later part of the day. If you don't prioritise your tasks, you may end up spending time on good work but leaving no time for the best ones.

It is important that you allow time for your body and mind to readjust and recuperate after each major life event. As much as possible, avoid crowding activities into a short period of time. You will only become disorganised and distracted. Decisions made under great stress are seldom great, as your anxious mind will only cloud your judgement.

Sharing your problems with someone who cares often offers an emotional buffer to the stress and strains of life. The purpose is to get it off your chest, so that you may not feel too bogged down. A problem shared is a problem halved. Moreover, others may be able to help you look at difficult situations differently, and you may also learn other ways of coping with stress.

The stress response produces muscle tension, which you would commonly experience as backache, neckache or tension headache at the end of the day. Often this is unconscious. So to relax these muscles, you need to consciously practise relaxation exercises. These could involve muscle relaxation, deep breathing exercises, body massage or guided imagery. Like any particular skill, you need to practise them regularly in order to reap the benefits.

Another way to relax is to maintain a quiet time as part of the daily routine. Quiet time refers to a time for yourself with no interruption from external sources or distractions. This is a time where you may choose to just think of nothing and relax, or read a passage of religious teaching, meditate and reflect on your life. If you have a religious faith, you may want to refresh yourself spiritually before you face the bombardment of daily living. Make sure others know and respect your time so that you will not be disturbed. If you can't find a place to have your quiet time at home, have it somewhere else.

Finally, you can always take up a hobby to help you relax. Do something you enjoy, be it listening to music, reading novels, watching movies, or even something physical like swimming, jogging, tennis, and badminton, etc. It need not be expensive golfing or tours to other countries. You can do it at home or just in the neighbourhood.

Not taking breaks in order to save time is a myth. Short breaks help everyone work better. Breaks improve performance while prolonged work leads to deterioration with time. Breaks are very important when you feel yourself responding out of emotion rather than reason. You will then offend fewer people or make fewer knee-jerk decisions.

You can see more about stress by using one of the search engines in the web browser and typing Exam Stress. A mine of information awaits browsers on stress.

D

EASE AWAY STRESS **C**

A **relaxing bath with aromatic oils can really soothe strung-out students exhausted from exams and facing another exam the next day. To lift the mood, Alan Hayes in *It's so Natural* (Gill & Macmillan) recommends diluting 30 drops of your chosen oil in 2 table-spoons of olive oil, and then adding 10 drops of this mixture to the bath while the taps are running. Try it and see how it works!**

TEST ANXIETY

Most students experience some level of anxiety during an exam. However, when anxiety begins to affect the exam performance it has become a problem.

Lack of preparation as indicated by cramming the night before the exam, poor time management, failure to organise text information and poor study habits can be a great source of anxiety. **B**

Past performance on exams, how friends and other students are doing and the negative consequences of failure are all factors which lead to a lot of worry.

During an exam, as in any stressful situations, a student may experience any of the following bodily changes: perspiration, sweaty palms, headache, upset stomach, rapid heart beat and tenseness of the muscles.

Having difficulty reading and understanding the questions on the exam paper, having difficulty organising your thoughts, having difficulty retrieving key words and concepts when answering essay questions can cause anxiety on exam day. This can cause a student to do poorly on an exam even though he or she has learned the material well. Relax!

EXERCISE 10

DOCUMENT ANALYSIS

The page to be analysed is from page 20 of the 'Student News', dated 11 June 2002. A photocopy of this page, which has been rescaled to 80% of the original can be seen on page 130.

Technical Analysis

Paper Size:

A4 – 210 mm. x 297 mm.

Margins:

Top, Bottom, Left and Right = 5 mm.

Column Widths:

The page is broken up into 4 text frames which I've named A, B, C and D.

- A's two columns = 75 mm. wide
- B's column = 40 mm. wide
- C's column = 75 mm. wide
- D's column = 25 mm. wide

Gutters:

- A's gutter = 5 mm.

Typeface Classification and Style:

- Page headline = sans serif, 28 pt, regular, left aligned, uppercase
- Main picture text = sans serif, 22 pt, bold, centre aligned, uppercase
- A's headline = sans serif, 10 pt, bold, left aligned
- B's headline = sans serif, 10 pt, bold, left aligned, uppercase.
- C's headline = sans serif, 10 pt, bold, left aligned, uppercase
- 4 lines of text above A's headline = sans serif, regular, left aligned, 9/11 pt leading
- A's body text = serif, regular, left aligned, 8/10 pt leading with an extra spacing between paragraphs of 6 pt

- B's and C's body text = sans serif, regular, left aligned, 8/10 pt leading. B's text has an extra spacing between paragraphs of 6 pt
- D's body text = sans serif, regular, centred, 6/7.5 pt leading

Visual Impact

Good Features in Design

Pick out any four of the following:

- All the headlines have sans serif typefaces. This is a good feature as it provides contrast to the serif body text. The uppercase lettering of two of the headlines provides contrast to the sans serif body text.
- The main body text frame is in serif typeface. The tiny 'feet' (serifs) at the edge of each letter guides the eyes from one letter to another – hence improving readability.
- All the body text is left aligned. This is a good design feature as left aligned text is easier to read than justified text. The ragged right edge creates more white space and improves readability. As the default leading is only slightly increased, it is important that the white space is created by aligning the text flush left.
- The extra spacing between paragraphs is a good design feature and improves readability. It adds extra white space and helps the reader to identify each paragraph more easily.
- The text across the bottom of the large picture, while not in typical caption form, does the work of a caption more effectively. Like a caption it integrates the picture with the body text, but does so more effectively.
- The reversed text across the main picture adds contrast to the page.

Document Analysis Chapter 10

- The body text in frames B and C is reversed on tinted backgrounds. Frame C is more effective than frame B as the reversed text stands out more on the darker tint. This is a good design feature. If not overdone on a page it adds contrast and makes the page more pleasing to the eye. The message gets special attention.

- Another message that the designer wants to stand out is the message inside the little oval. The designer did not choose to reverse this text and put it on a tinted background for fear of overdoing the reversing and tinting. Placing the text in the oval gives it the extra attention, while at the same time using a different approach.

- There is some consistency of text styles on the page. All the headlines are sans serif bold and left aligned, while nearly all the body text is left aligned with a leading of 8/10 pt. There is an extra spacing of 6 pt between the paragraphs in the two main body text frames.

- The text offset of 5 mm. to the left of the main picture improves readability as the eyes will not be distracted by the picture at the start of each line of text.

- The text run-around in the bottom right of the page is a good design feature as it adds variation and is a clever way of integrating the graphic with the text.

- Both picture bleeds (runs to the edge of the page rather than the margin) provide contrast.

- It could be argued that the following is either a good or bad point: The main picture looks slightly too large for the size of the page. This can take attention away from the message. However, it is offset by the fact that the reversed text across the picture integrates the picture with the body text effectively. The designer also has a choice to make. The picture size cannot be decreased slightly, as then it will invade only a very small portion of the second column. This may not look well. Otherwise it's a case of decreasing the picture size until it only extends to the right side of the first column. The picture may then be too small. It could of course be decreased slightly and centred between both columns. Then the effect of the bleeding to the left will not be present. Leaving it as it is seems the best idea.

Design Improvement

Identification and Alternative Treatment

Pick out any one of the following:

- Generally speaking the body text is done in a serif typeface. However, because of the small amount of text in frames C and D a sans serif typeface is OK. There is a case for saying that the typeface in frame B should be serif.

- The reversed text in frame B is difficult to read as the tinted background is far too light. The background here could have been darker to make the reversed text clearer. If by doing this the page is darkened too much, frame C could be altered. Perhaps then, black text on either a light tinted background or in a bordered text frame would do the trick for frame C.

- While there is some consistency of text styles on the page as mentioned in the *Visual Impact* section, nevertheless if all the body text were serif, none of the headlines would need to be in uppercase lettering. The sans serif headline, without being in uppercase lettering, offers enough contrast to the serif body text. The reason for the uppercase headlines is to offer contrast to the sans serif body text. If all the text frames were done like frame A, there would be more consistency of text styles and the appearance of the page would be improved.

- See the last point in the *Visual Impact* section. You can argue either a good feature or bad feature from it.

CHAPTER 11

DESIGNING A NEWSLETTER

NEWSLETTER TEMPLATE

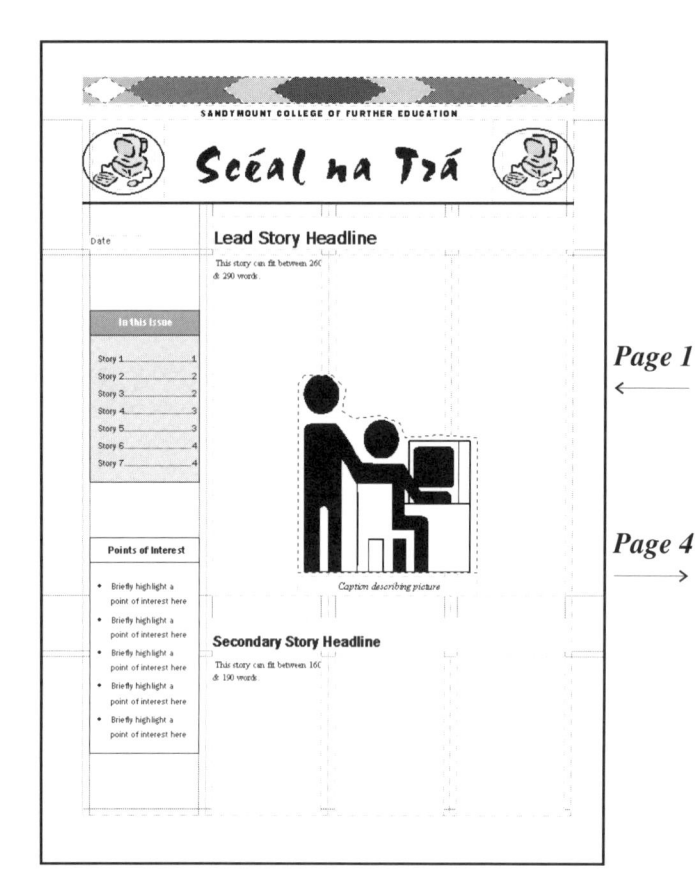

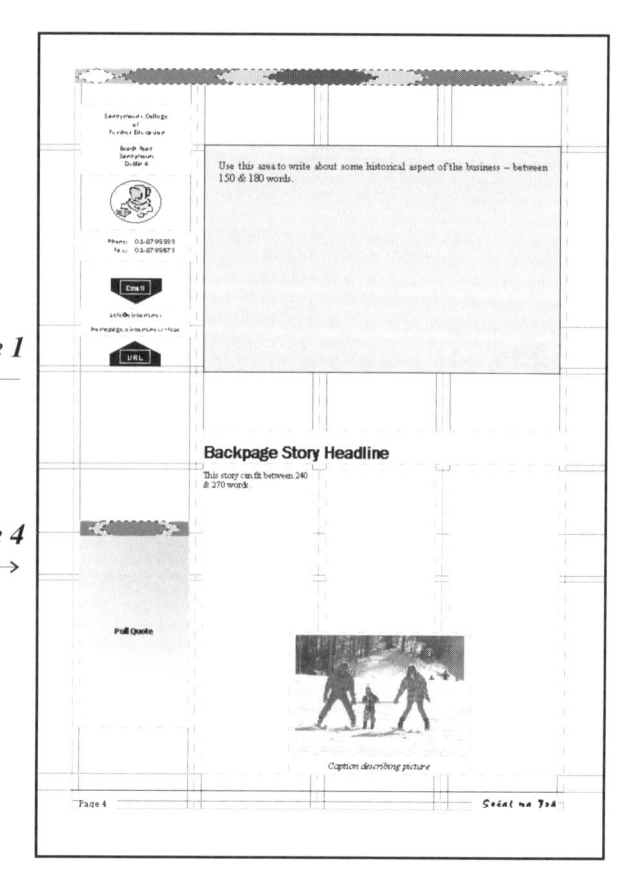

Page 1 ←

Page 4 →

Top border designed in Background

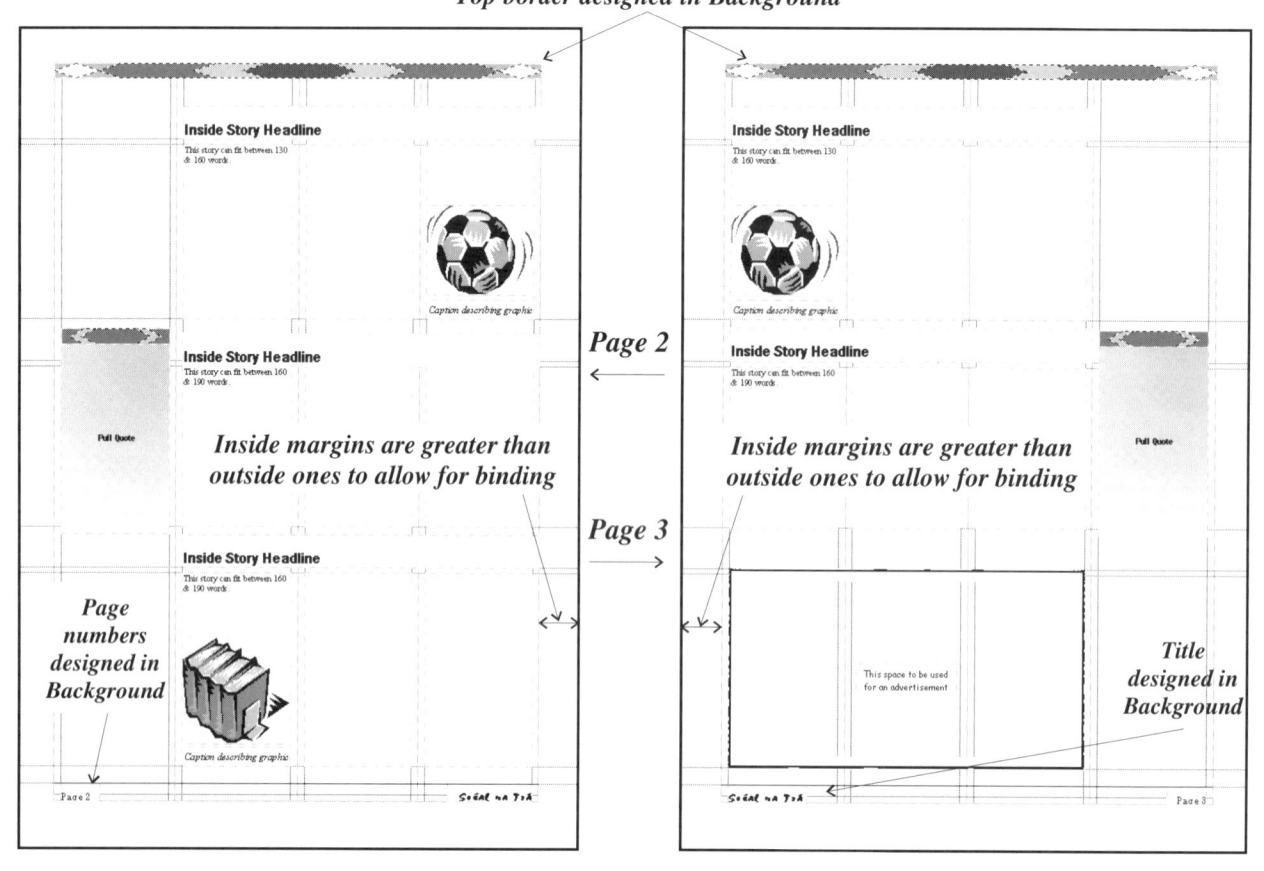

Page 2 ←

Inside margins are greater than outside ones to allow for binding

Page 3 →

Inside margins are greater than outside ones to allow for binding

Page numbers designed in Background

Title designed in Background

FINISHED NEWSLETTER

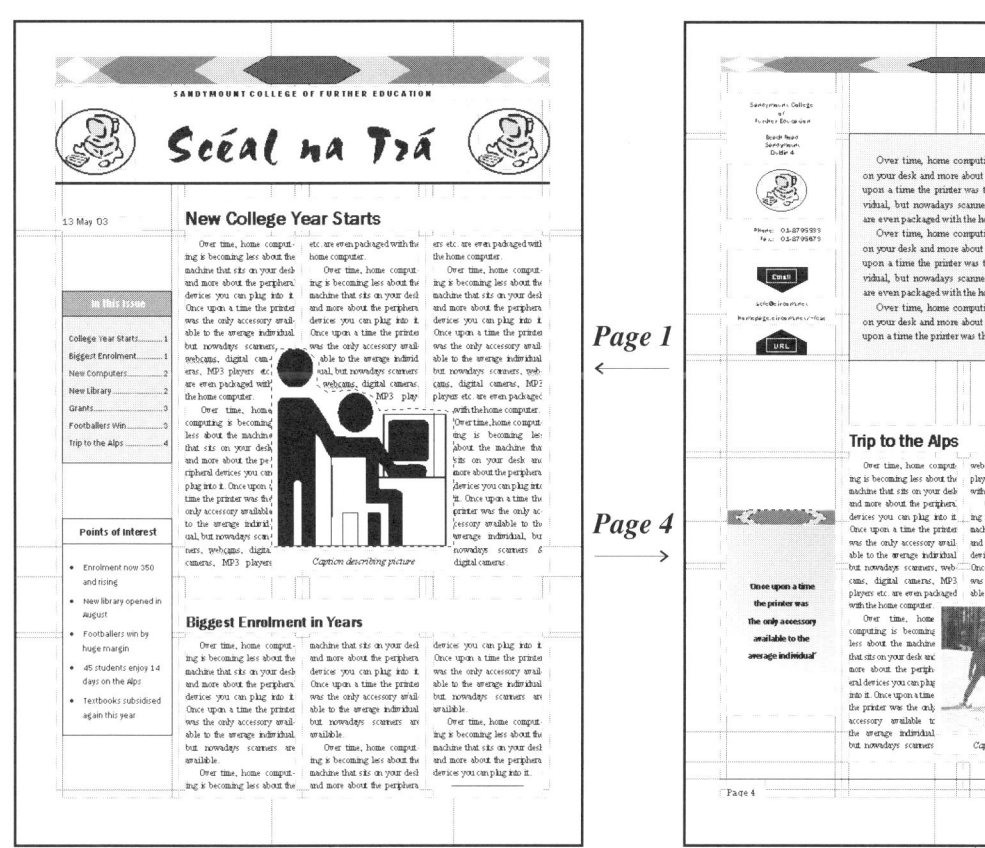

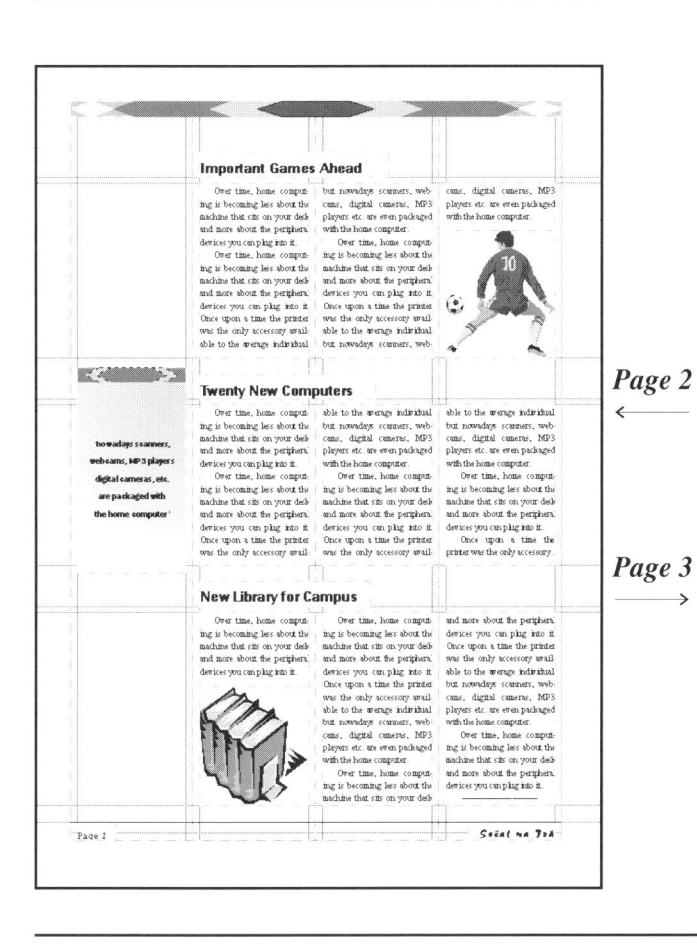

THE NEWSLETTER EXPLAINED

This is the final and by far the largest exercise to be completed. However, most of the skills needed to complete it have already been learned.

To design a four-page *A4* newsletter with pages 2 and 3 as facing pages we create two backgrounds, one for objects that will be repeated on the even numbered pages and the other for objects that will be repeated on the uneven numbered pages.

We shall design this newsletter in such a way as to make the structure of it available, so that a similar type newsletter can be produced on a monthly basis. First of all we have to design a template. Publisher will save this *as a template* in a special folder and make it available for every newsletter we want to create. When we open the template in future to complete the newsletter we will open a copy of it rather than the original. In that way we cannot save over it, but will be asked to give the publication a new name and location. *Templates* have been explained in Chapter 5.

Creating a newsletter has two stages:

(a) Designing the template and (b) Adding the text, graphics, etc to complete the newsletter.

There are also two stages to designing a template:

(a) Creating and positioning the objects in the background that will appear on all pages of the newsletter, (b) Finishing off the template by adding the text frames and picture frames etc. to indicate where the completed newsletter stories and pictures etc. will be inserted.

It will help to have a look at the four pages of the finished newsletter and the template from time to time on the previous two pages in order to understand how this newsletter is being designed. Part of the template contains the objects that are common to all the newsletter pages except the first page. Can you spot them? All such objects have to be created in the background.

The *Background* has also been explained in Chapter 5. It is where the objects that appear on all the pages of the publication are created. The foreground pages are like transparent pages letting you see all the background objects through them. The background objects can be ignored on any page of the newsletter and in our newsletter they are ignored on page 1. When ignored they are not visible anymore on that page.

The following will be done in the background: A top border, a bottom rule, a newsletter title, and page number and title text frames will be created, page numbers and title text will be inserted and formatted, and margins will be set. A two-page spread will be set up where the right background page will represent the uneven numbered pages and the left background page the even numbered pages. More about this later.

You know how to set margins, create text frames and draw rules, so we'll concentrate on creating the top border, inserting the page numbers and creating two backgrounds with mirrored guides for the even and uneven numbered pages – all of which will be created in the background.

DESIGNING A TOP BORDER FOR A NEWSLETTER

Creating the top border will give you a chance to display your design skills. You could of course create a simpler one, but it might not look as pleasing to the eye.

As this border will appear on every page of the newsletter, it will be designed in the background.

♦ *Go to Background* in the *View* menu.
♦ Set the appropriate margins in *Layout Guides* from *Arrange* on the Menu Bar.

This border is made up of 5 different sized shapes, all with different fills of black.

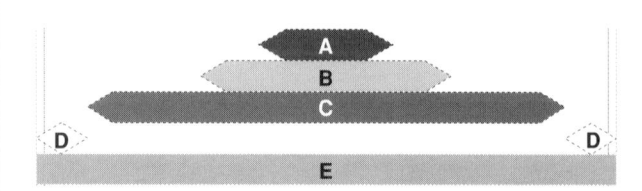

We need shape *A* to be at the top of the stack of shapes; otherwise it will be hidden. The secret is to create it last. See the tutorial on *Layering Objects* in Chapter 4. Create the shapes in this order: *E*, then *D*, then *C*, then *B* and finally *A*.

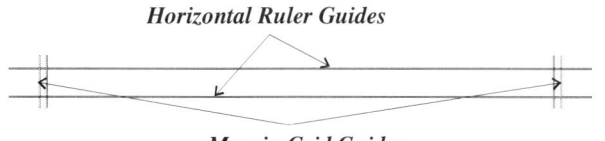

Chapter 11 *Designing a Newsletter*

Horizontal Ruler Guides

Margin Grid Guides

1. Place 2 horizontal ruler guides about 10 mm. apart as seen above. We can create all the shapes between these guides and the left and right margins.
2. Enable *Snap to Guides* and *Snap to Ruler Marks* from the *Tools* menu.

3. Click the *Rectangle* tool from the Tool Palette.

4. Draw rectangle *E* spanning the full page width and snapping in against both margin guides and both horizontal ruler guides.

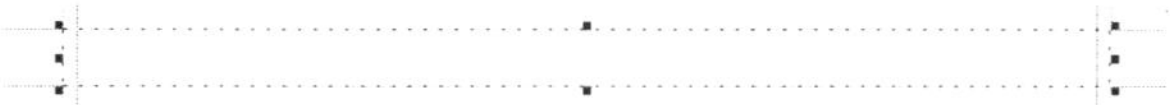

5. Remove the 1 pt border around the rectangle by clicking the *Line/Border Style* tool on the Formatting Toolbar and then clicking *None*.

6. Add a 30% fill of black.
7. Move the rectangle out of way to allow you to work on the other shapes.

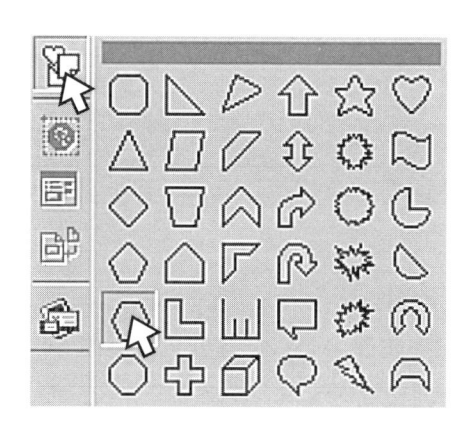

8. Click the *Custom Shapes* tool from the Tool Palette.
9. Click the first shape on the fifth row.

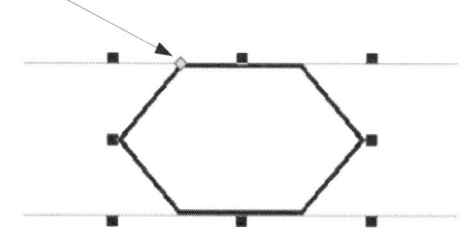

Adjust Handle

10. Draw shape *D* between the ruler guides and about 10 mm. wide.

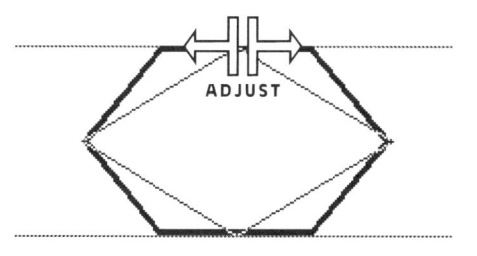

11. Position the mouse pointer over the adjust handle until it changes to an adjust pointer.
12. Drag the adjust handle back until a diamond shape has been created.

Using Microsoft Publisher Page 137

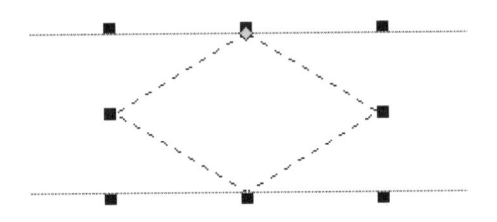

Designing a Newsletter Chapter 11

13. Remove the 1 pt border around the diamond by clicking the *Line/Border Style* tool on the Formatting Toolbar and then clicking *None*.

It is important that we create the same angle as in the diamond for the rest of the shapes.

angle

Ruler Guides

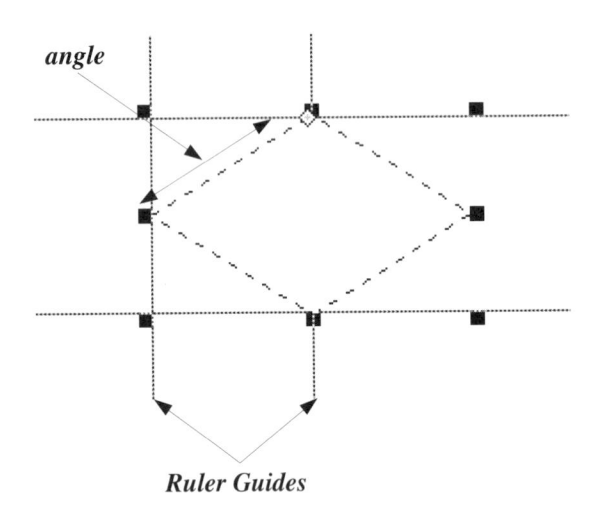

Use the vertical ruler guides to help create the same angle for the rest of the shapes.

14. Zoom in for more accuracy.
15. Place the first ruler guide at the left edge of shape. It will snap against it. Place the second ruler guide at its apex.

Ensure the same angle for each of the other shapes by placing its left edge against the first ruler guide and adjusting its angle by dragging the adjust handle over to the second ruler guide.

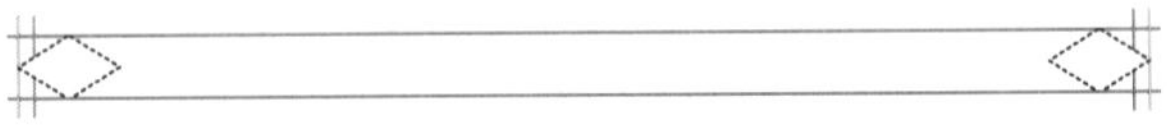

16. Copy the diamond shape and paste it.
17. Move one shape to the left and the other to the right of the page inside the horizontal ruler guides as above. Both will snap in against the margin guides.

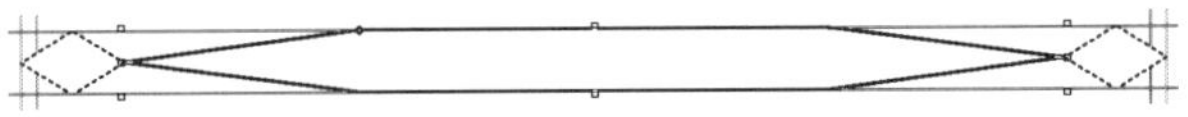

18. Selecting the same custom shape, draw the shape *C* between the ruler guides, stretching from the left diamond to the right diamond.

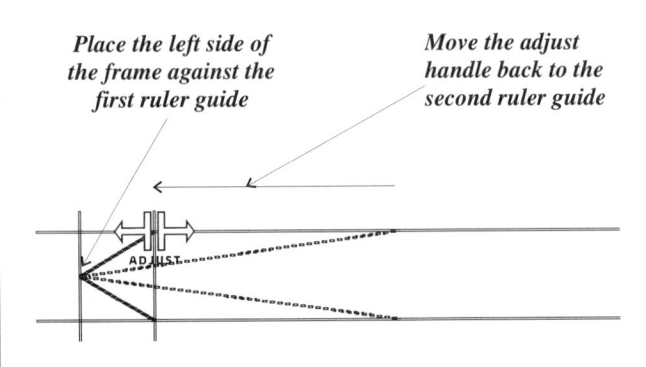

Place the left side of the frame against the first ruler guide

Move the adjust handle back to the second ruler guide

19. Remove the 1 pt border around the shape *C* by clicking the *Line/Border Style* tool on the Formatting Toolbar and then clicking *None*.
20. Move the left side of shape to furthest left ruler guide as shown above.
21. Adjust the angle by dragging the adjust handle back to the second ruler guide.

Vertical Ruler Guides

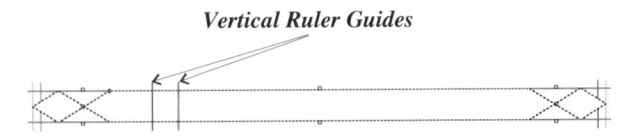

22. Move the shape *C* back between the first 2 diamond shapes.

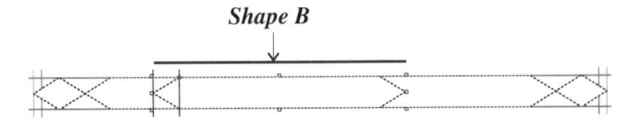

Shape B

23. Repeat each of the steps 18-21 for shape *B*, making it 80 mm. wide and not stretching from diamond to diamond.

Shape A

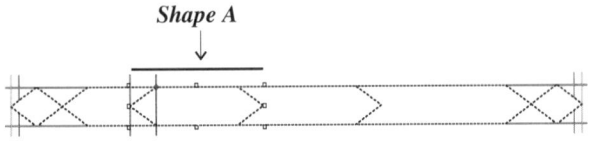

24. Repeat each of the steps 18-21 for shape *A*, making it 40 mm. wide and not stretching from diamond to diamond.

Page 138 Desktop Publishing Made Easy

Chapter 11 | *Designing a Newsletter*

Multiple-select these shapes

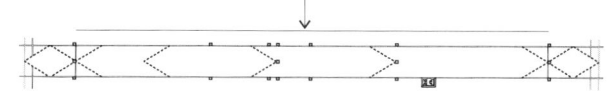

25. Multiple-select only shapes *A*, *B* & *C*.

26. Centre align the 3 shapes horizontally in relation to each other.

Having created shape *E*, the 2 shapes *D*, shape *C*, shape *B* and shape *A* in that order, there is no need to change the layering.

27. Select shape *C* by clicking on one of its angled sides.
28. Add a 60% fill of black.

29. Repeat step 27-28 for shapes *B* and *A*, adding 20% and 80% fills to each respectively.

30. Move the rectangle *E* back between the horizontal ruler guides.
31. Multiple-select all the shapes and group them.

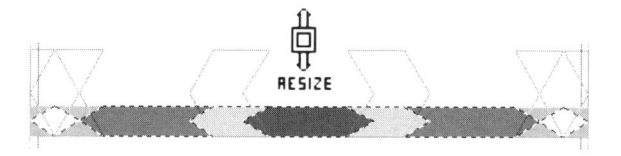

32. This top border can be resized to suit either the first page or the other pages by dragging from the centre top or centre bottom handles.

DESIGNING A PULL QUOTE BORDER

A pull quote is an excerpt from the main text that adds visual interest to the page and attracts the reader's attention. Bold text, shading and borders are associated with pull quotes.

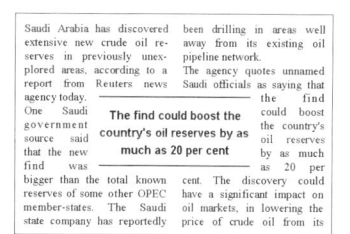

The pull quote border will not be created in the background. However, because it is similar to the last tutorial, it is appropriate to do it now. See the pull quote frames in the newsletter on page 135.

It is also important to note that in our newsletter this pull quote border will be created between the blue grid guides of one column.

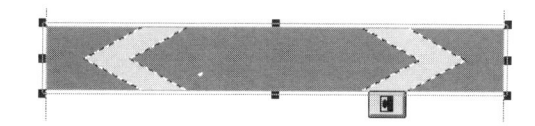

The pull quote border can be designed in the same way as the top border, using the horizontal ruler guides to control the depth and the vertical ruler guides to adjust the angle.

The pull quote border above is made from the 3 shapes below.

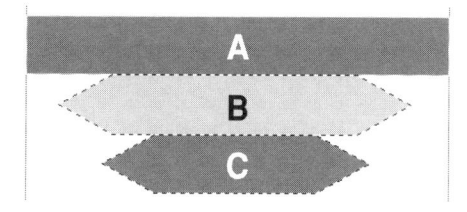

Ensure that you are working in the foreground.

1. Create the frames *A*, *B* and *C* in that order.
2. Widths: Place *A* between the blue grid guides in the appropriate right or left column of the newsletter, *B* = 32 mm. and *C* = 25 mm.
3. *A*, *B* and *C* have 60%, 20% and 60% fills of black respectively.

INSERTING PAGE NUMBERS

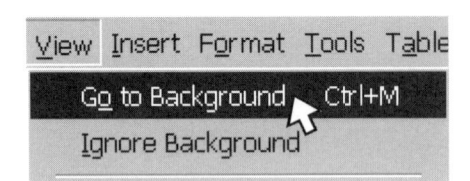

Page Numbers can be inserted on the foreground, in which case the current page only is numbered. However, if you want to insert page numbers for each page of a 4-page newsletter, you should do so in the background.

To do this:

1. Click *View* on the Menu Bar.
2. Click *Go to Background*.

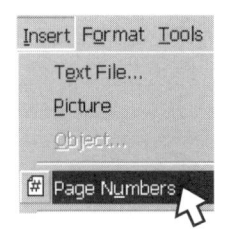

3. Create a text frame.
4. Type the word 'Page' and press the spacebar once.
5. Click *Insert* on the Menu Bar.
6. Click *Page Numbers*.

In the background a page number is represented by the page number mark '#'. However, when we *Go to Foreground* the '#' will change to the appropriate page number.

1. Click *View* on the Menu Bar.
2. Click *Go to Foreground*.

You are now out of the background and the proper page number will be displayed in the text frame you created.

TWO BACKGROUNDS WITH MIRRORED GUIDES

The background is a layer that appears behind every page. To repeat things on every page, such as headers, put them on the background. When you go to background you are working on one background page – the right one, marked with an *R* in the *Page Navigation Control* area – the bottom left of the screen.

However, you can choose to have 2 backgrounds – one to represent the right or the uneven numbered pages, and the other to represent the left or the even numbered pages.

In doing this you mirror all the objects and guides from the right to the left background page. Below you can see that the left page is a mirror of the right one. Having 2 backgrounds is used for a two-page spread, where the inside margin will be greater than the outside one to allow for binding.

In the background I will set the margins, create a top border, a text frame each for the title and the page number, a 1 pt rule just above the 2 text frames and insert grid guides to create 4 columns. Having done all of this in the right background page, I will then **create two backgrounds with mirrored guides**, which will mirror all the objects over to the left page. On the left page the text in the title text frame will have to be changed from left aligned to right aligned and the text in the page number text frame will have to be changed from right to left aligned. The tutorial for this is on page 141.

The left page is a mirror of the right page

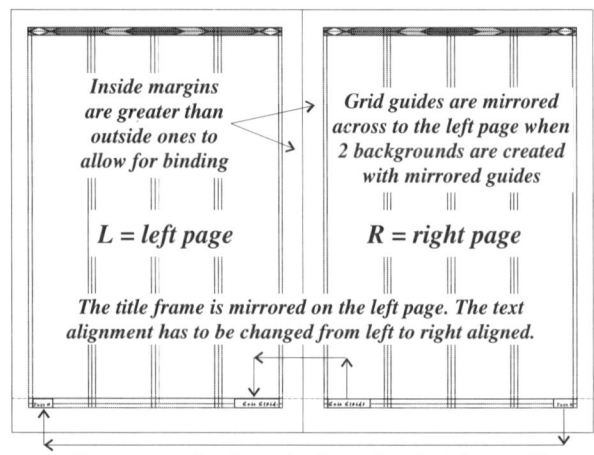

Inside margins are greater than outside ones to allow for binding

Grid guides are mirrored across to the left page when 2 backgrounds are created with mirrored guides

L = left page   *R = right page*

The title frame is mirrored on the left page. The text alignment has to be changed from left to right aligned.

The page number frame is mirrored on the left page. The text alignment has to be changed from right to left aligned.

CREATING 2 BACKGROUNDS WITH MIRRORED GUIDES

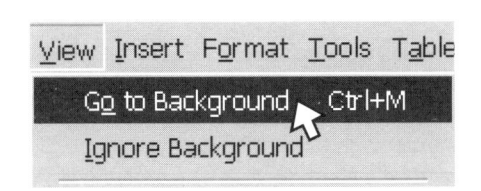

1. Click *View* from the Menu Bar.
2. Click *Go to Background*.

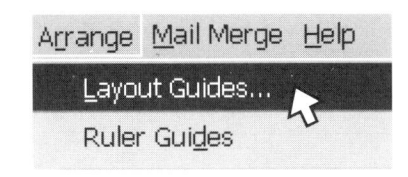

3. Click *Arrange* from the Menu Bar.
4. Click *Layout Guides*.

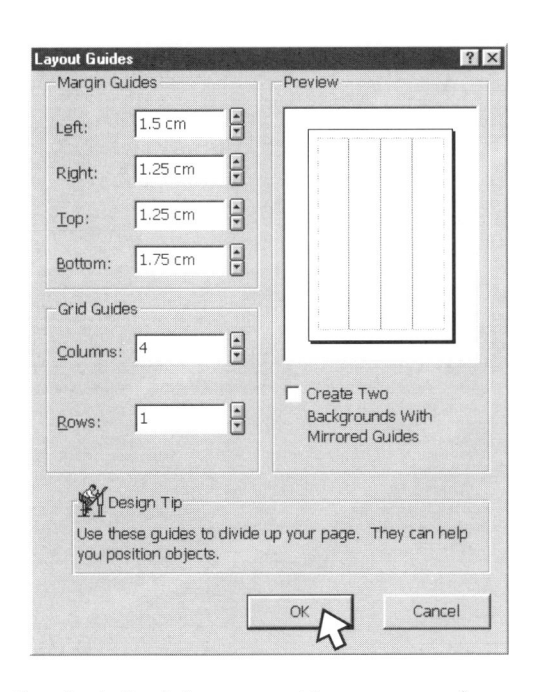

5. Set the left, right, top and bottom margins.
6. Type a value of *4* in the *Columns* box.
7. Click *OK*.

8. Create the background objects you want in the newsletter (e.g. border, logo, page numbers etc.) and place them in suitable positions.

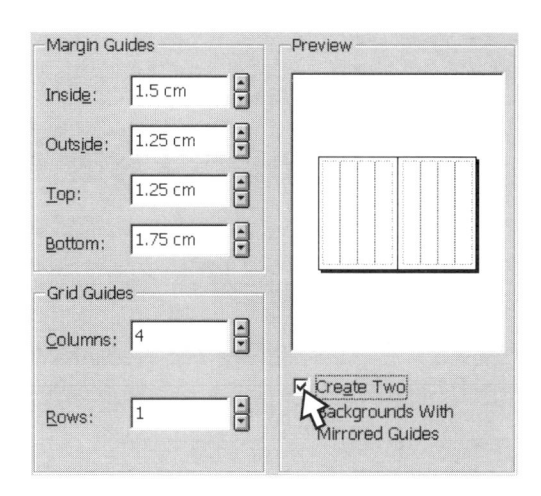

9. Click *Arrange* from the Menu Bar.
10. Click *Layout Guides*.
11. Click the *Create Two Backgrounds with Mirrored Guides* box to enable it.

You will notice that the *Left* and *Right* margins change to *Inside* and *Outside* margins.

A thumbnail of the two facing pages can be seen in the *Preview* section.

12. Click *View* from the Menu Bar.
13. Click *Two-Page Spread*.

Two facing pages will appear. A second *Page Navigation Control* button *L* appears at the bottom left of the screen, representing the left or the even numbered pages. The *R* button represents the right or the uneven numbered pages.

14. Click *View* from the Menu Bar.
15. Click *Go to Foreground*.

You are now out of the background. Any thing you create from now on will only appear on the page on which it was created.

Only one page appears in the foreground. You will insert the extra pages later.

Designing a Newsletter   Chapter 11

DESIGNING THE NEWSLETTER TEMPLATE
CREATING THE BACKGROUND OBJECTS

Carry out the instructions in numerical order

1. Open a new file and go to background.

2. Save the file as **Background**. We shall **Save as Template** later in the chapter when the template is completed. Save regularly.

3. Set the following margins: Left = 15 mm., Right = 12.5 mm., Top = 12.5 mm., Bottom = 17.5 mm. Set 4 columns in the **Grid Guides** section.

11. Save.

8. Create 2 backgrounds with mirrored guides.

9. Click **Two-Page Spread** from the **View** menu.

4. Design the border as shown in the tutorial stretching from the left to the right margin.

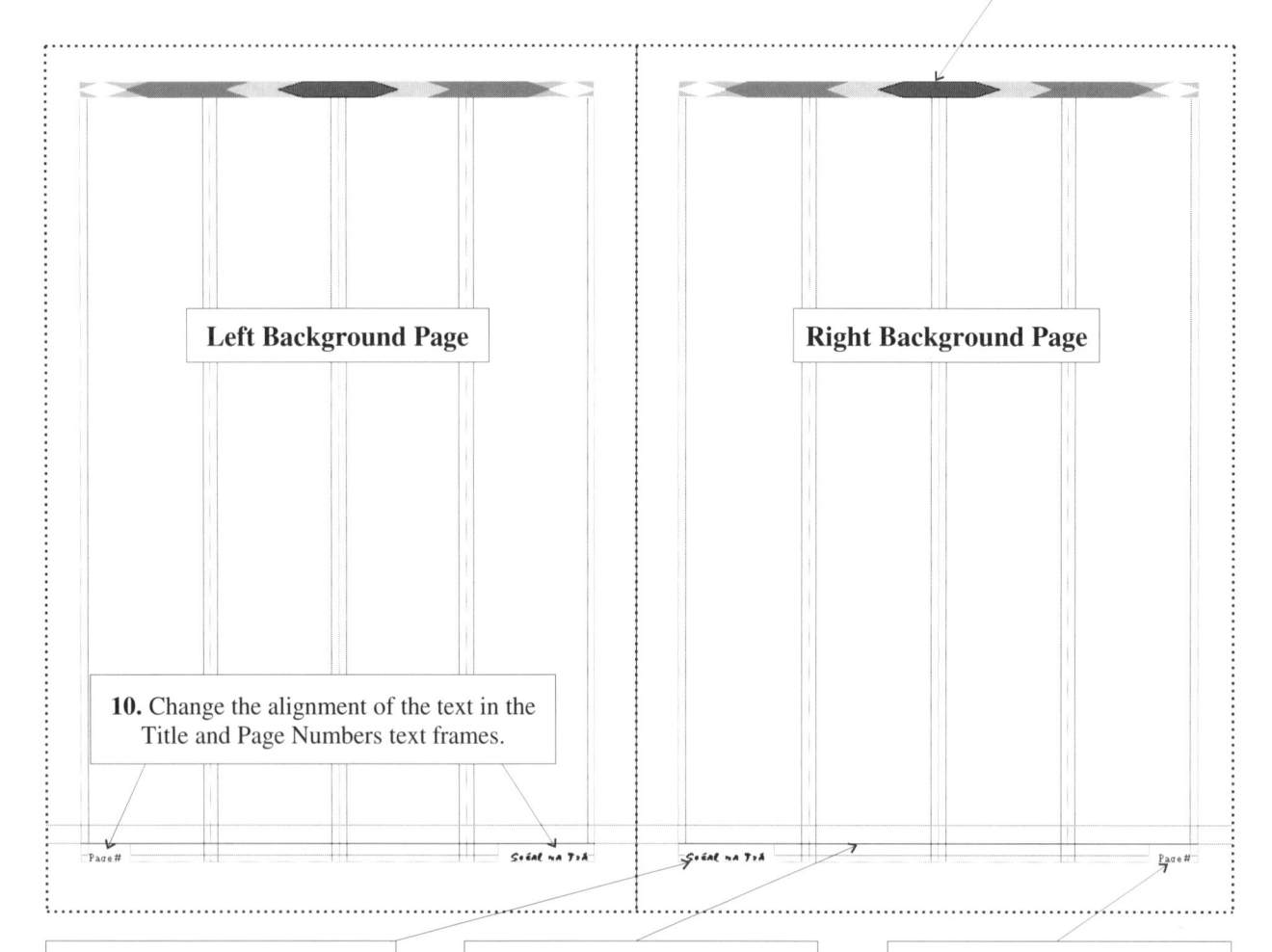

Left Background Page

Right Background Page

10. Change the alignment of the text in the Title and Page Numbers text frames.

6. Create a text frame and insert the newsletter title. Left align the text, resize the frame to suit the text and place it in the bottom left corner of the page.

7. Draw a 1 pt rule across the bottom of the page, just above the text frames and stretching from the left to the right margin.

5. Create a text frame and insert page numbers. Right align the text, resize the frame to suit the text and place it in the bottom right corner of the page.

Page 142   Desktop Publishing Made Easy

WHY LAYOUT GUIDES?

If you were building a house, you would have to line up everything properly. When you build a publication you want the design elements properly aligned vertically, horizontally and in relation to each other. The basic layout of a page is usually defined by a grid composed of horizontal and vertical layout guides. To this you can also add ruler guides. These guides define sections of the page and help you to align objects on the page with precision.

Layout guides exist on the background of every page, because no matter which page you are on when they are set, they apply to all the pages. Layout guides and ruler guides are visible on the screen, but are always obscured by text frames and other design elements that you place on the page. They do no print out. Publisher's layout guides are coloured pink, with blue guides at either side, a distance of 2.5 mm. away. The ruler guides are green.

Horizontal ruler guides, placed 2 mm. apart, can be used to separate the headings from the body text.

A pink layout guide in the middle has a blue guide at either side, a distance of 2.5 mm. away.

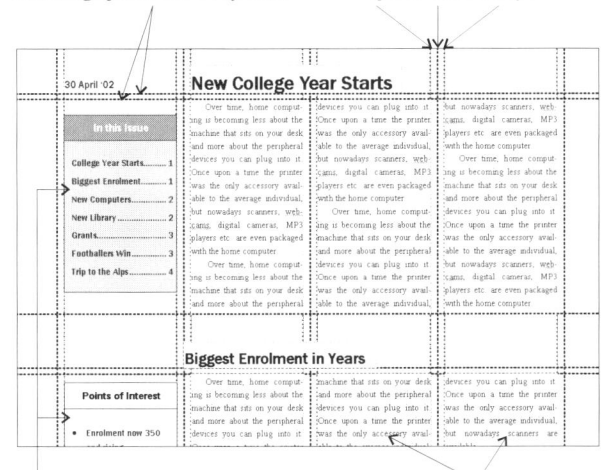

The page is broken up into 4 columns. The design elements are placed between the blue guides.

Text frames are placed between the blue guides, producing a gutter of 2 x 2.5 mm. = 5 mm.

See above how the layout guides and the ruler guides help to align the design elements. By placing frames between the blue guides a gutter of 5 mm. is created. A space of 2 mm. between the 2 horizontal ruler guides creates enough white space between the headings and the body text.

Having created in the background the design elements that will appear on all the pages of the newsletter, it is now time to create the elements that are peculiar to each separate page. To do this we have to go to foreground.

- Click *Go to Foreground* from the *View* menu.

INSERTING PAGES

Creating the 2 background pages allowed us to create a booklet with facing pages and greater inside margins to facilitate the binding. However, when we went back to the foreground we still only had one page. We have to insert the extra 3 pages to make up the 4 pages of the newsletter.

To do this:

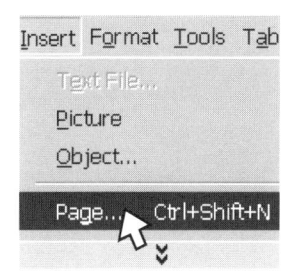

1. Click *Insert* from the Menu Bar.
2. Click *Page*.

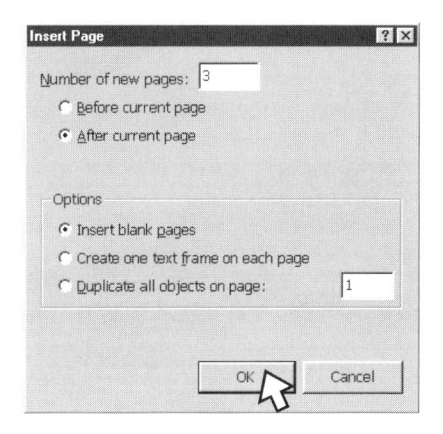

3. Type *3* in the *Number of new pages* box.
4. Click the *After current page* button.
5. Click the *Insert blank pages* radio button.
6. Click *OK*.

CREATING TEXT STYLES

A text style is a set of formatting properties that can be quickly applied to text. It contains the following formatting information: font, font size, font colour, indents, character spacing (*tracking*) and line spacing (*leading*), tabs, bulleted or numbered list etc.

You can apply the style prior to typing in the text or you can insert the text first and then apply the style later. By clicking a paragraph and choosing the style, only that paragraph receives the style. To apply the style to more than one paragraph you must first highlight the paragraphs. You will be shown how to apply a text style later.

The first style we're going to create is the style for the newsletter title. You may create your own style, but for the sake of these instructions let's choose the style: *Staccato555 BT, 54 pt, centred*.

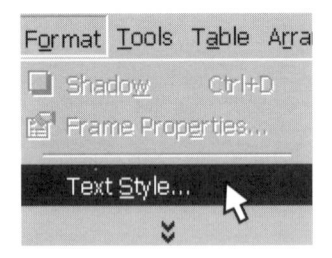

1. Click *Format* on the Menu Bar.
2. Click *Text Style*.

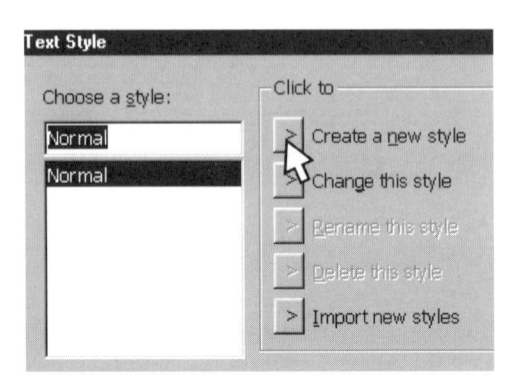

3. Click *Create a new style*.

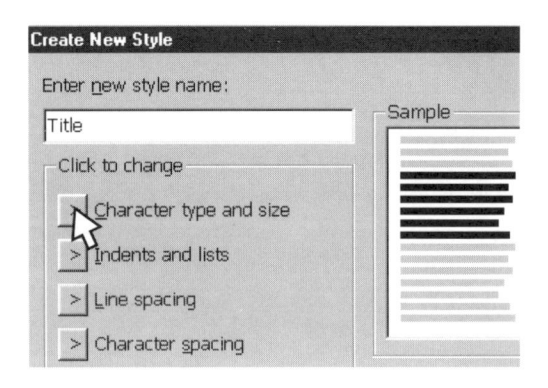

4. Type in the style name in the *Enter new style name* box.
5. Click *Character type and size*.

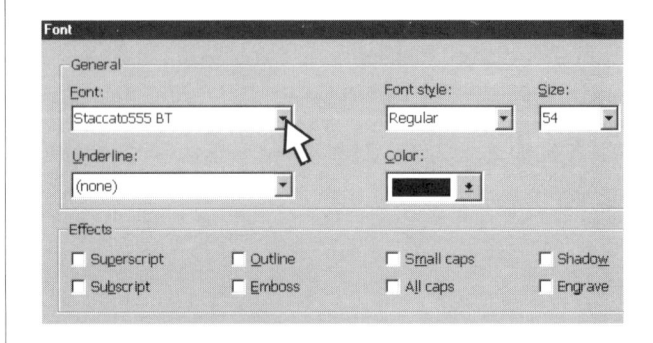

6. Scroll through the fonts in the *Font* box and choose an appropriate one.
7. As it is not italic or bold or underlined etc., the only other change you have to make here is to change the font size in the *Size* box. If the size is not included in the list, you can type it in.
8. Click *OK*.

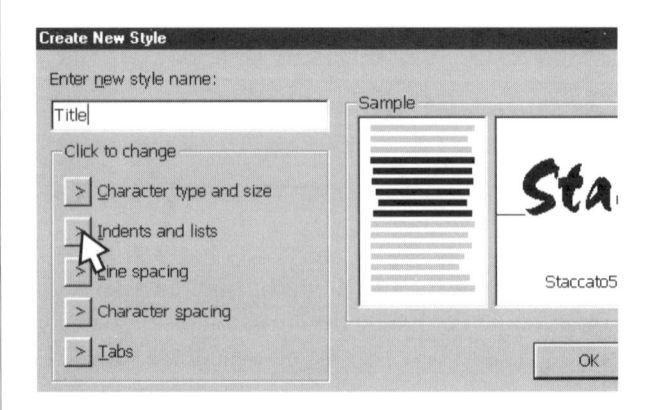

9. Click *Indents and lists*.

Chapter 11 *Designing a Newsletter*

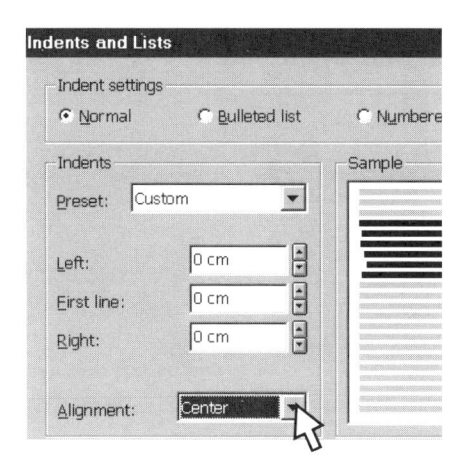

10. Choose **Center** in the **Alignment** box.
11. Click **OK**.

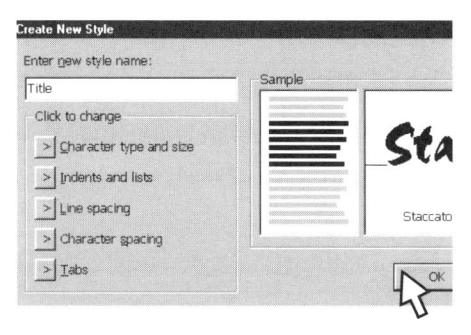

12. As all the **Title** text formatting is complete, click **OK**.

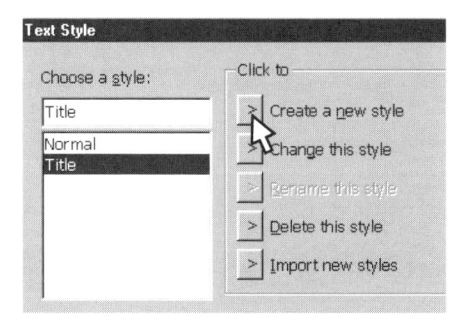

The first text style for the newsletter has been created and its name appears in the main part of the **Text Style** window. Don't click **Close** until all the text styles have been created.

When you create new styles, the previous style you created will be the default style unless you click **Normal**, which is the default Publisher style.

The next style is for the body text. For the sake of these instructions let's choose the style: **Times New Roman, 9/13 pt leading, justified, first line indent of 5 mm**.

13. Click **Create a new style** for the body text.

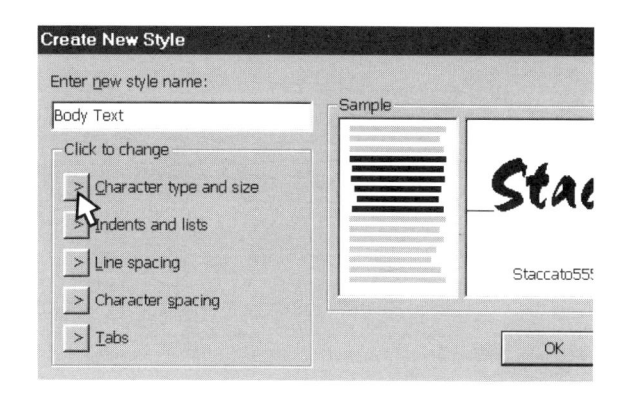

14. Type a name for the new style in the **Enter new style name** box.
15. Click **Character type and size**.

16. Follow instructions 6-8, but choose **Times New Roman** in the **Font** box, **Regular** in the **Font Style** box and **9** in the **Size** box.
17. Click **OK**.
18. Click **Indents and lists**.
19. Follow instructions 10-11, but choose **Justified** in the **Alignment** box, and insert value of 0.5 in the **First line** box.
20. Click the **Line Spacing** tab.

If the next style you create is not justified or does not have a 5 mm. first line indent, you'll have to change that formatting unless you choose **Normal** when you get back to the **Text Style** window.

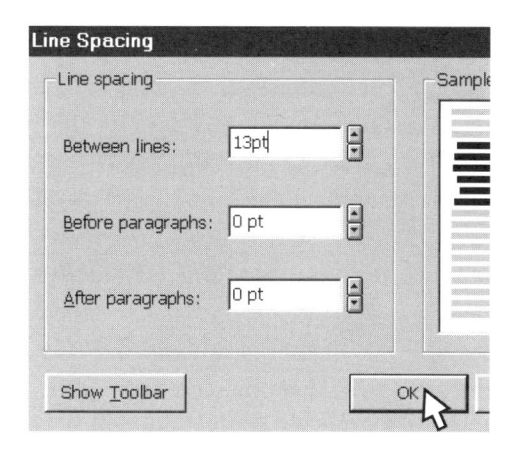

21. Type **13 pt**. in the **Between lines** box.
22. Make sure you include the *'pt'* after the *'13'*. Otherwise the program will assume you want to increase the spacing by a factor of **13**.
23. Click **OK**.

The font size of the body text is 9/13 pt leading.

Using Microsoft Publisher Page 145

Designing a Newsletter   Chapter 11

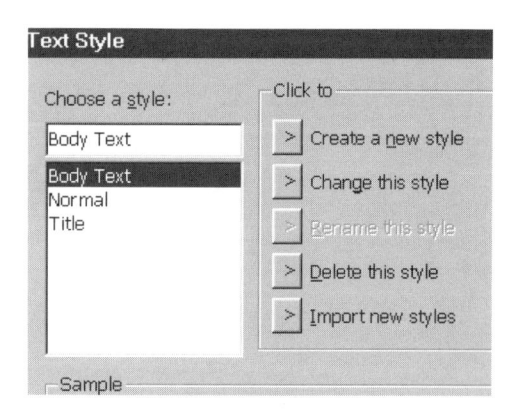

Your second style is now created. You are advised to select **Normal** here before you create a new text style. Selecting **Normal** changes from the **Body Text** style back to the default style, which speeds up the creation of the next new style.

Create the following extra text styles:

- Lead Story: Franklin Gothic Medium, bold, 20 pt, left aligned
- College Name: Franklin Gothic Heavy, 9 pt, centred, uppercase lettering. The uppercase lettering can be done by clicking the **All Caps** box in 6-8
- Inside Story: Franklin Gothic Medium, bold, 16 pt, left aligned. You can also use this style for the secondary story headline
- Back Story: Franklin Gothic Medium, bold, 18 pt, left aligned
- Issue: Franklin Gothic Medium, bold, 11 pt, centred. You can also use this style for the **Points of Interest** and the **Pull Quotes**
- Contents: Franklin Gothic Medium, 9 pt, left aligned
- Date: Franklin Gothic Medium, 10 pt, left aligned
- College History: Times New Roman, 11/15 pt leading, justified, first line indent of 5 mm.
- Address: Franklin Gothic Medium, bold, 6.5/9 pt leading, centred.

24. When all the text styles have been created click **Close** in the **Text Style** window.

APPLYING TEXT STYLES

Choose a text style here

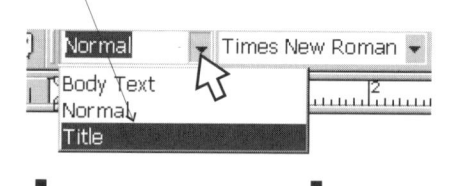

When you insert text in a text frame from now on you will have a range of text styles to choose from. Clicking the arrow to the right of the **Style** box on the Formatting Toolbar will present you with a list of styles. In the illustration above two of the styles you created appear.

To apply a text style:

1. Click anywhere within a paragraph or highlight more than a paragraph of text.
2. Choose a style from the **Style** box.

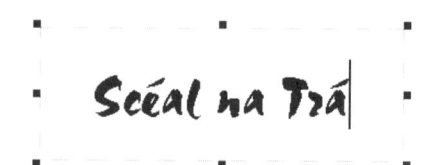

The newsletter title has a new text style.

Highlight more than one paragraph of the text.

See the body text below of size 9/13 pt leading, and a first line indent of 5 mm.

Page 146   Desktop Publishing Made Easy

Creating a Table of Contents

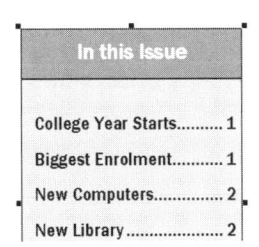

The newsletter table of contents on page 1 is a grouped object made up of the 4 objects below – 2 text frames, a box and a rule.

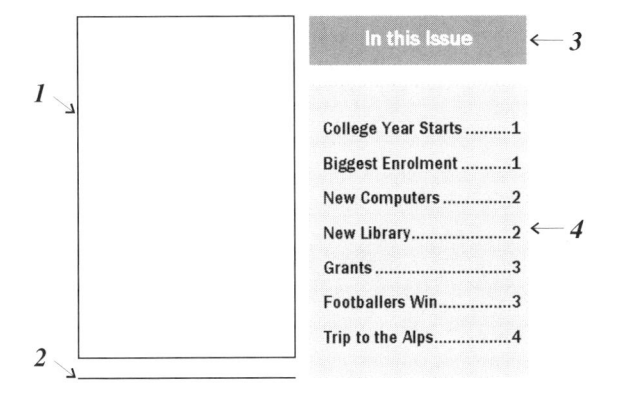

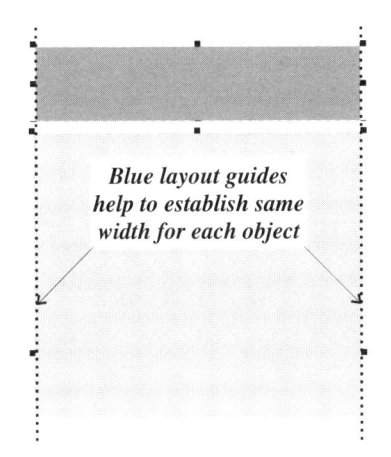

Blue layout guides help to establish same width for each object

The blue layout guides of one of the newsletter columns can be used to establish the width of each object in the designing of the table of contents.

1. Enable *Snap to Guides* and *Snap to Objects*.
2. Create 2 text frames, one 9 mm. deep and the other about 50 mm. deep, each stretching from one blue layout guide to the other.
3. Give the smaller frame a 40% fill of black and the other a 10% fill of black. 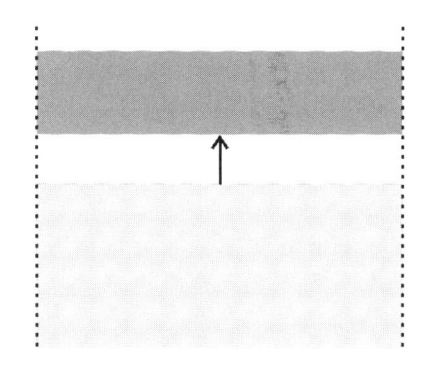
4. Move one of the text frames between the blue layout guides until it snaps in against the other text frame. 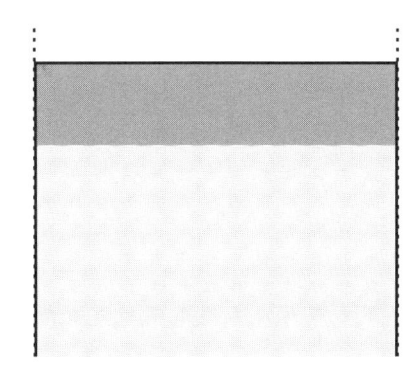
5. Using the **Rectangle** tool draw one box around both of the text frames.
6. Give it a 1 pt thickness.

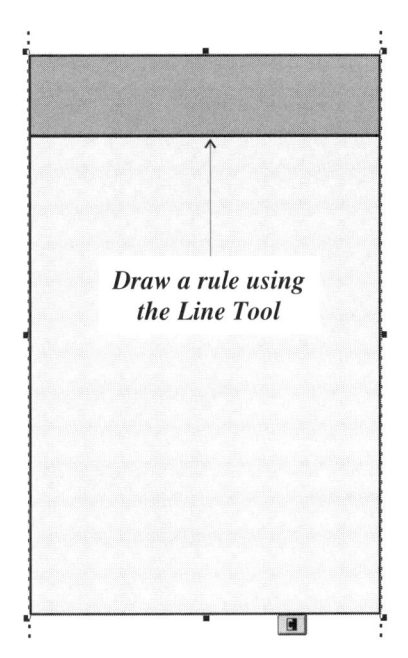

Draw a rule using the Line Tool

7. Draw a 1 pt rule from one blue layout guide to the other where the 2 text frames meet.
8. Group all 4 objects.

Designing a Newsletter — Chapter 11

9. Type the text into the smaller text frame.
10. Format the text or apply a text style.
11. Change the text colour to white.
12. Centre the text vertically in the frame.
13. Give the larger text frame a left margin of 25 mm. in the *Text Frame Properties* window. 
14. Click in the text frame and format the text or apply a text style to the text that you will be inserting later.
15. Set a left tab about 5 mm. from the right edge of the text frame.
16. Type in the text using the TAB key on the keyboard to tab to the position for each page number.
17. Centre the text vertically in the text frame. Increase leading to create more white space and to balance the text better in the frame.

In this Issue

College Year Starts	1
Biggest Enrolment	1
New Computers	2
New Library	2
Grants	3
Footballers Win	3
Trip to the Alps	4

FINISHING THE PULL QUOTE FRAME

You saw how to design the top border between the blue layout guides earlier in this chapter.

To finish off the pull quote frame:

1. Create the bottom text frame and make it about 65 mm. deep.
2. Move the text frame until it snaps in against the top border.
3. Group them.
4. Type in the text and format it or apply a style.
5. Centre the text vertically.
6. Group all the objects.

'nowadays scanners, webcams, MP3 players digital cameras, etc. are packaged with the home computer'

CREATING A POINTS OF INTEREST FRAME

Points of Interest

- Enrolment now 350 and rising
- New library opened in August
- Footballers win by huge margin
- 45 students enjoy 14 days on the Alps
- Textbooks subsidised again this year

Use the same blue layout guides as you did for the Table of Contents.

The Points of Interest objects are created in the same way as the Table of Contents objects. The only differences are:

1. Do not shade either frame.
2. Do not set tabs.
3. Create a bulleted list.

INVERTING TEXT IN A CUSTOM SHAPE WITH A TINTED BACKGROUND

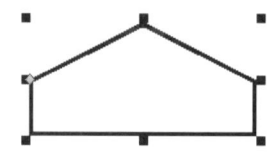

1. Click the *Custom Shapes* tool from the Tool Palette.
2. Click the second shape on the fourth row.
3. Draw the shape as shown above about 20 mm. wide and 9 mm. deep.

Chapter 11   *Designing a Newsletter*

4. Fill with black.

5. Create a text frame.
6. Type the word 'URL' into the text frame.
7. Format the text.
8. Resize the text frame to fit the text.

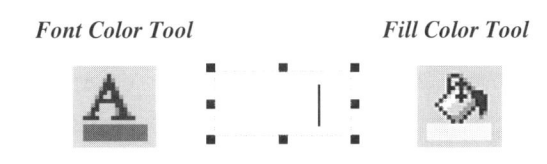

Font Color Tool   *Fill Color Tool*

9. Highlight the text.
10. Click the **Font Color** tool from the Formatting Toolbar.
11. Choose the white colour. See the white text on the white background above.
12. Click the **Fill Color** tool from the Formatting Toolbar.
13. Choose *No Fill*.

Choosing *No Fill* ensures that the text frame will not have a background colour to obscure part of the custom shape.

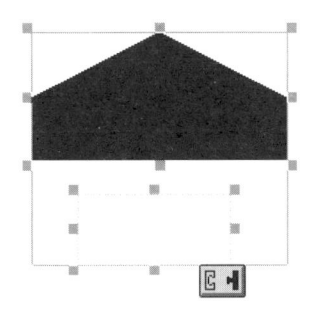

14. Multiple-select both objects.

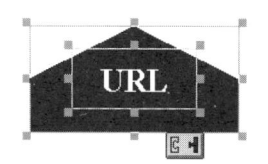

15. Centre both objects horizontally and vertically in relation to each other.

You may need to nudge the text frame down to give the text a more balanced appearance within the custom shape.

16. Click the text frame to select it.
17. Nudge it down slightly.

18. Group the objects.

The *Email* and *URL* grouped objects and the text frame with the addresses will be placed on page 4 of the newsletter as shown above.

Their completion instructions are on page 150.

Using Microsoft Publisher   *Page 149*

To finish off the Email and the URL addresses:

1. Copy and paste the *URL* grouped object.
2. Move the pasted object out of way.
3. Ungroup the pasted grouped object by clicking the *Ungroup* button.
4. Click the custom shape to select it.
5. Click the *Flip Vertical* tool on the Formatting Toolbar.
6. Nudge the custom shape down until the text is balanced within it.
7. Delete the text and type in the word 'Email'.
8. Group the objects.
9. Create a new text frame and type in the email address and the URL.
10. Format the text and increase the line spacing.
11. Resize the text frame to suit the text.
12. Place the text frame between the 2 grouped objects, leaving similar gaps between the top grouped object and the text and the bottom grouped object and the text.
13. Multiple-select the 3 objects.
14. Centre the 3 objects horizontally in relation to each other.
15. Group the 3 objects.
16. Place the grouped objects in an appropriate position in the newsletter.

CONNECTING TEXT FRAMES

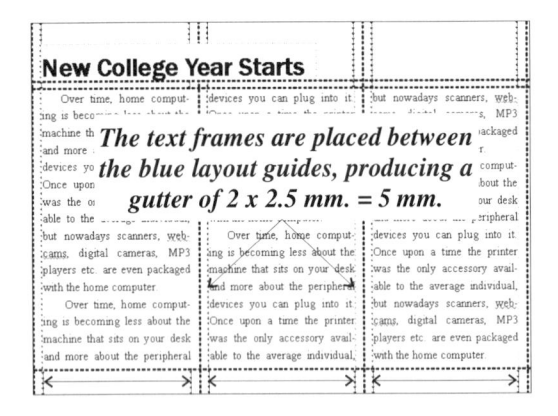

The text frames are placed between the blue layout guides, producing a gutter of 2 x 2.5 mm. = 5 mm.

Later in this chapter we'll see how to import text from another application into Publisher. We don't need to do it until the template is finished.

In this newsletter we can use 3 small text frames for each story. These frames are placed within the blue layout guides and opposite each other across the page. It is a good idea to connect these frames.

In the newsletter template we shall connect the 3 empty text frames across the page. Before we do this let's see what happens when text is imported into a text frame that is too small to hold the text.

When only one text frame has been created to accept the imported text:

> The inserted text doesn't fit in this frame. Do you want to use autoflow?

You are asked if you want to use autoflow to allow the text to flow from the overflow area into another text frame. The overflow area is an area where Publisher stores text that will not fit in a text frame. You cannot see this text unless you click *Yes* to the question. Clicking *No* leaves the text in the overflow area.

If you click *Yes*:

> Do you want Publisher to automatically create text frames?

You are asked if you want to allow Publisher to create text frames for you. If you click *Yes* to that, Publisher will create a new text frame covering the whole of the next available empty page and insert the text in it. Clicking *No* leaves the text in the overflow area.

Generally speaking it is preferable to click *No*, as doing that gives you more control over the positioning of your text frames.

When more than one text frame has been created to accept the imported text:

> The inserted text doesn't fit in this frame. Do you want to use autoflow?
>
> Autoflow to this frame?
>
> Do you want Publisher to automatically create text frames?

You are asked first if you want to use autoflow. If you click *Yes*, then for each of the other frames you are asked if you want to use autoflow into that particular frame. If after that there's still more text in the overflow area you'll be asked if you want to allow Publisher to create the extra text frames.

Connected text frames are treated as one text frame, which means that the *Autoflow to this frame* question is skipped until they are filled.

Chapter 11 — Designing a Newsletter

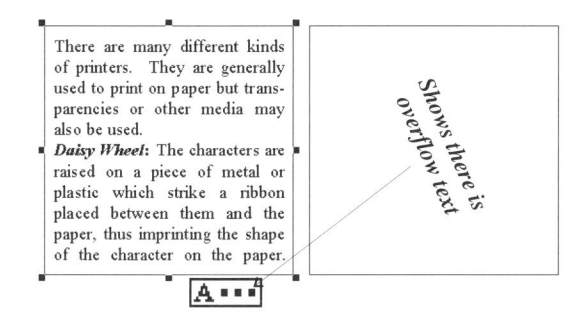

Let's say we've imported text into frame 1 of 3 adjacent text frames across the newsletter page. A *Text Overflow Indicator* appears at the bottom of the text frame if there is text in the overflow area.

To connect the frames:

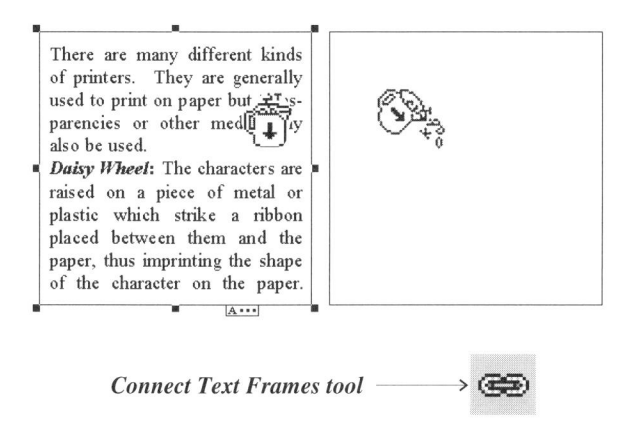

Connect Text Frames tool ⟶

1. Click the full text frame to select it.
2. Click the **Connect Text Frames** tool on the Text Frame Connecting Toolbar.

If this toolbar is not there, enable it by clicking it in the *Toolbars* submenu of the *View* menu.

3. Click text frame 2 when the mouse pointer changes to a slanted pitcher.

See the illustration above which shows that on clicking the **Connect Text Frames** tool the mouse pointer changes to a vertical pitcher in frame 1 and to a slanted pitcher in frame 2.

The overflow text flows into frame 2 below.

To spill the overflow text into frame 3:

4. Click frame 2 to select it.
5. Click the **Connect Text Frames** tool on the Text Frame Connecting Toolbar.
6. Click frame 3. See the result above.

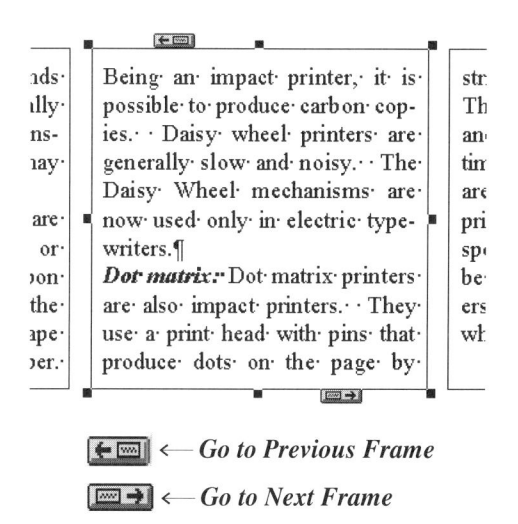

⬅ *Go to Previous Frame*

➡ *Go to Next Frame*

The 3 text frames are now connected. The middle text frame is connected to each of the other two. It has the *Go to Previous Frame* button on the top and the *Go to Next Frame* button on the bottom. Clicking either one of them brings you to the appropriate frame.

You can connect the text frames even if there's no text in them. The usual pitcher appears every time pouring imaginary text into the next text frame.

As the 3 connected text frames (considered one text frame in Publisher) will house each story in the newsletter, click *No* to allowing Publisher create new text frames for overflow text.

When the text is inserted you will have to make it fit the connected text frames. This will be dealt with later in this chapter.

Using Microsoft Publisher — Page 151

Designing a Newsletter   Chapter 11

DISCONNECTING TEXT FRAMES

There are many different kinds of printers. They are generally used to print on paper but transparencies or other media may also be used.
Daisy Wheel: The characters are raised on a piece of metal or plastic which strike a ribbon placed between them and the paper, thus imprinting the shape of the character on the paper.

Being an impact printer, it is possible to produce carbon copies. Daisy wheel printers are generally slow and noisy. The Daisy Wheel mechanisms are now used only in electric typewriters.
Dot matrix: Dot matrix printers are also impact printers. They use a print head with pins that produce dots on the page by

Disconnect Text Frames tool ⟶

1. Click the first text frame of the ones to be disconnected.
2. Click the **Disconnect Text Frames** tool on the Text Frame Connecting Toolbar.

PLACING PICTURES IN A NEWSLETTER TEMPLATE

Temporary pictures can be placed in the template to show where to insert the appropriate ones in the completed newsletter. The placement can be done to allow the insertion of the pictures into the completed newsletter with the minimum of fuss. Below we will see one way of doing that.

In our newsletter most of the pictures are placed between the blue layout guides of each column, but on pages 1 and 4 they are inserted between the 3 connected text frames. Ruler guides can be used to facilitate the easy insertion of these pictures in the completed newsletter.

To insert these pictures in the template:

1. Group the 3 connected text frames.
2. Create a picture frame and insert a picture.
3. With **Snap to Objects** enabled, create a caption frame the same width as the picture, type in the text and format it.
4. Snap the picture and caption frames together. Nudge the picture an appropriate distance away from the text frame. Group both objects.
5. Place these 2 grouped objects inside the 3 connected and grouped text frames.
6. Centre the 2 grouped objects horizontally in relation to, and align them at the bottom of the 3 connected and grouped text frames.

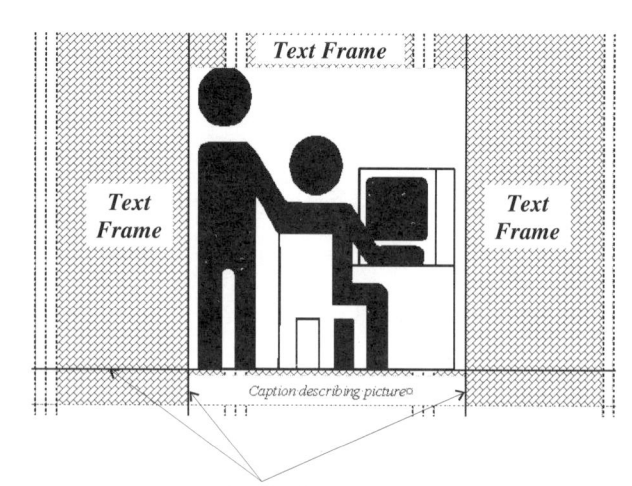

Ruler Guides

7. Place ruler guides under, to the left and right of the picture. In the completed newsletter these guides can be used to rectify any positional changes to the newly inserted pictures.

See how the pictures may be repositioned in the completed newsletter below.

If the picture has inserted as the one marked **A** has, resize it down until it snaps in against each of the blue layout guides. It will still sit on the horizontal ruler guide. Also, resize down the caption frame so that it too snaps in against the blue layout guides.

If the picture has inserted as the one marked **B** has, move it down onto the horizontal ruler guide, while keeping it between the vertical ruler guides.

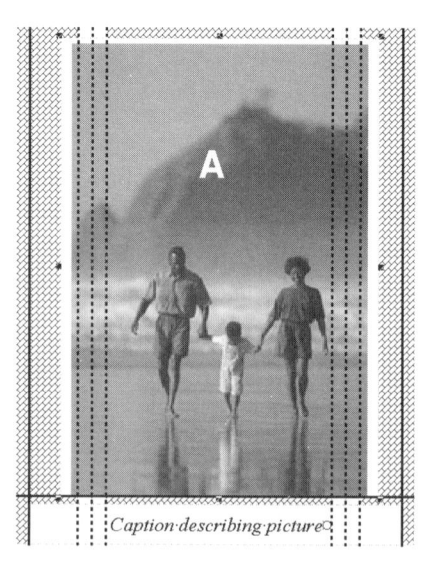

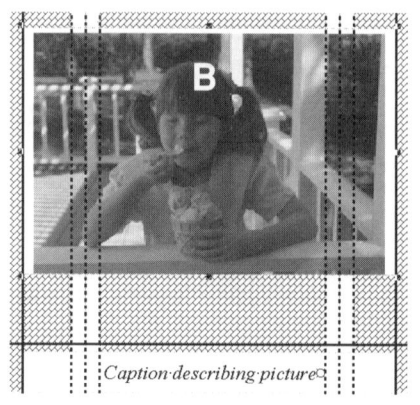

Page 152   Desktop Publishing Made Easy

Chapter 11　　　　　　　　　　　　　　　　　　　　　　　　Designing a Newsletter

FINISHED TEMPLATE INSTRUCTIONS (PAGE 1)

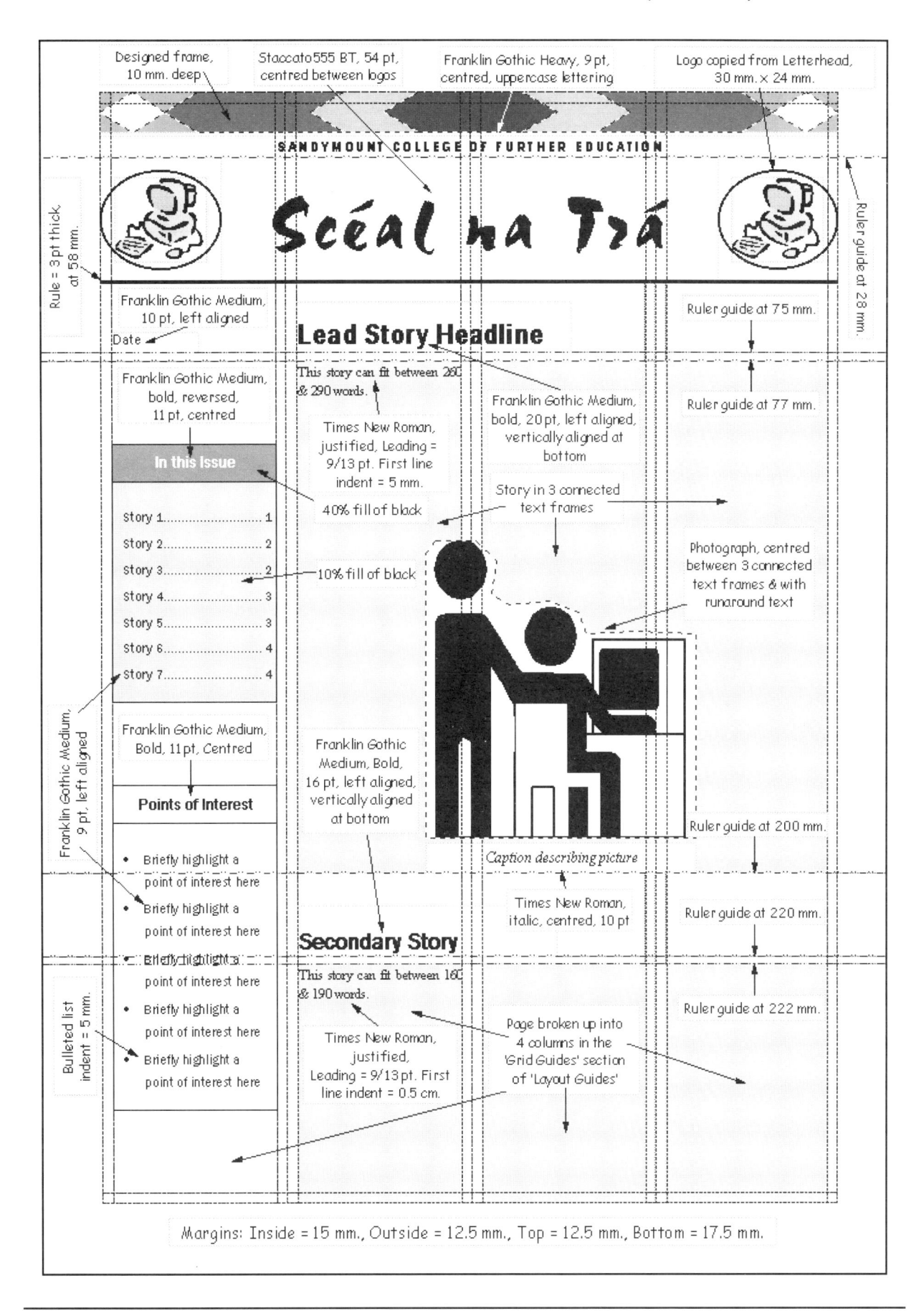

Designed frame, 10 mm. deep

Staccato555 BT, 54 pt, centred between logos

Franklin Gothic Heavy, 9 pt, centred, uppercase lettering

Logo copied from Letterhead, 30 mm. x 24 mm.

SANDYMOUNT COLLEGE OF FURTHER EDUCATION

Scéal na Trá

Rule = 3 pt thick, at 58 mm.

Ruler guide at 28 mm.

Franklin Gothic Medium, 10 pt, left aligned
Date

Lead Story Headline

Ruler guide at 75 mm.

Franklin Gothic Medium, bold, reversed, 11 pt, centred

This story can fit between 260 & 290 words.

Franklin Gothic Medium, bold, 20 pt, left aligned, vertically aligned at bottom

Ruler guide at 77 mm.

In this Issue

Times New Roman, justified, Leading = 9/13 pt. First line indent = 5 mm.

40% fill of black

Story in 3 connected text frames

Story 1 1
Story 2 2
Story 3 2
Story 4 3
Story 5 3
Story 6 4
Story 7 4

10% fill of black

Photograph, centred between 3 connected text frames & with runaround text

Franklin Gothic Medium, 9 pt, left aligned

Franklin Gothic Medium, Bold, 11 pt, Centred

Points of Interest

Franklin Gothic Medium, Bold, 16 pt, left aligned, vertically aligned at bottom

Ruler guide at 200 mm.

• Briefly highlight a point of interest here
• Briefly highlight a point of interest here
• Briefly highlight a point of interest here
• Briefly highlight a point of interest here
• Briefly highlight a point of interest here

Caption describing picture

Times New Roman, italic, centred, 10 pt

Ruler guide at 220 mm.

Secondary Story

This story can fit between 160 & 190 words.

Page broken up into 4 columns in the 'Grid Guides' section of 'Layout Guides'

Ruler guide at 222 mm.

Bulleted list indent = 5 mm.

Times New Roman, justified, Leading = 9/13 pt. First line indent = 0.5 cm.

Margins: Inside = 15 mm., Outside = 12.5 mm., Top = 12.5 mm., Bottom = 17.5 mm.

Using Microsoft Publisher　　　　　　　　　　　　　　　　　　　　　　　　Page 153

Designing a Newsletter · Chapter 11

FINISHED TEMPLATE INSTRUCTIONS (PAGE 2)

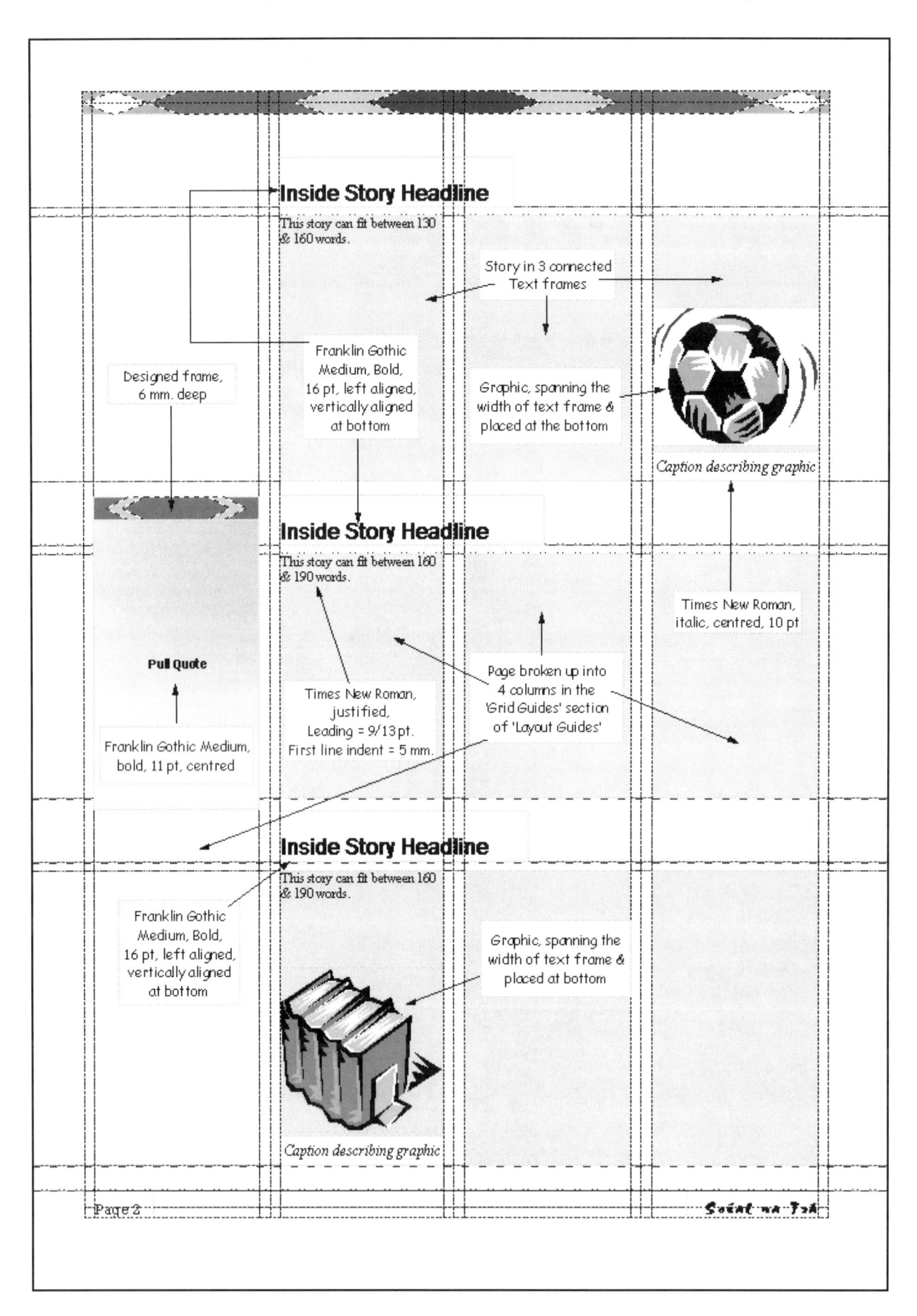

Inside Story Headline

This story can fit between 130 & 160 words.

Story in 3 connected Text frames

Designed frame, 6 mm. deep

Franklin Gothic Medium, Bold, 16 pt, left aligned, vertically aligned at bottom

Graphic, spanning the width of text frame & placed at the bottom

Caption describing graphic

Inside Story Headline

This story can fit between 160 & 190 words.

Pull Quote

Times New Roman, italic, centred, 10 pt

Franklin Gothic Medium, bold, 11 pt, centred

Times New Roman, justified, Leading = 9/13 pt. First line indent = 5 mm.

Page broken up into 4 columns in the 'Grid Guides' section of 'Layout Guides'

Inside Story Headline

This story can fit between 160 & 190 words.

Franklin Gothic Medium, Bold, 16 pt, left aligned, vertically aligned at bottom

Graphic, spanning the width of text frame & placed at bottom

Caption describing graphic

Page 2

Page 154 · Desktop Publishing Made Easy

Chapter 11 — Designing a Newsletter

FINISHED TEMPLATE INSTRUCTIONS (PAGE 3)

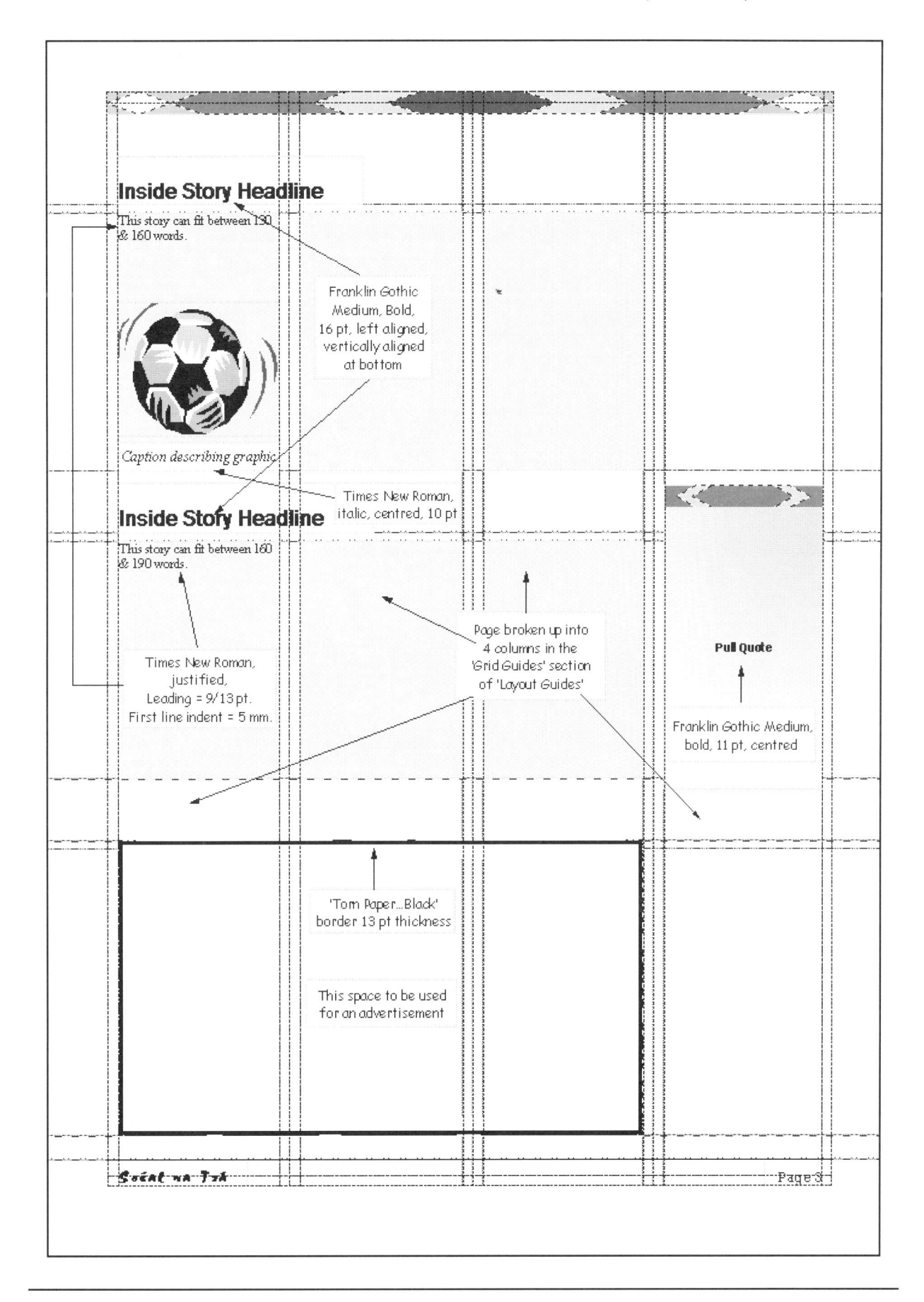

Inside Story Headline

This story can fit between 150 & 160 words.

Franklin Gothic Medium, Bold, 16 pt, left aligned, vertically aligned at bottom

Caption describing graphic

Times New Roman, italic, centred, 10 pt

Inside Story Headline

This story can fit between 160 & 190 words.

Times New Roman, justified, Leading = 9/13 pt. First line indent = 5 mm.

Page broken up into 4 columns in the 'Grid Guides' section of 'Layout Guides'

Pull Quote

Franklin Gothic Medium, bold, 11 pt, centred

'Torn Paper...Black' border 13 pt thickness

This space to be used for an advertisement

Scéal na Tvá — Page 3

Using Microsoft Publisher — Page 155

Finished Template Instructions (Page 4)

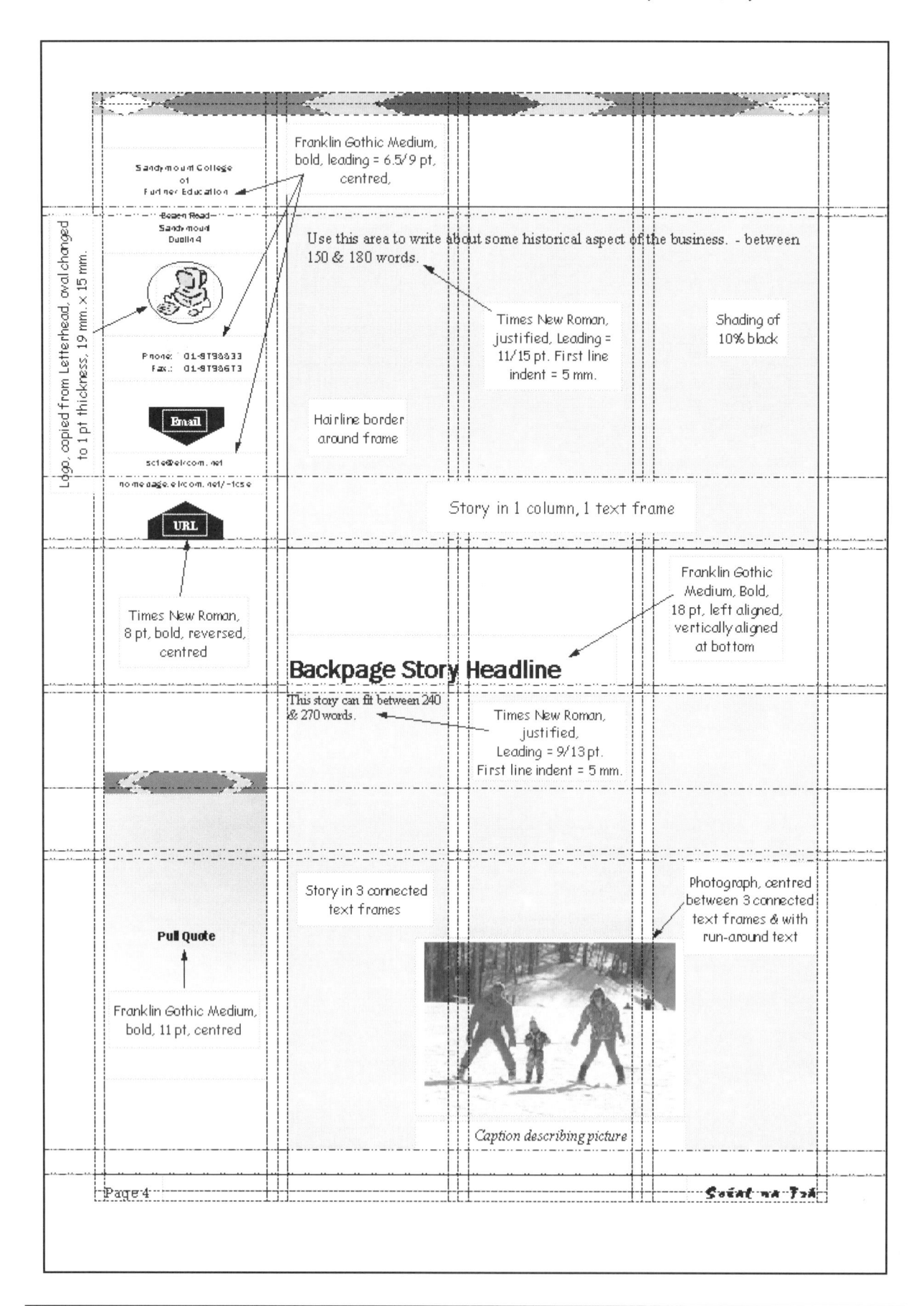

Annotated page 4 template with the following labels:

- **Sandymount College of Further Education** / Bothar Road, Sandymount, Dublin 4 / Phone: 01-8798833, Fax: 01-8798673 / Email: scfe@eircom.net / homepage.eircom.net/~fcse — Franklin Gothic Medium, bold, leading = 6.5/9 pt, centred
- Logo, copied from Letterhead, oval changed to 1 pt thickness, 19 mm. x 15 mm.
- Use this area to write about some historical aspect of the business. - between 150 & 180 words. — Times New Roman, justified, Leading = 11/15 pt. First line indent = 5 mm.
- Shading of 10% black
- Hairline border around frame
- Story in 1 column, 1 text frame
- Email / URL labels — Times New Roman, 8 pt, bold, reversed, centred

Backpage Story Headline

- Franklin Gothic Medium, Bold, 18 pt, left aligned, vertically aligned at bottom
- This story can fit between 240 & 270 words. — Times New Roman, justified, Leading = 9/13 pt. First line indent = 5 mm.
- Story in 3 connected text frames
- Photograph, centred between 3 connected text frames & with run-around text
- **Pull Quote** — Franklin Gothic Medium, bold, 11 pt, centred
- Caption describing picture

Page 4 — Scéal na Ts̄ı

Chapter 11 — *Designing a Newsletter*

FINISHING THE NEWSLETTER TEMPLATE
PAGES 1 AND 4

Carry out the instructions in numerical order

1. Insert horizontal ruler guides to help in the placement of the heading and the body text frames. Place them in the following positions: Page 1: 75 mm., 77 mm., 200 mm., 220 mm., and 222 mm. Page 4: 40 mm., 120 mm., 150 mm., 152 mm. and 267 mm. The 2 mm. space between the ruler guides is the space between the heading and body text frames. You can choose your own ruler guide positions if you wish.

2. Copy and paste the border from the background, resize to make deeper and place here.

3. Insert the business name here.

4. Copy the logo from the *Letterhead* file, resize, copy and paste again, and place both logos in appropriate positions under the top border.

5. Insert the title *Scéal na Trá*.

6. Draw a 3 pt rule across the width of the page underneath the logos.

12. Create Email and URL text frames and place here.

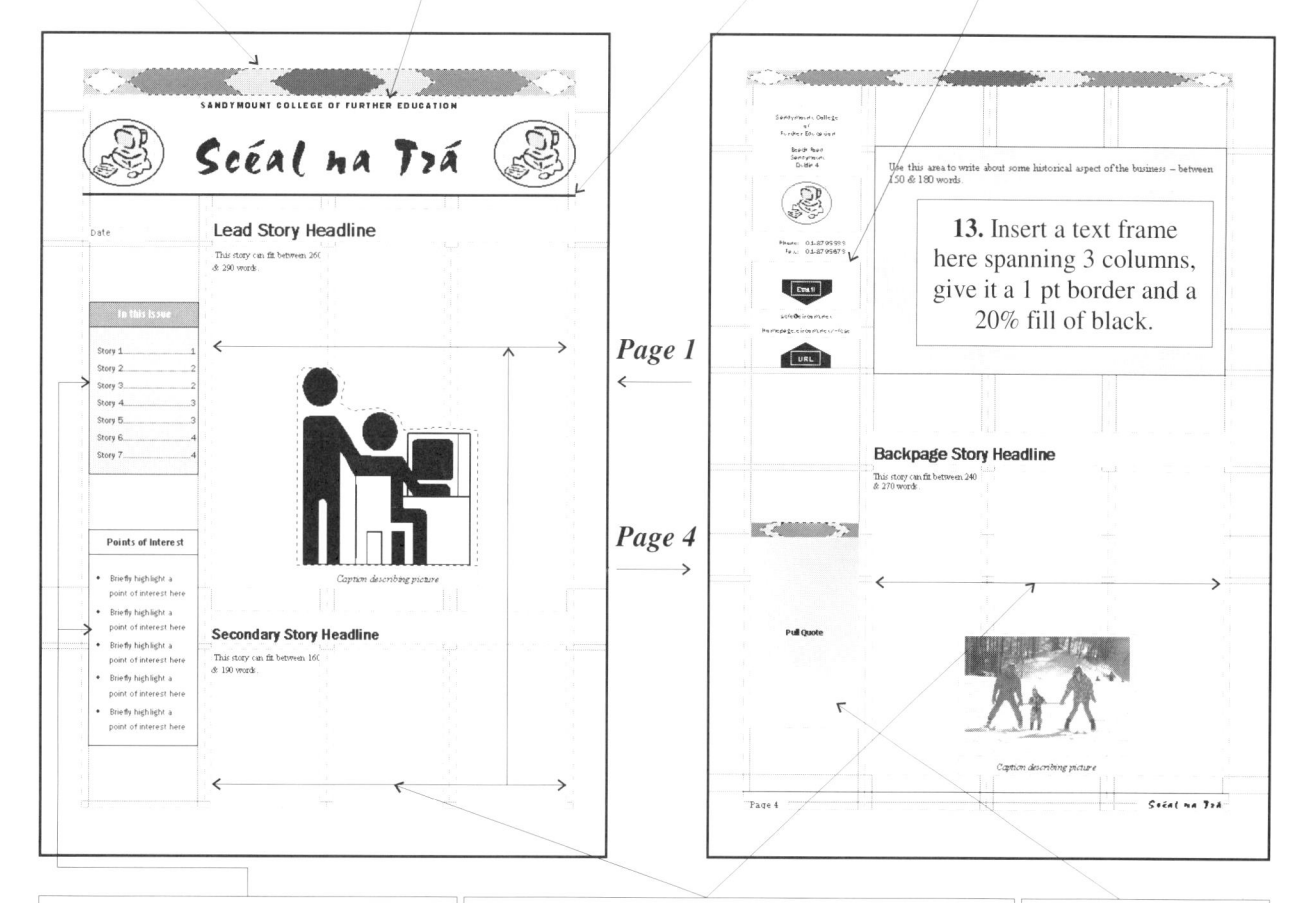

13. Insert a text frame here spanning 3 columns, give it a 1 pt border and a 20% fill of black.

7. Create Table of Contents and Points of Interest frames and place here.

8. Insert 3 rows of 3 text frames, connect and group them. Give the frames margins of 0 mm. all around.

11. Create Pull Quote frame and place here.

9. Insert the pictures and caption text frames.

10. Insert the heading text frames.

14. Insert a text frame for the company name and address in the top left corner of page 4. Type in the text and format it.

Using Microsoft Publisher

Designing a Newsletter   *Chapter 11*

FINISHING THE NEWSLETTER TEMPLATE
PAGES 2 AND 3

Carry out the instructions in numerical order

Set margins all around to 0 mm. for all the text frames of the newsletter by clicking **Text Frame Properties** *from the* **Format** *menu. This ensures that the body text will only have a gutter (space between frames) of 5 mm., that the headings will be aligned with body text, that the date will be aligned with Table of Contents frame etc.*

Choosing the same ruler guide positions for pages 2-4 doesn't necessarily mean they will be structured exactly the same. You will notice that on page 3 we created an advertisement covering 3 columns. On page 4 we created a bordered text frame with a tinted background spanning 3 columns.

15. Insert horizontal ruler guides to help in the placement of the heading and the body text frames. Place them in the following positions: 40 mm., 42 mm., 105 mm., 120 mm., 122 mm., 180 mm., 195 mm., 197 mm. and 267 mm. The 2 mm. space between the ruler guides is the space between the heading and body text frames. You can choose your own ruler guide positions if you wish.

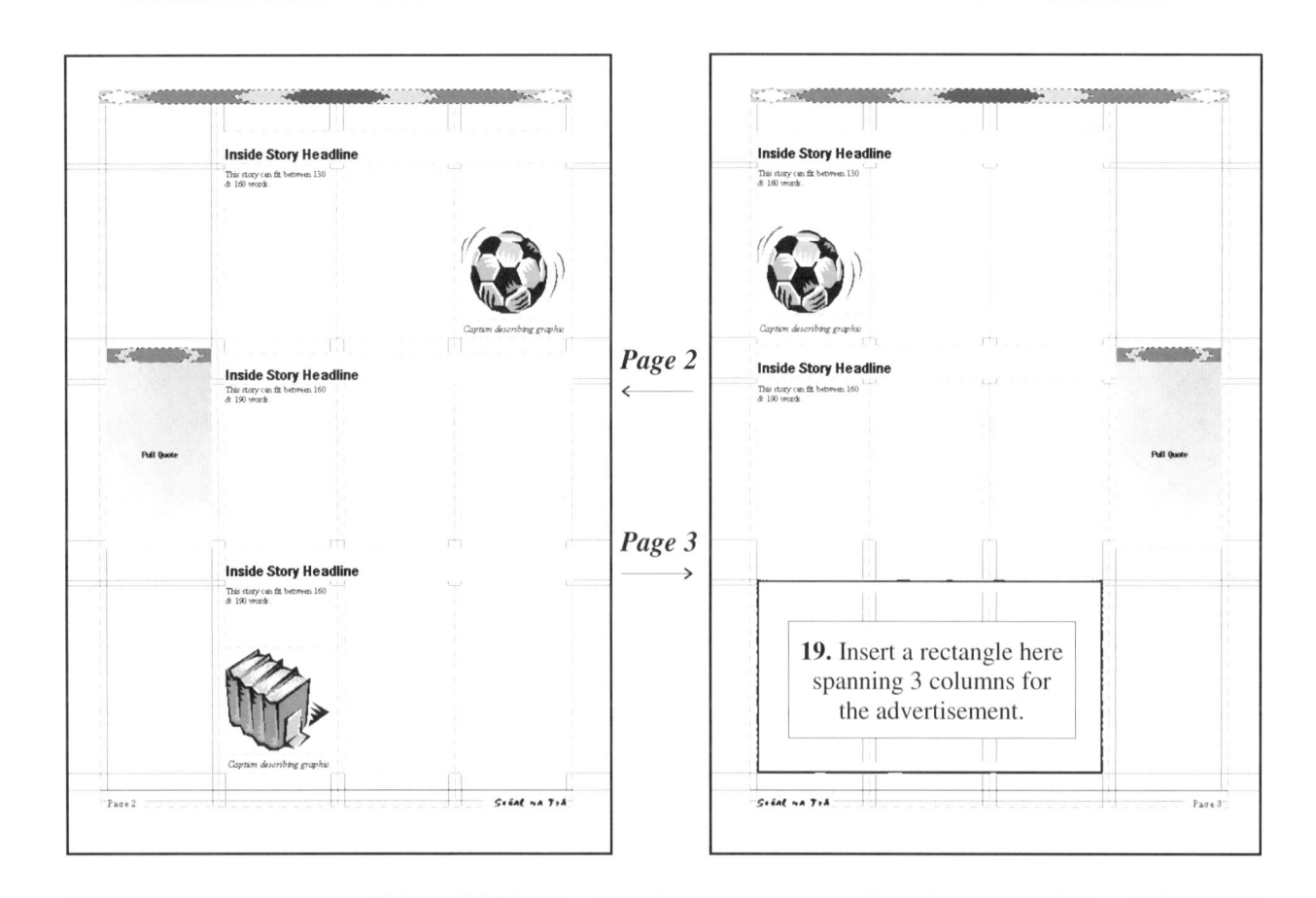

Page 2 ←

Page 3 →

19. Insert a rectangle here spanning 3 columns for the advertisement.

16. Insert the pictures and caption text frames.

17. Create Pull Quote frames and place them.

21. Print.

18. Insert 5 rows of 3 text frames. Connect and group them.

20. *Save as Template*. Name it *Newsletter*.

Page 158   **Desktop Publishing Made Easy**

SAVING FILES AS TEXT ONLY FILES

Saving a file in a word-processing application as a *Text Only* file saves it but does not preserve any text formatting such as font type, emboldening, line spacing, indentation, alignment etc.

It is better to save files as *Text Only* so that all the formatting is done within the Desktop Publishing application. Formatting unformatted text is easier to do than re-formatting formatted text.

To save as text only:

1. Type the text into a word-processing application.

2. Click the *Save* tool on the Standard Toolbar.

3. In the *Save in* box choose the drive in which you want to save the file.
4. Click the destination folder in the main part of the window and click *Open*. The folder's name should now appear in the *Save in* box.

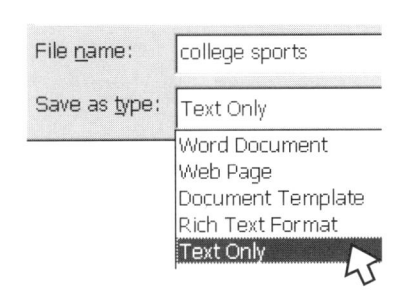

5. In the lower part of the window click in the *File Name* box.
6. Type in the file name.
7. In the *Save as type* box choose *Text Only*.
8. Click *Save*.

A message appears telling you about the possible loss of formatting.

9. Click *Yes* to save without the formatting.

IMPORTING TEXT INTO THE NEWSLETTER

We touched on this subject in the *Connecting Text Frames* tutorial earlier in this chapter.

In the newsletter we shall be importing text into 3 connected text frames, which Publisher treats as one text frame.

To do that:

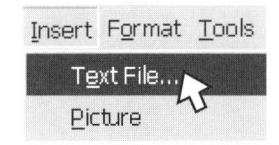

1. Click the first of the 3 connected text frames to select it.
2. Click *Insert* on the Standard Toolbar.
3. Click *Text File*.

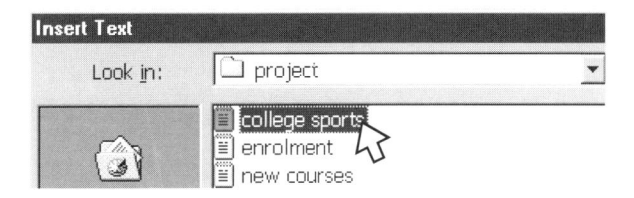

4. In the *Insert Text* window click in the *Look in* box for the drive containing the file.
5. In the main part of window click the appropriate folder and click *Open*.
6. Click the appropriate file to select it.
7. Click *OK*.

The inserted text doesn't fit in this frame. Do you want to use autoflow?

8. If the text doesn't fit in the last frame, you are asked if you want to use autoflow. Click *No* as we only want to use 3 connected frames for any particular story. We can make the text fit the frames later in this chapter.

Designing a Newsletter — Chapter 11

ANOTHER WAY TO CREATE TEXT COLUMNS

1. Import text into a text frame in the usual way.

2. Click *Format* from the Menu Bar.
3. Click *Text Frame Properties*.

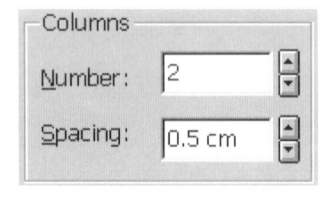

4. In the *Columns* section insert *2* in the *Number* box.
5. Insert *0.5* in the *Spacing* box. This gives a gutter of 0.5 cm. or 5 mm.
6. Click *OK*.

Gutter

The illustration above shows 2 columns of text in the one frame with a gutter of 5 mm.

In the newsletter I could have created a wide text frame spanning the 3 columns for each story, but decided to use 3 narrow connected text frames instead. Each text frame has margins of 0 mm. all around in the *Text Frame Properties* window, is within the blue layout guides and is 5 mm. apart.

This space between the text frames is the gutter.

SPELL CHECKING

Spellings should always be checked before the newsletter is completed. This can be done in the Word-processing or the Desktop Publishing application. In Word 2000 click *Spelling and Grammar* from *Tools* on the Menu Bar.

Below is how to do it in Publisher 2000.

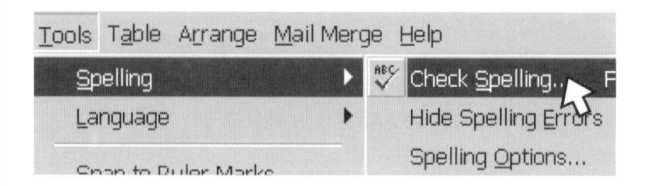

1. Click in the story (text frame) you want to spell-check.
2. Click *Tools* from the Menu Bar.
3. Click *Spelling*.
4. Click *Check Spelling*.

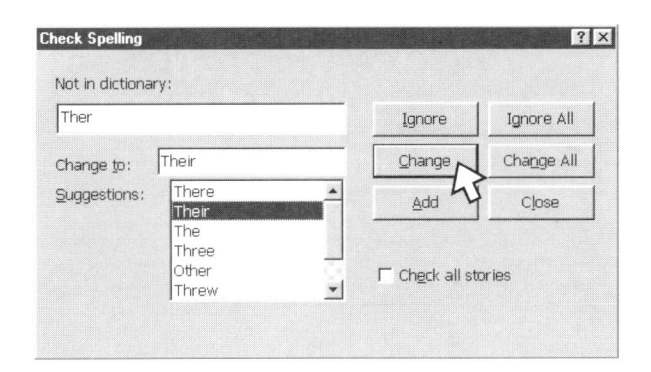

Chapter 11   Designing a Newsletter

If the word isn't recognised it will appear in the *Not in dictionary* box. A number of suggested spellings may appear in the *Suggestions* box.

5. Click the correct spelling and it will appear in the *Change to* box. If there is only one suggested spelling it will automatically appear in the *Change to* box.
6. Click *Change* if you want to change it.
7. Click *Change All* to change all future examples of the same word in the same way.
8. Click *Ignore* if you don't want to change the spelling.
9. Click *Close* to close the spell checker before it completes the checking.
10. Click the *Check all stories* box to spell-check all the text frames in your publication.

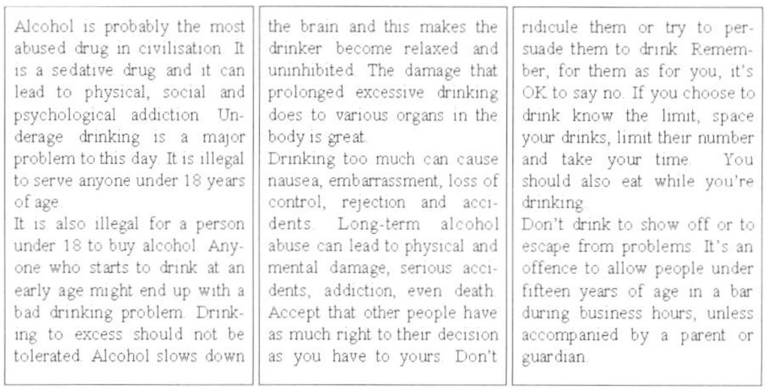

The story above is broken into paragraphs and fills the frames. The paragraphs should of course be logical ones. There are many other ways to make text fit in a text frame.

Whether there is too much text or too little text in a text frame, it can be made to fit as follows:

♦ Change the leading slightly.
♦ Change the tracking (to be used sparingly).
♦ Change the font size.
♦ Change the text frame size.
♦ Delete or insert words.
♦ Substitute one word or phrase for another.
♦ Split or join paragraphs.

You must be careful to have consistency of style for the body text in the newsletter, which rules out some of the points in the list above.

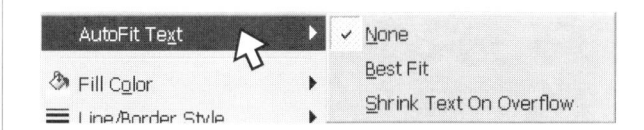

MAKING TEXT FIT INSIDE A FRAME

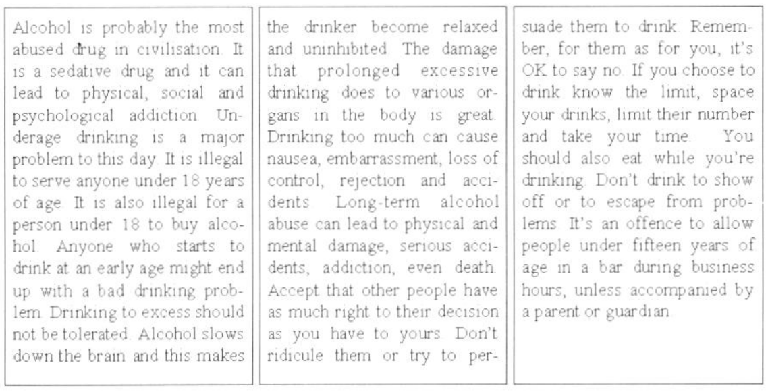

If the text imported into a text frame or connected text frames doesn't fill the frame(s):

1. Type in more text or
2. Increase the leading or
3. Break up the story into paragraphs.

Publisher 2000 (not earlier versions) has special features for making text fit in a frame, but as it changes the font size it is not suitable to be used on body text in a newsletter.

Here's how to do it:

1. Click the text frame to select it.
2. Click *Format* on the Menu Bar.
3. Click *AutoFit Text*.

• By clicking *Best Fit* the text is expanded or shrunk to suit the size of the text frame.

• By clicking *Shrink Text On Overflow* the text is shrunk to suit the smaller size of the text frame. The size of the text will not increase beyond its original size on expanding the text frame.

Using Microsoft Publisher   Page 161

Designing a Newsletter   Chapter 11

CROPPING PICTURES

1. Click the picture to select it.
2. Click the *Crop* tool from the Formatting Toolbar.

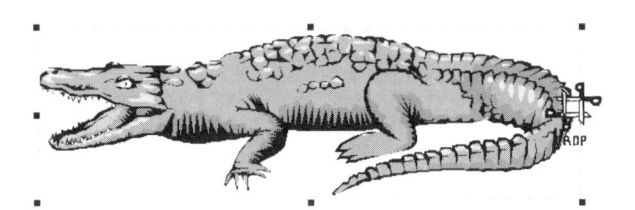

3. Place the mouse pointer over one of the selection handles.
4. When it changes to a facing pair of scissors drag inwards.

Cropping can make the picture more dramatic. See the result below.

5. Dragging out achieves extra white space. It is useful for creating space (offset) between the picture and the text.

INSERTING PICTURES INTO THE NEWSLETTER

Ruler Guides

Earlier in this chapter we placed pictures in the template to show us where to insert them into the completed newsletter. We also placed ruler guides around the template pictures to help rectify any positional changes to the newly inserted ones.

We've seen in Chapter 4 how to insert a picture. Double-clicking on an existing picture will also open the *Insert Picture* window.

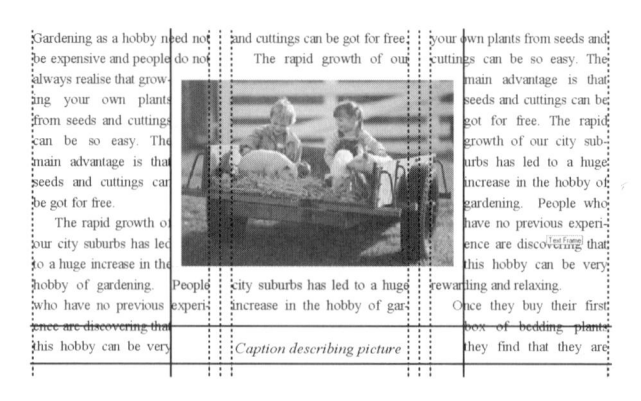

The picture above, of greater width but less depth than the template one, has been inserted over the existing picture. When moving the picture down onto the horizontal ruler guide, the vertical ruler guides help to maintain its horizontal alignment, while the horizontal ruler guide maintains the consistent space between it and the caption text.

Page 162   Desktop Publishing Made Easy

Chapter 11 — Designing a Newsletter

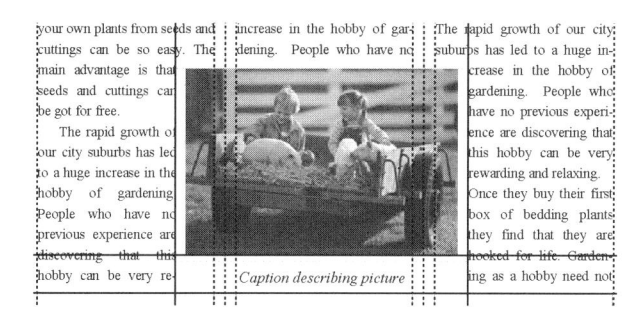

The picture above has been moved down onto the horizontal ruler guide and kept inside the vertical ruler guides.

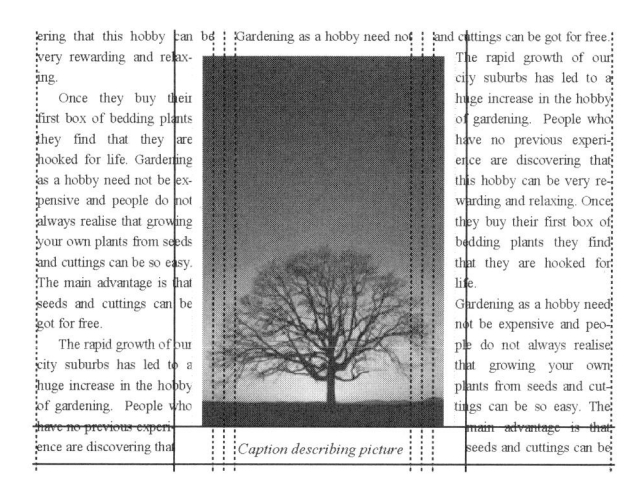

The picture above, of greater depth but less width than the template one, has been inserted over the existing picture and rests on the horizontal ruler guide. Resize down the picture proportionately from one of the top corner handles until it snaps in against each of the blue layout guides.

As the resized picture will rest between the blue layout guides, these guides will create the text offset. See the resized picture below and also the next tutorial on how to create a text offset.

CREATING A TEXT OFFSET

When inserting a picture over text, there should always be a text offset – a space between the picture and the text.

As in the illustration above where there is no text offset, it is very difficult to read the text. As the eye approaches the picture when reading a line of the text it will be attracted away from the text and onto the edge of the picture. The omission of an offset here is a very bad design flaw.

The following are 2 ways of creating a text offset:

1. Insert a picture over text without an offset.
2. Crop out from the picture on the top, left and right. This creates a space between the picture and the text – a text offset.

You can crop the same space on opposite sides of the picture simultaneously by pressing the CTRL key on keyboard while using the *Crop* tool.

Designing a Newsletter — Chapter 11

Another way of creating an offset:

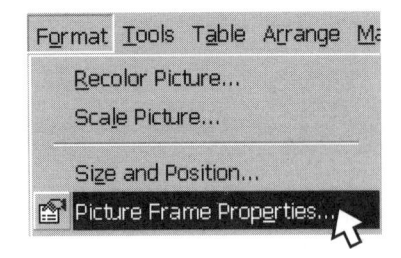

1. Click the *Picture Frame* tool from the Tool Palette.
2. Click *Format* on the Menu Bar.
3. Click *Picture Frame Properties*.

A text offset is created by setting margins in the *Picture Frame Properties* window.

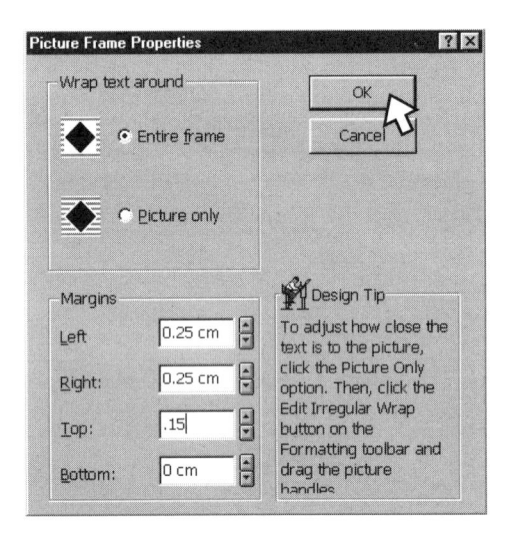

4. Insert the margins as shown in the illustration.

As there is extra white space between each line of text, the top margin does not have to be as great as the other margins. If there is no text beneath the picture, the bottom margin can be set to 0 cm.

5. Click *OK*.
6. Create the picture frame and insert the picture.

See the result on the top of the next column.

Set the *Picture Frame Properties* before inserting the picture, because setting them afterwards may distort the picture. If they are set before creating the picture frame these properties will apply to all future picture frames in the publication, until they are changed.

WRAPPING TEXT TO PICTURES

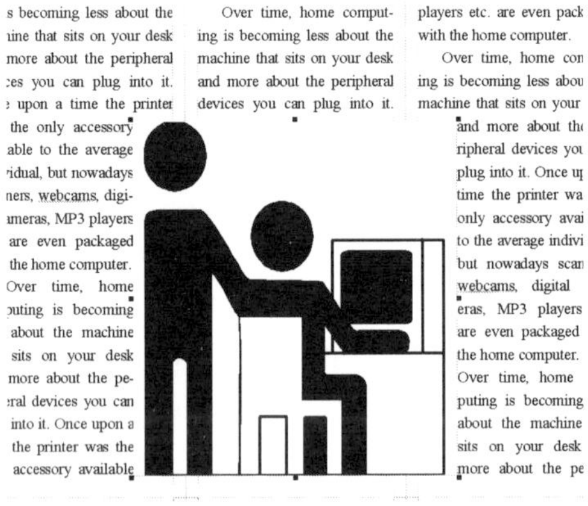

When a picture is inserted over text, the text wraps to the the picture frame rather than to the picture. See the illustration above.

Wrapping text to a picture can integrate the picture more effectively with the text.

When the *Wrap Text to Frame* tool is clicked the *Crop* tool can be used.

1. To wrap the text to the picture click the *Wrap Text to Picture* tool on the Formatting Toolbar.

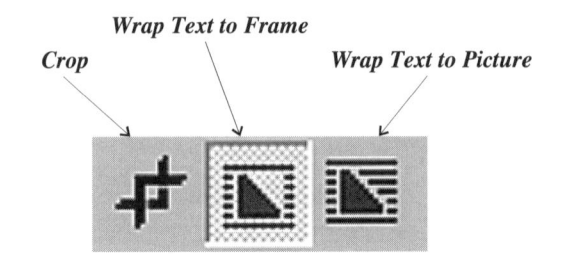

Crop   *Wrap Text to Frame*   *Wrap Text to Picture*

Chapter 11 — Designing a Newsletter

If you clicked the *Wrap Text to Picture* tool twice, you will be asked if you want to create a new wrap boundary.

2. Click *Yes* to allow Publisher create the new wrap boundary.

Otherwise skip this.

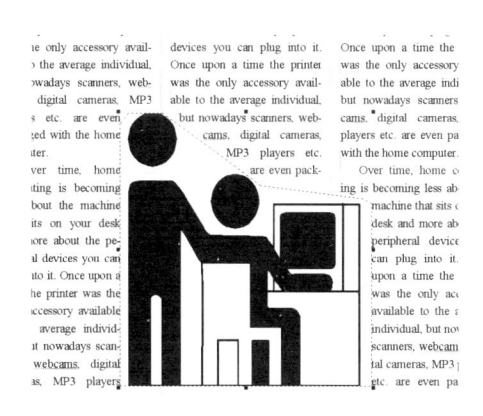

The wrap border on the picture has changed.

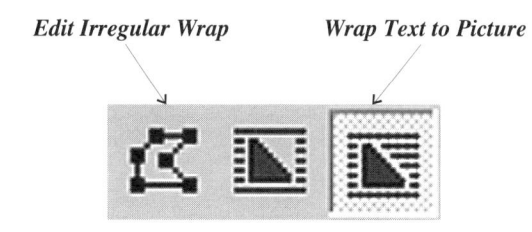

Edit Irregular Wrap   *Wrap Text to Picture*

The Crop tool changes to the Edit Irregular Wrap tool

3. Click the *Edit Irregular Wrap* tool on the Formatting Toolbar.

Notice the extra adjust handles.

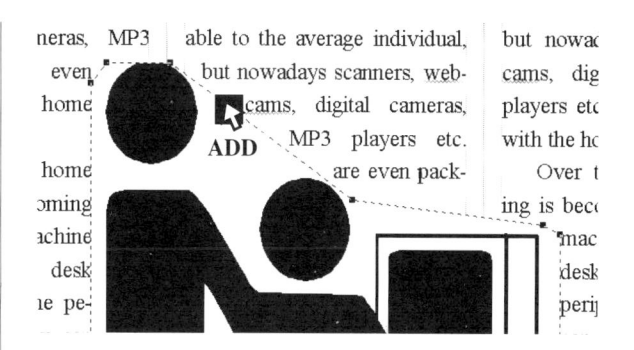

In order to increase the accuracy of the wrap you may want to add adjust handles. To do that:

4. Click on the wrap border and away from the other adjust handles, while pressing the CTRL key on the keyboard.

To delete an adjust handle click an existing one, while pressing the CTRL key on the keyboard.

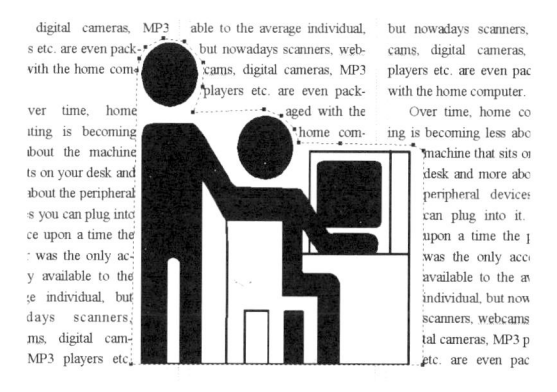

5. Add as many adjust handles as you need.
6. Click on any adjust handle where the border needs adjusting and drag it to an appropriate position until the wrap border is in the same shape as the picture.

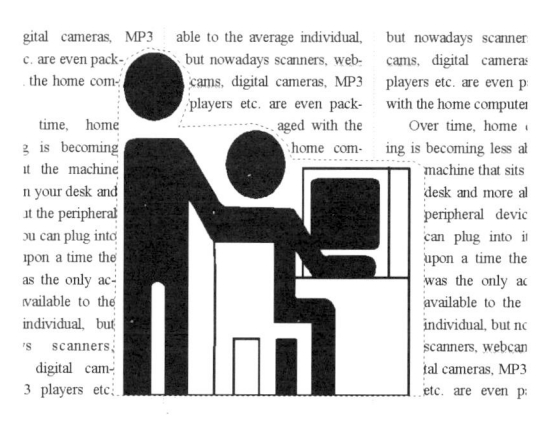

7. Click the *Edit Irregular Wrap* tool on the Formatting Toolbar to get rid of the frame handles and to see the finished product.

Using Microsoft Publisher

Designing a Newsletter   *Chapter 11*

SCANNING PICTURES

A scanner is a hardware device which digitises artwork or photographs and stores the image as a file which in turn can be integrated with text in a Desktop Publishing program.

Every scanner is supplied with scanning as well as other related programs and in this tutorial we shall use the scanning and the graphics editing ones. The programs you have may not be the same as the author's, but they may have graphics handling features similar to the following:

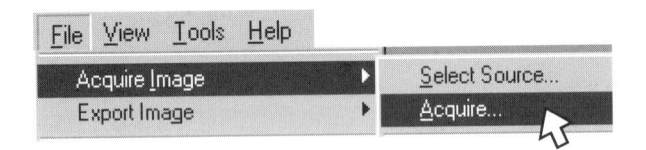

1. Click *File* from Menu Bar.
2. Click *Acquire Image*.
3. Click *Acquire*.

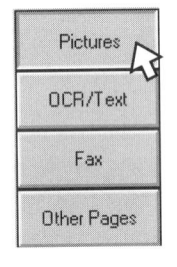

The next window may invite you to select a scan type and then may invite you to scan.

4. Ensure that it is a picture you are going to scan. Above I clicked the *Pictures* button.
5. Click *Scan*.

As the preview of the picture is being scanned a progress meter may appear to show you how the scanning job is progressing.

A preview of the whole page will be scanned, with a selection marquee around any pictures.

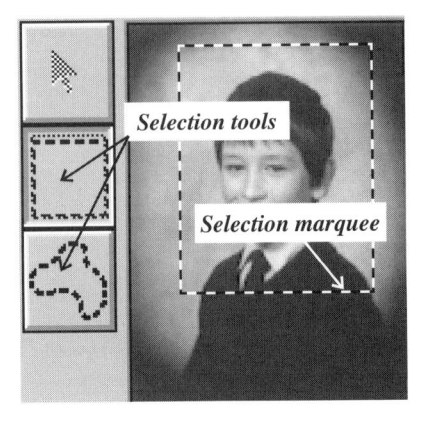

6. You can resize this selection marquee to suit the portion of the picture you want.
7. You can also click the *Selection* tool and create your own selection marquee.

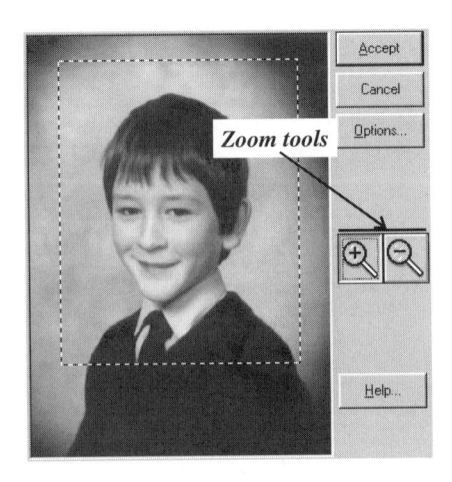

8. Click the *Zoom* tool to zoom in on the portion of the picture selected.

Page 166   **Desktop Publishing Made Easy**

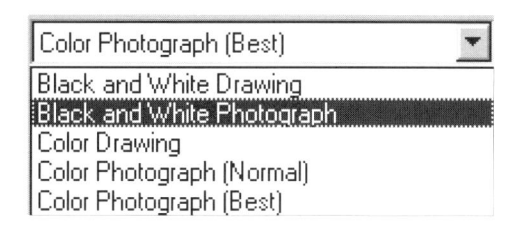

There may be an *Options* button on your Task Manager window to allow you perform some editing before the final scan.

9. If you use a mono laser printer it is better to convert the picture from colour to *black and white photograph*. This cuts down greatly on the file size. The conversion can be also done from within the graphics editing package, but is better if done during the scanning process.

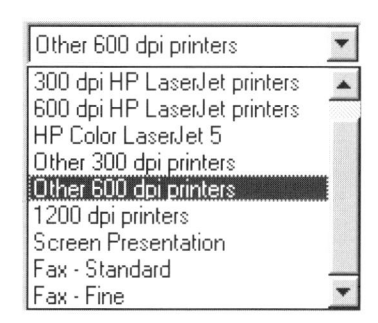

10. You will also have an option of changing the scanning resolution. This will affect the file size. If the printer resolution is 600 dpi, then a scan of 150 dpi will suffice.

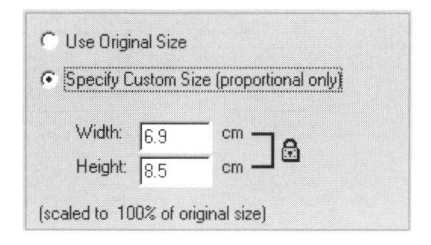

11. The physical dimensions of the picture can be altered proportionately, which will either decrease or increase the file size.

Make the scanned picture size greater than the picture frame size in Publisher, as increasing the picture size in Publisher beyond the scanned size may sacrifice the quality of the picture.

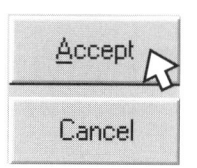

12. When all the alterations are completed, click the *Accept* or *Final Scan* button to scan the picture into the graphics editing package. Clicking *Cancel* will allow you to start the scanning process again without exiting the Task Manager window.
13. More picture editing can be done in the graphics editing package.

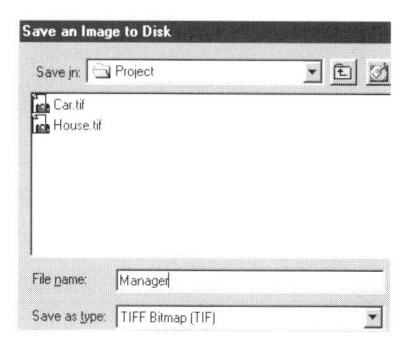

It's now time to save the picture from the graphics editing package. Make sure to save it in a format compatible with Publisher.

14. Click *Save* from the Standard Toolbar.
15. In the *Save in* box choose the destination folder for the picture file.
16. Type a file name in the *File Name* box.
17. Click in the *Save as type* box.
18. Choose a file extension that is compatible with Publisher, e.g. *'bmp'* or *'tif'*.
19. Click *Save*.

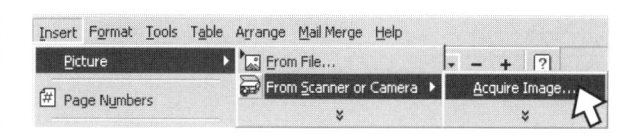

If the scanner software is set up properly on your computer, you will also be able to scan directly from Publisher.

1. Click *Insert* from the Menu Bar.
2. Click *Picture*.
3. Click *From Scanner*.
4. Click *Acquire Image*.
5. Follow the previous steps up to step 12.

Designing a Newsletter Chapter 11

FINISHING THE NEWSLETTER
PAGES 1 AND 4

Carry out the instructions in numerical order

1. Open the template *Newsletter*. The *Opening a Template File* tutorial is in Chapter 5.

2. Save as *Newsletter*. A new file *Newsletter* is saved.

3. Change the date of the publication.

4. Import the text into each of the 3 connected text frames. Apply a text style and make the text fit in the text frames.

5. Type in each of the headings.

7. Insert the pictures and adjust them as is necessary.

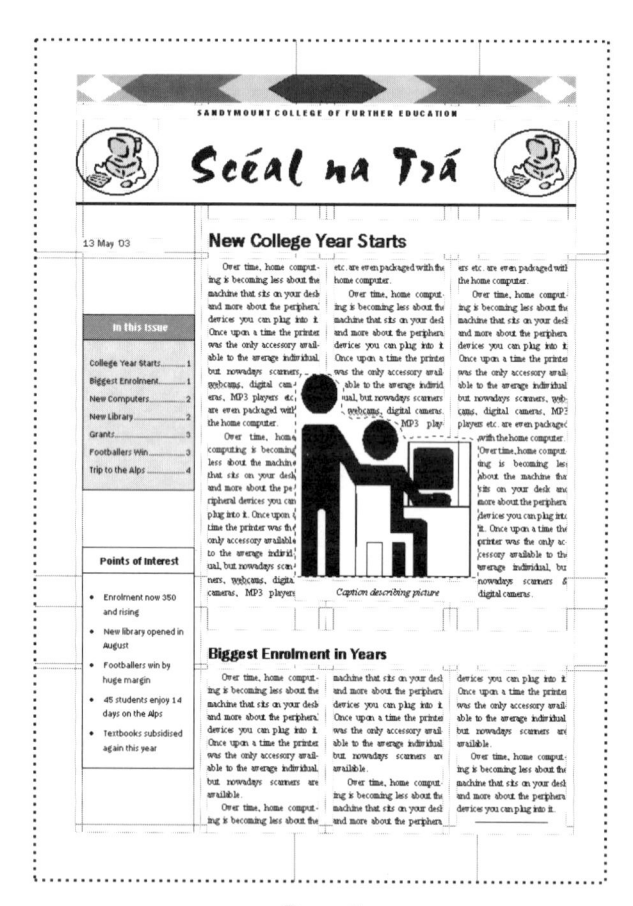

Page 1

Page 4

6. Insert the text into the Table of Contents and Points of Interest text frames. You may have to adjust the leading to balance the text in the frames.

8. Change the text in the captions.

9. Insert the text into the Pull Quote frame.

10. Import the text into the bordered and shaded text frame.

11. Save.

Page 168 Desktop Publishing Made Easy

Chapter 11 Designing a Newsletter

FINISHING THE NEWSLETTER
PAGES 2 AND 3

Carry out the instructions in numerical order

12. Import text into each of the 3 connected text frames.

13. Type in each of the headings.

14. Insert the pictures and adjust as is necessary.

15. Insert the text into the Pull Quote frames.

16. Design the advertisement by creating picture frames and inserting pictures, creating text frames, inserting text and formatting it. Balance the advertisement area by positioning the objects properly.

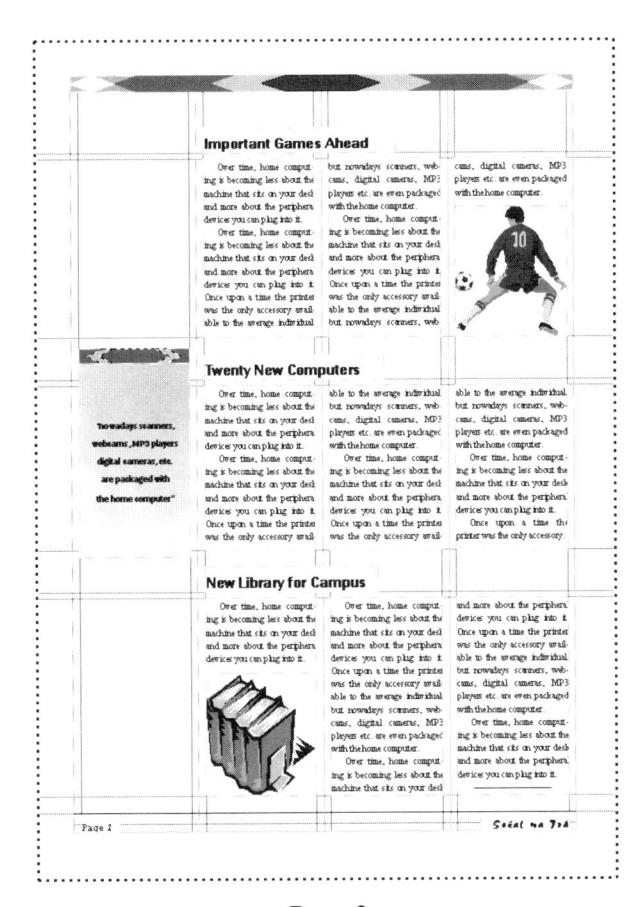

Page 2

Page 3

17. Save the publication.

18. Print.

Extra Newsletter Exercises

Design Newsletters for a Building Contractor and a Garage

The pages are broken up into 4 columns

1 pt border around the margins

Transparent text frame on oval with 20% fill of black

Design the other 3 pages of each newsletter

IN CHAPTER 11 YOU HAVE DONE THE FOLLOWING:

- Understood the stages in the setting up of a newsletter.
- Designed a top border for a newsletter.
- Designed a Pull Quote border.
- Inserted page numbers in the newsletter.
- Created two backgrounds with mirrored guides.
- Learned about layout guides.
- Created text styles.
- Applied text styles.
- Created a Table of Contents frame.
- Created a Pull Quote frame.
- Created a Points of Interest frame.
- Inverted text in a custom shape with a tinted background.
- Connected text frames.
- Disconnected text frames.
- Placed pictures in a newsletter template.
- Saved files as Text Only files.
- Imported text into a newsletter.
- Applied two columns to a text frame.
- Used the Spell Checker.
- Made text fit inside a frame.
- Cropped pictures.
- Created a text offset.
- Wrapped text to pictures.
- Scanned pictures.

INDEX OF TUTORIALS

DESIGNING A FORM

Setting Margins 16
Creating a Table 16
Highlighting Cells 16
Highlighting Column(s)/Row(s) 17
Highlighting a Table 17
Highlighting One Cell 17
Adding a Border to a Table 18
Adding a Border to a Cell 18
Adding a Border to a Range of Cells 19
Borders of Different Thickness 19
Deleting Borders 20
Resizing a Table 20
Adjusting Rows and Columns 20
Adjusting Multiple Rows and Columns 21
Shading Cell(s) 21
Merging and Splitting Cells 22
Moving a Table Frame 22
Adding Rows and Columns 23
Deleting Rows and Columns 23
Inserting Text into Cells 24
Highlighting Text in a Cell 24
Deleting Text in a Cell 24
Deleting a Table 24
Changing Cell Properties 25
Aligning Text Vertically 25
Aligning Text Horizontally 25
Copying and Moving Text 26
Bold/Italic/Underline 26
Changing a Font in a Cell 27
Changing the Font Size 27
Format Painting Text 27
Format Painting a Cell 28
Snapping to Guides etc. 28
Changing Page Orientation 28
Saving a File 29
Opening a File 30
Printing 30

DESIGNING A LOGO

Opening a New File 38
Nudging Objects 38
Zooming In and Out 38
Using Ruler Guides 39
Creating a Picture Frame 39
Inserting a Picture 39
Resizing a Picture Frame 40
Moving a Picture Frame 40
Creating a Text Frame, Inserting Text,
Resizing a Text Frame 41
Highlighting Text in a Text Frame 42
Deleting Text in a Text Frame 42
Text Frame Properties 43
Moving a Text Frame 43
Deleting Objects 43
Creating an Oval 44
Creating Custom Shapes 44
Multiple Selections 45
Aligning Objects 45
Layering Objects 46
Changing the Layering 46
Copy and Paste Objects 47
Cut and Paste Objects 48
Pixel Editing 48
Enclosing an Object in an Oval,
Grouping and Resizing them 51

DESIGNING A BUSINESS LETTERHEAD

Template (Style Sheet, Master Page) 60
Saving as a Template File 60
Opening a Template File 60
What is a Background? 61
Creating a Background 61
Copying a Logo from One File to Another 62
Ungrouping the Logo and the Text Frame,
Deleting the Text Frame 62
Using WordArt to Create a Text Design 62

INDEX OF TUTORIALS

Inserting a WordArt Object inside an Oval
of the Same Dimension as the Logo 64
Reversing Text on a Tinted Background 65
Creating a Rectangle 67
Using a Custom Shape as a
Tinted Background for Text 67

DESIGNING A BUSINESS CARD

Page Setup 74
Creating Rules 74
Aligning Rules with Text 74
Ungrouping Logo, Changing Oval
Thickness and Re-grouping 75

DESIGNING A COMPLIMENT SLIP

Tracking 83
Kerning 83

DESIGNING A GREETING CARD

Paper Sizes 90
Using a Pre-defined Layout to
Set Up a Greeting Card Page 90
Manually Setting Up a Greeting Card Page 91
Alignment within Panels 93
Rotating Objects 94

DESIGNING A BROCHURE

Gatefold Brochure 101
Setting Up the Front Side of a
Gatefold Brochure 102
Bulleting and Numbering 103
Indenting Paragraphs 104
Inserting Tabs 105
Line Spacing (Leading) 106

Shadowing Frames 107
Inserting Extra Pages 108
Inserting WordArt around the Logo 108

DESIGNING A NEWSLETTER

The Newsletter Explained 136
Designing a Top Border for a Newsletter 136
Designing a Pull Quote Border 139
Inserting Page Numbers 140
Two Backgrounds with Mirrored Guides 140
Creating 2 Backgrounds
with Mirrored Guides 141
Why Layout Guides? 143
Inserting Pages 143
Creating Text Styles 144
Applying Text Styles 146
Creating a Table of Contents 147
Finishing the Pull Quote Frame 148
Creating a Points of Interest Frame 148
Inverting Text in a Custom Shape
with a Tinted Background 148
Connecting Text Frames 150
Disconnecting Text Frames 152
Placing Pictures in a Newsletter Template 152
Saving Files As Text Only Files 159
Importing Text into the Newsletter 159
Another Way to Create Text Columns 160
Spell Checking 160
Making Text Fit inside a Frame 161
Cropping Pictures 162
Inserting Pictures into the Newsletter 162
Creating a Text Offset 163
Wrapping Text to Pictures 164
Scanning Pictures 166